Beauty
AND
THE
Beast

From *Beauty and the Beast: or a Rough Outside with a Gentle Heart,
a Poetical Version of an Ancient Tale*, attributed to Charles Lamb, 1811.
By permission of the Department of Special Collections,
University of Chicago Library.

Beauty AND THE Beast

VISIONS AND REVISIONS
OF AN OLD TALE

BETSY HEARNE

With an Essay by Larry DeVries

The University of Chicago Press
Chicago and London

Betsy Hearne, a former storyteller and librarian,
is now a member of the faculty of
the University of Chicago and editor of
the *Bulletin of the Center for Children's Books.*

The University of Chicago Press, Chicago 60637
The University of Chicago Press, Ltd., London
© 1989 by The University of Chicago
All rights reserved. Published 1989
Printed in the United States of America

98 97 96 95 94 93 92 91 90 89   54321

Library of Congress Cataloging-in-Publication Data
Hearne, Betsy Gould.
Beauty and the beast : visions and revisions of an old tale /
Betsy Hearne : with an essay by Larry DeVries.
p.   cm.
Originally presented as the author's thesis.
Bibliography: p.
Includes index.
ISBN 0-226-32239-4 (alk. paper.)
1. Le prince de Beaumont, Madame (Jeanne-Marie) 1711–1780.
Belle et la bête. 2. Le prince de Beaumont, Madame (Jeanne-Marie),
1711–1780—Influence. 3. Children's literature, English—History
and criticism. 4. Children's literature, French—History and
criticism. 5. Beauty and the beast (Tale) 6. Fairy tales—History
and criticism. 7. Oral tradition in literature. 8. Folklore in
literature. I. DeVries, Larry. II. Title.
PQ1995.L75B434   1989   89-30266
398.2'1—dc19   CIP

∞ The paper used in this publication meets the minimum requirements
of the American National Standard for Information Sciences—Permanence
of Paper for Printed Library Materials, ANSI Z39.48-1984.

To the students of
THE GRADUATE LIBRARY SCHOOL
first graduated, 1929
last admitted, 1989

Contents

Illustrations

Color Plates

Following page 112

Preface

The study of fairy tales is by nature interdisciplinary, requiring some familiarity with folklore, literature, art, history, psychology, and education. Although researchers must guard against thin scholarship in dealing with so many diverse canons of knowledge, they otherwise risk limitations of vision within a narrow specialty. Numerous recent essays by scholars of widely differing backgrounds attest to the importance of a holistic approach.

In this respect, the tradition of children's literature in librarianship provides a logical springboard for the study of fairy tales. Librarianship is by nature interdisciplinary in its goals of gathering, organizing, and preserving knowledge of all kinds, in many forms. That knowledge includes oral narrative, and for many years, children's librarians have been staple tradition bearers. Before the turn of the century, they pioneered storytelling programs to which children all over the country had free access. The first library schools, established in the early 1900s, included storytelling and children's literature—long before education or English departments offered such courses or recognized them as academically worthwhile. Those early courses emphasized a common core of folklore and mythology, and they stressed both the theoretical and the practical aspects of studying fairy tales. Children's librarians were also crucial, in the 1920s and early 1930s, to the establishment of children's book publication, which is now the primary medium for the popular dissemination of fairy tales. The first children's book editors were either children's librarians or in close working relationship with children's librarians, who were often consulted on publishing decisions and, as primary consumers and critics, always crucial to the success of a book.

While I have pursued "Beauty and the Beast" through thickets of reading in various disciplines, my fundamental appreciation for the tale is that of a storyteller. I grew up in a time and place that included many illiterate adults for whom storytelling and story singing were art forms. I have told stories to children and adults for twenty-five years, reviewed children's books professionally for twenty, and written some as well. Throughout my study of "Beauty and the Beast," it was the artistry of the story's tradition bearers that sustained and refreshed me. Each teller/interpreter recreates the tale anew. Every listener/reader hears a different story, according to his or her life experience. It is not a correct reading that I seek here, but an exploration of the multiple dimensions embodied in any great work of art, whether it is oral, visual, or literary.

This is a study of the art and artifice of the story rather than an analysis of its meaning. In paying more attention to the forms of the story's regeneration than to its interpretation, I am exposing myself to charges of staying on the story's surface. In this introspective era, the study of a story's meaning sometimes overshadows the story itself. We must remember that the story is fundamental and irrepressible, the meaning secondary and chameleon in that it shifts with time and culture. A story can be appreciated for one meaning, for many, or for none on an interpretive level. It is the art of a story that moves us, not the Freudian, Jungian, or other conceptualization of it. In fact, explaining a metaphor can sometimes limit its meaning more than expand it. The art and the idea of a great story, the outside and inside, are synonymous. As Shakespeare has Antony describe the crocodile to Lepidus: "It is shaped, sir, like itself, and it is as broad as it hath breadth; it is just so high as it is, and moves with its own organs; it lives by that which nourisheth it; and the elements once out of it, it transmigrates. . . . Of its own colour too. . . . 'Tis so; and the tears of it are wet." (2. 7. 42–49). This brings to mind the words with which C. S. Lewis accused Jung of explaining one myth only by creating another: "Surely the analysis of water should not itself be wet" (*Of Other Worlds: Essays and Stories*, 71). The art of the story is the heart of the story.

Any analysis, of course, creates an interpretive environment. Interpretation is implicit in the analysis of form and will suggest itself to readers. Moreover, I have occasionally but inevitably touched on interpretation in discussing point of view, style, plot, characterization, and historical nuance, as has Larry DeVries in his appended essay on the folkloristic structure of the tale. The study begins with an overview of the story's survival in oral and literary traditions and proceeds with an analysis of selected versions from the eighteenth through the twentieth centuries. The first appendix consists of Larry DeVries's structural analysis of the folk narrative. The second provides the Beaumont text, the third presents an oral version collected by Paul Delarue and Marie-Louise Tenèze, and a fourth appendix provides a list of nineteenth-century printed versions. The bibliography is divided into story sources and critical sources. I have tuned my comments for general as well as academic readers because "Beauty and the Beast" appeals to several levels of interest, aesthetic and emotional as well as intellectual. The most fruitful scholarship I encountered in the course of this study acknowledged all three levels.

Parts of the manuscript have been presented previously, first during a *Booklist* Open Forum at the American Library Association Conference in 1978 and later as essays in *New Observations* and in *The Lion and the Unicorn* 12 (2) 1988, reprinted by permission of Johns Hopkins University Press. I am deeply grateful to Zena Sutherland for her championship of children's literature and of this study in its original dissertation form. I have benefited, as well, from discussions with Hazel Rochman and Roger Sutton on aspects of cultural myth in children's and young adult literature. Alan Dundes provided helpful criticism of the manuscript in an earlier stage, although he is of course not responsible for errors and omissions in the finished book. Thanks also to Larry DeVries, who strengthened my knowledge of oral narrative, contributed a folkloristic essay, and stimulated ideas related to the "Cupid and Psyche" variants he has studied. I am indebted to Don Swanson, who, during his deanship, supported my humanistic interests at the Graduate Library School when his own were scientific. The Joyce Foundation gave a grant making possible the reproduction of color plates that are crucial to discussions of the art. Catharine Lange photographed many of the illustrations and did so clearly, cheerfully, and on time. Finally, thanks to my family for their love of story and their patience with its development.

There is no one true version of which
all the others are but copies or distortions.
Every version belongs to the myth.
Claude Lévi-Strauss, "The Structural Study of Myth"

ONE
The Survival of a Story

"Beauty and the Beast" offers proof of simple story as a powerful form of complex statement. It is a story told to children but echoed in literary and artistic elaborations through hundreds of years. Based on an ancient folktale with global variants, the story has not petrified as a relic of the past but has adapted constantly to reflect new variations of culture and creativity. The core of motifs, images, characters, and conflicts remains constant. Yet the changes of form, detail, and tone show the tale's elasticity. Its endurance of transition proves it to be one of the great metaphors of oral and written tradition.

The very survival of the story raises a host of questions. What is its source? What makes it persist while other stories fade from memory? What has happened to it through the two hundred and fifty years since its publication in the 1700s? Which of its versions are most effective? What central aspects are most often retained? How does one reconcile conflicting interpretations? The study of fairy tales has generated many psychological, historical, cultural, and aesthetic theories. A close look at the variations and constants of one tale over a long period of time shows it to have kaleidoscopic implications for all these areas.

In the story of "Beauty and the Beast," a wealthy merchant with three beautiful daughters, the youngest incomparably lovely and good-hearted, loses everything through misfortune. Hearing of one cargo ship's safe return, the merchant sets off to straighten out his finances. His older girls clamor for rich gifts, but Beauty requests only a rose. After a fruitless journey, the merchant turns homeward, gets lost in a storm, and discovers a magic palace, where he plucks from the garden a rose. This theft arouses the wrath of a terrible Beast, who demands he either forfeit his life or give up a daughter.

Beauty insists on sacrificing herself but becomes, instead, mistress of a palace and develops an esteem for the Beast. In spite of her growing attachment to him, however, she misses her ailing father and requests leave to care for him. Once home, she is diverted by her two sisters from returning to the palace until nearly too late. She misses the Beast, arrives to find him almost dead with grief, and declares her love, thereby transforming him into a prince who makes her his bride.

Animal groom and bride stories have varied as widely across time and culture as versions of the Cinderella theme. Traditional tales bearing striking parallels with "Beauty and the Beast" have been collected from India and Central Asia, Europe, and Africa. The tale of "Cupid and Psyche," one of the earliest recorded predecessors of "Beauty and the Beast," was available in published form to French writers by the middle of the seventeenth century. The most familiar version of "Beauty and the Beast" is the one written by Madame Le Prince de Beaumont in 1756 in *Magasin des enfans, ou dialogues entre une sage gouvernante et plusiers de ses élèves de la première distinction* and translated into English several years later in *The Young Misses Magazine, Containing Dialogues between a Governess and Several Young Ladies of Quality, Her Scholars* (reproduced in appendix 2). The wife of a minor French aristocrat, Beaumont emigrated to London in 1745 and established herself as a tutor and writer of educational and moral books, which were to amount to some seventy volumes before her death. The story of "Beauty and the Beast" is buried in the midst of tedious, didactic conversations among figures such as Mrs. Affable and Lady Witty. There are other stories that appear in the same series, none of which has ever drawn the same following as "La Belle and la Bête."

Beaumont's story is based on the first known literary version of "Beauty and the Beast," a 362-page romance by Gabrielle Susanne Barbot de Gallon de Villeneuve, who wrote *La jeune amériquaine, et les contes marins* in 1740, not for children but for the entertainment of court and salon friends ("J'aime les jeux innocents avec ceux qui ne le sont pas").[1] Various other ladies of the court played with similar tales, among them Madame D'Aulnoy in "Le Mouton."

These eighteenth-century versions were followed in the nineteenth century by a profusion of chapbooks and collections that featured "Beauty and the Beast" and imprinted it on the cultural subconscious of French, English, and Americans, among others. This is a story with levels of meaning for all ages. Its audience has always fluctuated between children and adults. Children absorb the symbolic dimensions through the literal, while both aspects offer possibilities for elaboration that attract sophisticated adults. Although some versions clearly are created for children and others for adults only, the broad age appeal is an important aspect of the tale's popularity with readers and its perpetuation by writers and artists who find it challenging.

Listed in Mary Eastman's *Index to Fairy Tales* are sixty-eight printed editions of "Beauty and the Beast," from single editions to rare old collections. A 1984 On-line Computer Library Center (OCLC) printout of publications, films, and recordings under the title entry ran to 257 items. There are at least twenty different single editions of the story dated from 1804 to 1900 in the British Museum, Victoria and Albert Museum, Pierpont Morgan, and Newberry Libraries.[2] These range from the most pedestrian samples of text and illustration to work by writers such as Charles Lamb (1811) and Andrew Lang (1889) and artists of the caliber of Walter Crane and Eleanor Vere Boyle (both 1875). One of the richest blends of art and text is anonymous and undated, part of the Aunt Mavor's Toy Books series, published by George Routledge in London during the 1860s for sixpence (plate 1).

Nineteenth-century forms of the story vary as greatly as the physical editions. All the nineteenth-century versions, however, are faithful to the narrative surface of the story, whereas many of the twentieth-century versions abandon narrative surface for an emphasis on internal themes. Charles Lamb's 1811 "Beauty and the Beast," for instance, is a chronicle in iambic tetrameter; John Heath-Stubbs' 1943 "Beauty and the Beast" is a lyrical poem that extracts the tone and images of the story in order to beam an existential spotlight on the two main characters. J. R. Planché's 1841 "Grand, Comic, Romantic, Operatic, Melo-dramatic, Fairy Extravaganza in Two Acts" is embroidered with witty dialogue but takes none of the liberties Fernand Nozière does in his 1909 "Fantasy in Two Acts." There the merchant-father, his lover, the two sisters, their suitors, Beauty, and the Beast weave elaborate sexual repartee and games from the simple erotic threads of the original. Jean Cocteau's 1946 film projects the duality of nature and magic into a surrealistic vision much more introverted than Andrew Lang's room of mirrors, where Beauty sees multiple reflections of herself.

Versions of "Beauty and the Beast" expanded during the twentieth century to include opera, dance, film, radio, and television productions in addition to drama, poetry, novels, picture books, and science fiction stories. Popular dissemination has affected the tale but not necessarily weakened it. Eighteenth-century versions, for instance, are affected by the forging of folk narratives with a new literary tradition; nineteenth-century versions, by innovations in bookmaking and printing; and those in the twentieth century, by the influence of psychological interpretations, new media techniques, and mass market distribution. Yet the fact remains that "Beauty and the Beast" translates flexibly and successfully. Central aspects of the story endure from century to century, medium to medium, culture to culture, artist to artist. The content of the tale to some extent defies the form, or remains basic despite variations of form.

Whether the variations are textual, with realistic or fantastical elaboration, or visual, as in the contemporary spate of picture books illustrating Beaumont's story, "Beauty and the Beast" is still identifiable by its core elements. The tale's survival through so many re-creations would seem to demonstrate the fact that plurality does not dissipate a story but may in fact be healthy and even essential to its continuation. Living things change. Printing and reproduction have not frozen these tales. Before printing, every telling varied around a central pattern. Now multiple printed and illustrated versions still vary around a central pattern. Acting, dancing, filming, painting, cartooning have not decreased the imaginative power of the story.

Roger Sale in *Fairy Tales and After* seems to idealize the oral tradition as a high point after which the literary tradition became self- and audience-directed. The old tradition bearers, he claims, shared "a power that has been lost or debased in the latter days."[3] Yet there is little evidence that storytelling in illiterate cultures is not audience- and self-directed. Texts do not include body language, tempo, nuances of successful or unsuccessful adjustment. Storytelling at its best has always been a sophisticated craft, whatever the medium. The technological era is similar to the oral tradition in many ways. There are simply too many parallels across time among storytellers, whether they are talking, singing, acting, writing, painting, or dancing, to identify some set point of development or deterioration in the total artistic spectrum.

Jane Yolen contends in her provocative essay on Disney's version of "Cinderella" that "the magic of the old tales has been falsified, the true meaning lost, perhaps forever."[4] Although she cites persuasive evidence from current media, the effects of mass market dissemination on the shaping of a story may not justify quite such a sense of doom. We have developed a fairy tale about fairy tales, that in print or film they become culturally, textually, and graphically fixed. Some critics, including J. R. R. Tolkien and Bruno Bettelheim, have even deplored the illustration of fairy tales as further limiting them to a frozen confine. Of course, what can become fixed is, by implication, fixable, perfectible. The version of the tale closest to the oral tradition, or most compatible with a set theory, or best suited to an aesthetic definition, or simply dearest to a childhood memory is the truest. This assumption of an ideal, in either form or meaning, is not neccessarily a bad thing and may in fact figure in the story's perpetuation. Yet the power of radically different versions, the elastic nature of story, is undeniable, and, as we shall see, common to printed as well as oral versions.

Following this tale through its first centuries of printed history, in the countries that shared the earliest and greatest impact of its publication, shows that literary versions have varied in storytelling patterns reflective of the oral tradition. Certain central elements of structure have supported a range of differences in style and meaning. One can hypothesize that the same kinds of storytelling variation would surface in studies of printed versions in other languages, but this remains to be shown.[5] The following study traces "Beauty and the Beast" from its printed birth in France through its migration to England with its "author," Madame Le Prince de Beaumont, and its subsequent dissemination in primarily English and American publications often but not always considered the realm of children's literature.

Stories pass back and forth between oral and literary traditions, are told, written down, read, remembered, retold. Books go in and out of print. Celluloid deteriorates, the images made upon it fall out of fashion. A film is considered old after ten years. A book is considered old after twenty-five years, rare after seventy-five. Over the course of a hundred years, literary versions differ substantially. By folkloristic standards that is a short time. We have barely arrived at a point when enough time has elapsed to allow perspective on a story's development in literate societies. Cartoon versions can make a story affecting—or disembowel it. The criticism of popularized versions is sometimes justified. But powerful new forms accompany them as well. There is also the growing factor of mass production; as more of everything becomes available, good as well as bad, quantity itself comes under fire as potentially depersonalizing. Many criticisms of cheap, gutted, or bowdlerized versions seem based on an objection to something originally commonplace—now accepted because of age and tradition—becoming newly commonplace.

Folktales are not always profound or even coherent, much less moving. No telling is above modification. Wilhelm Grimm's tidying up tales to suit society had an impact as pervasive as Disney's. And the Grimms, needless to say, did not "fix" them, either in the sense of freezing them or in the sense of achieving a terminal ideal. It was the Grimms' versions that touched off rebellious new forms such as Anne Sexton's fairy tale poetry and Tanith Lee's fictional reworkings. The strong story is greater than any of its tellings. The core elements remain because they are magnetic to each other, structurally, and to people, variably but almost universally.

To some extent, scholars of the fairy tale have added their voices to the storytellers'. Interpretations vary as widely as versions of the tale: Freudians, Jungians, Marxists, feminists have all attributed different meanings to it. Usually these meanings are both insightful and contradictory; sometimes they are limited by an attempt to fit story into theory rather than generate theory from story; and often they do not take into account the tale's multiple variants. Whether it appears in the form of a Buddhist moral tale, a Scandinavian folktale, a French romance, an English chapbook, or an American picture book, "Beauty and the Beast" has a nucleus of elements that has survived cultural, historical, economic, and aesthetic change. The flexibility of the metaphor allows for a range of adaptation and interpretation. The story has outlived many theories and will outlast many more.

A close look at representative examples of "Beauty and the Beast" from its first printed appearance in 1740 to current editions reveals not only the persistence of intrinsic elements despite great variation of treatment, but also some patterns common to each historical period. The versions on which this book concentrates are selected for qualities both typical of the period represented and important in the tale's aesthetic development through the eighteenth, nineteenth, and twentieth centuries. Although other relevant versions, from chapbook to television production, are not excluded from the discussion, those listed below provide the main focus of examination.

    Madame Gabrielle de Villeneuve, 1740 (story)
    Madame Le Prince de Beaumont, 1756 (story)
    Comtesse de Genlis, 1785 (play)
    Charles Lamb, 1811 (poem)
    J. R. Planché, 1841 (play)
    Walter Crane, 1875 (picture book)
    Eleanor Vere Boyle, 1875 (illustrated novella)
    Andrew Lang, 1889 (story)
    Fernand Nozière, 1909 (play)
    Sir Arthur Quiller-Couch/Edmund Dulac, 1910 (illustrated story in collection)
    Margaret Tarrant, 1920 (illustrated story in collection)
    John Heath-Stubbs, 1943 (poem)
    Jean Cocteau, 1946 (film)
    Philippa Pearce/Alan Barrett, 1972 (picture book)

Diane Goode, 1978 (picture book)
Marianna Mayer/Mercer Mayer, 1978 (picture book)
Robin McKinley, 1978 (novel)
Angela Carter, 1979 (short story)
Angela Carter/Michael Foreman, 1982 (illustrated story in collection)
Deborah Apy/Michael Hague, 1983 (picture book)
Tanith Lee, 1983 (short story)
Warwick Hutton, 1985 (picture book)

The pattern of analysis for the twenty-two versions is based on a listing and labeling of every detail in Beaumont's basic story. These details fall naturally into structural functions: character (and characterization); narrative structure (action, event, plot); narrative voice (style, description, tone, point of view, theme); and symbols, objects, and images. Reorganizing the elements from their order of appearance in the story into groups according to structural function provides a prototype for examining the variations in each version and for judging its effectiveness as a whole, along with its publication format and illustration or visual realization.

There is no question that a story's sociohistorical context influences the selection and detail of its telling. Yet a story like "Beauty and the Beast," which has flourished in so many contexts, has some claim to an aesthetic examination beyond context. Although each of the next chapters reveals patterns common to versions of a group or period, the historical organization here serves primarily to trace the intrinsic elements that have made the story survive so many generations of variation and to put those elements in critical perspective. The story tells its own story.

TWO

Oral and Literary Traditions:
The Eighteenth Century

Once there was a travelling merchant who was rescued from a thieves' attack by a large dog, who nursed him back to health. In thanks the merchant promised the dog his most precious possession, never guessing the dog would choose not his fish that spoke twelve languages, not his goose that laid golden eggs, not his mind-reading mirror, but his daughter. The daughter went to the dog's house, became lonely, and pleaded to return home. The dog agreed, asking her first to tell him what she called him. "A great, foul, small-tooth dog," she said, and that was the end of the trip. Later she repented and called him "Sweet-as-a-honeycomb," which got her partway home . . . till she jeered at him and found herself back at his house. Three times they tried to make the trip. At last she got hold of the door-latch and could jeer at him safely. But then she saw how grieved he was and, remembering his kindness, called him "Sweet-as-a-honeycomb," though she need not have. At that he reared up on his hind legs, threw off his dog's head, shed his fur, and became a handsome young man, whom she married and lived with happily ever after.[1]

Once again, there was a merchant with three daughters. Setting out to buy wares, he asked them what they might like to have. While the older two asked for coats, the younger wished for a red flower. On the way back from his travels the man saw a palace garden, but just as he tore off the flower for his daughter, a winged snake with three heads appeared, threatening the merchant unless he promised to give up whatever met him first on his arrival home. The merchant's youngest daughter ran to meet him. She agreed to go to the palace of the snake, where her every wish was fulfilled. The snake even suggested she visit her family, whereupon her sisters rubbed their eyes with onions to make tears and dissuaded her from returning to him. When she finally did, he was almost dead. In grief she pulled him from the pool where he lay and, with a kiss, redeemed "The Enchanted Tsarévich."[2]

From England to Russia, versions of "Beauty and the Beast" have appeared in the European oral tradition. Among world-wide variants of the animal groom cycle, "Beauty and the Beast" is classified as tale type 425C, which Jan-Öjvind Swahn establishes in his comparative study of "Cupid and Psyche" (tale type 425A) as "entirely dependent upon literary influence."[3] "Beauty and the Beast," while undoubtedly influenced by oral tradition, became a literary tale that returned to oral tradition as a new variant. Swahn analyzes which motifs in the Villeneuve and Beaumont versions are retained by or omitted from oral tradition[4] and concludes that "Beauty and the Beast" is a subtype which entered the folk tradition from the literary, with evidence of overlapping geographical distribution of oral and printed versions. He also suggests that the influence on Villeneuve's authoring of "Beauty and the Beast" in 1740 was primarily Madame d'Aulnoy's "Le Mouton" (1721), a story containing "some motifs which are rather closely connected with folk tradition, others which seem entirely literary."[5] In "Le Mouton," the heroine is too late to save her lover, enchanted in the form of a sheep, and he dies brokenhearted. Another closely aligned literary fairy tale from the same period is Perrault's "Riquet à la Houppe," in which the ugly hero and stupid heroine redeem each other from their respective deficiencies.[6]

Tale type 425 has become one of the most intensively studied categories of Indo-European folklore.[7] *The Motif-Index of Folk Literature* identifies "Beauty and the Beast," under Disenchantment of animal by a kiss (D735.1), as related to tale types 402 (The mouse, cat, frog, etc. as bride), 425 (The search for the lost husband), 433A (A serpent carries a princess into its castle), and 440 (The frog king or Iron Henry).[8] The Aarne-Thompson *Index of Tale Types* lists "Beauty and the Beast" within section 400–459 (Supernatural or enchanted husband [wife] or other relatives), as 425C:

> Beauty and the Beast. Father stays overnight in mysterious palace and takes a rose. Must promise daughter to animal (or she goes voluntarily). Tabu: overstaying at home. She finds the husband almost dead. Disenchants him by embrace. (No search, no tasks). Analysis I b, c, d, II, III c³, V b.[9]

The analysis of 425C is this:

425. The Search for the Lost Husband
    I.   The Monster as Husband

(b) He is a man at night.
(c) A Girl promises herself as bride to the monster
(d) or her father promises her
II.   Disenchantment of the Monster
III. Loss of the Husband
      (c³) Staying too long at home
V.   Recovery of Husband
      (b) Disenchants him by affectionate treatment[10]

The Aarne-Thompson listing of variants by geographical distribution, though limited, gives some idea of "Beauty and the Beast's" range:

Finnish 12, Finnish-Swedish 3, Estonian 3, Lithuanian 30, Swedish 2, Spanish 3, Catalan 2, Dutch 1, Flemish 8, German 24, Italian 12 (incl. Tuscan and Sicilian), Rumanian 1, Hungarian 7, Czech 10, Slovenian 1, Serbocroation 1, Polish 15, Russian 8, Greek 13, Indian 1, Franco-American 3, English-American 4, West Indies (Negro) 5.[11]

Paul Delarue and Marie-Louise Tenèze cite forty-two French versions of 425C, in which they mention the most frequent supernatural spouses as being a bear, dog, serpent, pig, wolf, and "Bête" or "Monstre."[12] (The sample variant of "La Belle et La Bête" included in the Delarue and Tenèze book, in which the rose bleeds when it is plucked, appears in appendix 3.) Katharine Briggs discusses a number of British variants of 425C, among them "The Small-Tooth Dog," "Sorrow and Love," "The Stove," and "The Three Feathers," and under 425A, "The Glass Mountain" and "The Red Bull of Norroway."[13]

Versions of 425A focus on the tasks of the bride, while 425C emphasizes the beast and its transformation, an important point to remember in the upcoming comparison of "Cupid and Psyche" with "Beauty and the Beast." In an Irish version of "The Roarin' Bull of Orange" (425A), for instance, the daughter must redeem her animal lover after a long, difficult journey at the end of which she swaps magic objects acquired along the way for a night with her enchanted husband. Other Irish versions include "The Daughters of King O'Hara" and "Sgiathán Dearg and the Daughter of the King of the Western World."[14] Several subtypes of 425 abound in Scottish folklore—"The Hedgehurst," for instance, or "Kemp Owyne," Child no. 34, in which a lady transformed into a "thing of horror" is released by the kisses of her lover.[15]

Some of the related tales to appear most popularly in published form are

"The Frog Prince," "Snow White and Rose Red" (both Grimm), "East of the Sun and West of the Moon" (Scandinavian), "The Black Bull of Norroway" (British), and "Cupid and Psyche" (Greco/Roman). However, here is a sampling of others that are readily available in collections or single editions: "Belinda and the Monster" (Italian);[16] "The Lilting Leaping Lark" (German); "The Enchanted Pig" (Rumanian); "The Monkey Son-in-law" (Japanese); "Prince White Hog" (Missouri French); "Bully Bornes,""The Enchanted Cat," "Whitebear Whittington," and "A Bunch of Laurel Blooms for a Present" (Appalachian); "Monyohe" (Basotho); "Mufaro's Beautiful Daughters" (Zimbabwe); "The Princess and the Pig" (Turkish); and "The Serpent and the Grape-Grower's Daughter" (French) (fig. 1).[17]

Obviously, we are surrounded by Beauties and Beasts of every form and both genders (there is an animal bride type as well, in which a female

1. "The Serpent and the Grape-Grower's Daughter," from *French Fairy Tales*, selected and edited by Paul Delarue, translated by Austin E. Fife, illustrated by Warren Chappell. Copyright © 1968, 1956 by Alfred A. Knopf, Inc. Reprinted by permission of the publisher.

creature is transformed by a man). Although 425C is a comparatively new European variant, its relatives are very old and widely distributed in Asian, African, and Native American lore. Seen in its broadest context, this and related tale types test the boundaries between folktale, fairy tale, mythology, and literature. The elements of Greek mythology in "Cupid and Psyche," for instance, were assuredly added by Apuleius to an older folktale.[18] Amidst furious academic debates over the sources of oral lore and the revisions of art, two scholars writing from different traditions and decades stand out in their convergent perspectives.

> The märchen [fairytale] may be a myth, and that possibility brings before us the startling, and it would seem incontrovertible fact, that the myth is also a märchen, that the sanctions it has over human feelings, the appetites it satisfies are derived from the fact that—whatever else it may be—it is a good story. Its episodes are concretions of desires, at times obscure and only partly understood, which grow out of situations which are frequent in the experience of all times and places. (R. D. Jameson, 1932)[19]

> Poetry is a kind of speech which cannot be translated except at the cost of serious distortions; whereas the mythical value of the myth remains preserved, even through the worst translation. Whatever our ignorance of the language and the culture of the people where it originated, a myth is still felt as a myth by any reader throughout the world. Its substance does not lie in its style, its original music, or its syntax, but in the *story* which it tells. It is language, functioning on an especially high level where meaning succeeds practically at "taking off" from the linguistic ground on which it keeps on rolling. (Claude Lévi-Strauss, 1955)[20]

The interplay of folk and literary traditions behind "Beauty and the Beast" has a history of scholarly attention. In his discussion of the folkloristic lineage of "Beauty and the Beast" in an 1878 issue of *The Nineteenth Century*, W. R. S. Ralston cites a number of stories in which the bride or groom destroys the animal skin to keep a mate in human form. These include, from India and Central Asia, a Hindu Monkey Queen, several serpent spouses, a frog bride (from the *Mahābhārata*), marriage to an ass, and a third-century B.C. variant from Tibet in which a Buddhist philosopher turns a "husk-myth" into a moral tale about a Beauty and a Beast. In it, a lion prince with the eighteen marks of ugliness and an exceedingly powerful frame is married to a wife who is only allowed to visit at night. She sees him finally and runs but is reconciled eventually because of his merits, especially military. However, the prince sees himself reflected in a stream one day, determines to kill himself by hanging, and is saved only when Indra from heaven tells him to take courage and gives him a jewel to wear on his forehead to efface his ugliness and make him look like other men. Thereafter he returns to Beauty, who has already forgiven him his ugliness. (The Pali Kusa Jātaka is discussed in appendix 1.)

Ralston, from a nineteenth-century perspective, concludes his article with a consideration of possible origins.

> The Story of "Beauty and the Beast"—to return to the point from which we started—is evidently a moral tale, intended to show that amiability is of more consequence than beauty, founded upon some combination of a story about an apparently monstrous husband with another story about a supernatural husband temporarily lost by a wife's disobedience. And the romance of "Cupid and Psyche" seems to be a philosophical allegory based upon a somewhat similar combination of tales of an apparently Oriental character.[21]

In his discussion of "Cupid and Psyche" and related animal/groom stories, Stith Thompson declares,

> It would be much fairer and honester to say that we have no idea, and probably never will have, as to the original form of this tale and as to who made it up. And we certainly have no way of finding out what was the particular psychological state of the unknown and unknowable person who invented this story.[22]

Although the enchanted animal spouse appears almost universally, it is impossible to know what tales were familar to d'Aulnoy, Villeneuve, and Beaumont in eighteenth-century France. We can trace certain stories to a fairly specific time or place. One legend tells of a beautiful woman, Mélusine, who supposedly used magic powers to build her husband a castle at Lusignan in the Loire Valley. However, he disobeyed her prohibition against entering her room one day each week and thereby witnessed her becoming a snake, after which she disappeared.[23] Jean d'Arras incorporated the legend into a long prose romance in 1387 and Couldrette, into an early fifteenth-century poem. We know that "Cupid and Psyche" (425A) was published in France by 1648[24] and that it was disseminated through La Fontaine's "Amours de Psyché et de Cupidon" in 1669. Also popular was *Psyché, a tragedie-ballet* with text by Molière, Quinault, and Corneille and music by Lulli (court production, 1670; public, 1671). The story was commonly known in England

2. "Eros and Psyche," from *Thoughts on Outline, Sculpture, and the System That Guided the Ancient Artists in Composing Their Figures and Groupes,* by George Cumberland, engraving by William Blake, 1796. By permission of the Department of Special Collections, University of Minnesota Library.

as well. (William Blake's 1796 engraving of "Eros and Psyche" appears in figure 2.) Since "Cupid and Psyche" was generically important to the evolution of "Beauty and the Beast," a comparison of the two stories is revealing.

"Cupid and Psyche" is centered on a woman remarkably beautiful, far more so than her two sisters. Men speak of her in the same breath as Venus but do not approach her for marriage. The jealous goddess of love sends her son to punish this blossoming rival, but Cupid instead falls in love with Psyche. An oracle directs her parents to deliver her, upon a mountainous crag, to a "bridegroom . . . fierce and wild and of the dragon breed."[25] She is wafted away by the western wind to an exquisite palace, visited at night by a lover she cannot see, and eventually persuaded by her sisters to take a torch and knife to the creature ("He that lies secretly by your side at night is a huge serpent with a thousand tangled coils").[26] The light reveals Cupid but burns him as well, whereupon he flies back to Venus, who haunts Psyche mercilessly, assigning her four impossible tasks. Helped through the first three by ants, a reed, and an eagle, she nevertheless fails in the last and is rescued by Cupid, who makes a deal with Jove to arrange a legalized union, with Psyche and her baby deified, in return for Cupid's delivering the next lovely young mortal he happens upon to Jove.

The tale of "Cupid and Psyche" was incorporated by the Roman writer Apuleius into a novel, *The Golden Ass*, in the middle of the second century A.D. Georgios Megas has found Greece to be the source of the tale,[27] but similar stories may have been influential, Indian and African among them. In these the mysterious husband actually took the form of a serpent (the "viperum malum" prophesied as Psyche's fated groom), rather than remaining invisible with the sisters' merely accusing him of being a serpent. "Cupid and Psyche" is a literary tale based on folklore and serves as a good early western base for analysis in contrast to its eighteenth-century literary counterpart by Villeneuve and Beaumont. The latter reflects not only the immediate concerns of these authors and their times, but also a profound shift in the direction of contemporary attitudes. "Beauty and the Beast" is one of our most magnetic fairy tales precisely because it retains powerful old elements expressed with some profound new considerations. These at first appear to be simply a civilizing cloak of manners. It is obvious in "Cupid and Psyche," for instance, that the burning issue is sex. The mysterious husband crawls into Psyche's couch the first night and makes her his bride. She not only gets used to this situation but likes it, looks forward to her nights with him, and immediately becomes pregnant.

The aristocrat Villeneuve and the "Discreet Governess" Beaumont have firmly consigned such impulses and activities to the unconscious, from which they arise transformed into the niceties of romantic love. While the heroine's perfect beauty and virginity represent the same archetype, Psyche is helplessly unhappy that men leave her alone, but Beauty has refused offers and chosen not to marry in order to remain with her father. The mournful tone of separation from the parents and the luxurious transfer into the palace are remarkably alike in the first part of the tales. Thereafter comes a divergence: Psyche is left no choice; she is taken, while Beauty's encounter with the Beast is entirely in her own hands. Her control of the situation is emphasized over and over in the Beast's assurance that everything in the palace is hers to command, in his nightly but gentlemanly request that she consent to be his wife, and in her final realization of the affection for him upon which their union depends.

Psyche's happiness depends on compliance, first to parental force, then to her invisible lover's commands, and to her jealous future stepmother. The result of her rebellion is nearly fatal, while Beauty has the time and power to make her own decision without threat or pressure other than the Beast's proposal, which she asks him kindly to stop repeating. The ancient power of the Beast's presence, controlled by a gentle nature and respect for another individual, makes "Beauty and the Beast" appealing to modern readers. Irrepressible instincts allied with good intentions are so palatable.

In spite of the same eventual resolution—the legitimized union of male and female in marriage—the conditions determining the two women's fate are totally different. Beauty's is a test of the perception of heart and mind, while Psyche, repeatedly characterized as simple of mind, is tested for blind obedience. Curiosity consistently gets her in trouble.

Notably absent from "Beauty and the Beast" is the motif that so often appears in other subtypes, the requirement that the female obey the male in not looking at him or betraying the secret of his identity. No tasks are set for her. She is allowed to come and go, is indeed asked at first whether she came of her own free will, and is *requested* to return for the Beast's sake. The Beast assumes a passive role and Beauty an active one. The Beast basically sits around waiting to be rescued by the handsome princess as soon as she loosens her ties with home and family, especially her father (in modern coinage, resolves her oedipal dilemma). In fact, all the males in the tale—Beauty's father, brothers, and future husband—are assigned passive roles, all of them giving up Beauty, at one point or another, without asserting themselves beyond an ineffectual protest.

One point affecting the element of obedience, of course, is the acknowledgment, by the eighteenth century, that gods and royalty are two different articles. Psyche is dealing with heavenly forces, while Beauty is dealing with earthly enchantments. Still, the Greek and Roman gods were all too human, and Beauty's independence owes more to the glimmering developments of individual and female freedoms than to the dethronement of supernatural forces.

Indeed, several of the female writers of the court seemed determined to exercise certain powers of independence. Madame d'Aulnoy, a contemporary of Perrault and earlier habitué of literary circles similar to those that surrounded Villeneuve and Beaumont, carried this to an extreme. She supposedly plotted to have her husband executed for treason. Interestingly enough, "Le Mouton," her variant of "Beauty and the Beast," has the animal suitor, a ram with golden horns, killed off at the story's end. He dies pining at the palace gates while his intended is telling her story. According to a study by

Jane Mitchell, "This female dominance is found all through Mme. d'Aulnoy's tales. Even in the *contes* with titles bearing the hero's name, it is the heroine who motivates the action."[28]

After examining the text of "Beauty and the Beast" and some of Beaumont's other writings, it is impossible not to notice the conflict between her lip service to traditional feminine subservience and her surprised, ill-concealed recognition that such a condition is alterable. She is very much aware of writing for girls.

> Some will think, that the morning instructions to be given here are too serious for ladies from fifteen to eighteen years of age. But, to satisfy this objection, I need only acquaint my readers, that I have merely writ down the conversations that have passed between me and my scholars; and experience has taught me that those instructions are not above their reach. Among my young people there are children of twelve years of age that will not let a sophism be passed upon them for a syllogism, and they will tell you very gravely of a book they are reading: "The author has taken leave of his subject; he says very weak things. His principle is false; his inferences must be so." What is more my young ladies will prove it. We don't frame a true judgment of the capacity of children; nothing is out of their reach, if they are taught by little and little to form their argument, or rather to discourse on a subject. Now-a-days ladies read all sorts of books, history, politicks, philosophy and even such as concern religion. They should therefore be in a condition to judge solidly of what they read and able to discern truth from falsehood. Before I resolved to publish any thing concerning this matter, I tried two years successively what young ladies were capable of, and, after repeated trials, was fully convinced, that we are all born geometers, and that it is no such hard task to bring soon to light and to display the connate geometrical ideas of children twelve years old. To give still farther satisfaction to the reader, nothing shall appear in this work, that was not well understood by eight young ladies of that age. Their objections shall be repeated as they made them; if they are found too much above their years, the blame must not fall upon me but the young ladies, who have too much wit for their age. But as I write chiefly for their benefit, I cannot be dispensed from writing what, I know, is agreeable to them, and no ways above their reach.[29]

Beaumont's suggestions of female perspicuity are compounded, in *Letters from Emerance to Lucy*, by advice from a "fictitious" governess to one of her "fictitious" charges, who chooses an older, wiser, kinder husband after investigating the handsome profligate intended for her by her parents and finding him cruel-hearted under an imposing title and visage. There is undeniably something of "Beauty and the Beast" in this exchange, and one cannot help speculating on the influence that Beaumont's own unhappy marriage, subsequent move to England, successful career in letters, and happy remarriage had in her emphasis on Beauty's self-determination.

Beauty herself has been carefully tutored, a point reiterated in many printed versions ("Il n'épargna rien pour l'éducation de ses enfans, & leur donna toutes sortes de maîtres")[30] and does a lot of reading in her spare time. The Beast, on the other hand, characterizes himself as not only ugly, but also without wit, a reversal of Psyche's clever lord.

In view of Beauty's enlightenment, it is interesting to note the fate of her two sisters, both of whom are turned to stone, just as Psyche's sisters are destroyed by stones when they fling themselves into the abyss that has previously led them to Cupid's palace. It is jealousy that drives these two sets of wicked ladies to their fate; none of them has a life of her own, but all are dependent on a miserable bunch of husbands to fulfill their existence. Psyche's sisters complain of playing nursemaid to decaying old age, while Beauty's sisters suffer vanity and sarcasm. More explicitly, Beauty's sisters never work as Beauty does (or even play the clavichord), but simply rise at ten with empty heads, waiting for dukes to propose marriage. They are not, of course, satisfied with what they get, having neglected their inner development.

The mother figures or older women, in each of the tales, show a marked contrast to each other. Venus is as jealous as Psyche's sisters, stuck in her adolescence and loath to advance to grandmotherly status; and though as a goddess she does not suffer their fate, she nevertheless loses her campaign in the inevitable passing of time and production of her son's offspring. The "fine lady" or good fairy who advises Beauty in a dream, on the other hand, encourages an alliance with the Beast and enjoys the reunion of Beauty with her family after Beauty's acceptance of a husband. She's obviously secure in her own role—the job of encouraging and rewarding youngsters for their "judicious choices" of growing up, and does not envy Beauty's becoming queen. Had she appeared as Beauty's mother, there would have been the problem of how she could encourage her daughter to leave home to be eaten by a beast. And of course Beauty's conflict between caring for her father and caring for the Beast would not have been so clear-cut. Beauty's key oedipal dilemma is totally missing from Psyche's story, though it crops up strongly in Cupid's. As it is, the older woman in Beauty's life represents quite a reformation of the archetypal jealous mother-in-law to the archetypal fairy godmother. The French tutor had a different point to make than the Roman traveler, and the woman saw the story differently from the man.

Secondary characters aside, it becomes clear how much the myth of "Cupid and Psyche" has diverged, in "Beauty and the Beast," into the delicacies of amour courtois: the male serving female, the female saying no, the male suffering faithfully of lovesickness, the female saying yes. Cupid is indeed burned by love, but much against his will, and by the light of Psyche's forbidden awareness, not by any sensibility of his own. Psyche is brought to happiness by obedience and trial; hers are outer obstacles while Beauty's are inner conflicts resolved by free will. However deceptive such advances may appear to some modern feminist commentators,[31] the change is profound and undeniable.

The literary tale of "Beauty and the Beast" both affected and was affected by oral tradition. There is much debate over the literary recasting of folklore to include newly created dimensions. Marguerite Loeffler-Delachaux says in *Le symbolisme des contes de fées* about the purpose of archetypes:

> L'Absence des archétypes ou "images ancentrales" dénonce d'une manière absolument claire le conte truqué ou le conte inventé par des auteurs naïfs qui ont cru pouvoir substituer leur propre imagination aux produits du psychisme universal.[32]

> [The absence of archetypes or "ancestral images" exposes with absolute clarity the false tale or the story invented by those naive writers who believe they can substitute their own imagination for the products of the universal psyche.]

Beaumont's archetypes in "Beauty and the Beast" seem intact: neither the principles nor the supporting cast have been weakened from archetype to stereotype, nor have they been confined to an era by overspecification. But her heroine has discovered a room of her own in her alliance with the Beast. As was written on her door in his palace,

> Welcome Beauty, banish fear,
> You are queen and mistress here:
> Speak your wishes, speak your will
> Swift obedience meets them still.[33]

Psyche may have become a goddess, but Beauty became a relatively free human being—one reason, perhaps, that Beaumont's fairy tale has traveled so widely in the twentieth century. She has not lost traditional forms by incorporating too many refined details but has emphasized a basic new element in the story.

There is no question that the eighteenth-century version of "Beauty and the Beast" homogenized elements from ancient animal groom or bride stories and, in publication, dominated geographical, cultural, and historical variants orally transmitted in most parts of the world. That domination crystallized certain aesthetic, psychological, and social implications of the story, only a few of which have been pointed out in this comparison to "Cupid and Psyche."[34] While the focus of this book is on more subtle aesthetic changes in published versions of "Beauty and the Beast" through the eighteenth, nineteenth, and twentieth centuries, it is important—for a full understanding of the story as we know it today—to bear in mind its background, age, and the widely scattered appearance of its motifs. For despite dissimilar details and themes, "Beauty and the Beast" does share with "Cupid and Psyche" (1) a lead cast of Bride, Groom, and Bride's family and (2) a plot involving the Bride's journey that tests the strength of her love through either endurance or perception. Both characters and narrative structure common to the stories provide strong symbolic support for cultural, historical, and thematic variation. Even more important than the differences in the stories is the fact that the elemental story survived these changes.

Of course, the tale type index has long shown such patterns for a widely varied spectrum of oral narrative. Many candidates for the tale type index have not survived in literary treatment, however, and the fact that "Beauty and the Beast" has done so is significant in itself. Moreover, the question remains as to what effect the modern *printed tradition*, with its emphasis on the individual invention of author and artist, has on the respect for and retention of a story's basic elements.

The three eighteenth-century versions of "Beauty and the Beast" examined next, all French and all published in English translation, are as dissimilar as their folkloric and literary ancestors were. Yet each of the three prefigures later versions by writers who, in some cases, could not possibly have known about them. Perhaps, as Northrop Frye claims,

> art has not evolved or improved: it produces the classic or model. One can still buy books narrating the "development" of painting from the Stone Age to Picasso, but they show no development, only a series of mutations in skill,

Picasso being on much the same level as his Magdalenian ancestors. Every once in a while we experience in the arts a feeling of definitive revelation.[35]

Although Madame Gabrielle de Villeneuve's 1740 version of "Beauty and the Beast" was the first, Madame Le Prince de Beaumont's 1756 version became the classic model for most later works, including, almost immediately, a play by Genlis in 1785 and an opera by Marmontel and Grétry. The opera, *Zémire et Azor*, gained a great reputation

> and even gave rise to a tragedy at Marseilles. There, in 1788, the public insisting upon two daily representations of the opera instead of one, something like one of our own O.P. riots took place. Soldiers were introduced into the theatre, making their appearance during a duet sung by the Beauty and the Beast. The pit resented the intrusion and insulted the military, who replied by a volley which killed some of the audience and wounded more. The next day the piece was prohibited.[36]

Madame Gabrielle de Villeneuve's version appeared in *La jeune amériquaine, et les contes marins* and was reprinted in volume 26 of *Le cabinet des fées, et autres contes merveilleux* (1786), an unillustrated book of which "Beauty and the Beast" takes up 187 pages. One of the few unabridged English translations now available is Ernest Dowson's 1908 *Story of Beauty and the Beast*, used here for analysis.

Villeneuve's development of a complex explanation, 75 out of 187 pages, of the Beast's enchantment and Beauty's lineage complicates the number of characters and their relationships. The large cast includes the merchant-stepfather, twelve children (six sons and six daughters—all unnamed except Beauty), Beauty herself, the Beast/Dream Prince, a Dream Lady/fairy, a queen (the prince's mother), the King of the Happy Isles (Beauty's father), the Queen of the Happy Isles (Beauty's mother/Dream Fairy's sister), the Bad Fairy, the Mother of Seasons (grouchy old fairy), and the Queen of Fairies and her young daughter by the sage Amadabat. This group is extensively described if not developed. The prince's haughty queen mother, for instance, shocked at what she believes to be Beauty's low birth, exclaims after all Beauty's redeeming love for the prince, "What! You are only a merchant's daughter!" The Dream Fairy reprimands her.

> For you, Queen, the little value that you set upon virtue, unadorned by empty titles, which is all you esteem, would justify my heaping the bitterest

reproaches on you. But I pardon you your fault, on account of the pride which your rank inspires in you. . . .[37]

There is a mixed message in the Dream Fairy's insistence on Beauty's deserving an engagement to royalty by virtue of her goodness, however. On the next page, the truth comes out.

> . . . Beauty is no other than your niece, and what should render her still more worthy of your regard is that she is my niece as well, being the child of my sister, who did not, like you, worship rank, when virtue was absent from it. This fairy, then, knowing how precious was true worth, did the King of the Happy Islands, your brother, the honour of marrying him. I preserved the fruit of this union from the fury of another Fairy, who wanted to be the child's step-mother [and later, lover]. (P. 69)

If this seems complicated, it is a mere nutshell version of a very complex story within a story, as the plot outline shows.

1. Father's loss of wealth
2. Beauty's request for the rose
3. Father's journey to recover wealth
4. Storm and Beast's castle
5. Father's plucking of the rose and Beast's demand for retribution
6. Beauty's journey to the castle and father's departure
7. Beauty's first dream of a recurring series
8. Palace life and Beast's nightly proposals
9. Beauty's two-month leave at home
10. Beauty's return and revival of Beast
11. Queen Mother's arrival
12. Prince's story, told with the Dream Fairy's help
    a. Prince's king/father died
    b. Queen Mother campaigned against attacking monarch for many years
    c. Bad Fairy was appointed prince's protector, journeyed away several years
    d. Bad Fairy returned to seduce prince as he came of age
    e. Prince rejoined queen, rejected Bad Fairy's proposal
    f. Bad Fairy turned him into Beast with conditions of enchantment

13. Arrival of King of the Happy Isles (Beauty's father)
14. Beauty's story, told by Dream Fairy
    a. King married fairy-shepherdess (sister of Dream Fairy), had baby
    b. Fairy Queen was cast out of fairy circle for marrying someone of lesser powers; kept from returning to husband; baby (Beauty) sentenced to marry a monster
    c. Disguised as neighboring widowed queen, Bad Fairy tried to seduce bereft king, assume Beauty's education
    d. Bad Fairy conspired to kill Beauty, marry king
    e. Dream Fairy in shape of bear killed would-be assassins, abducted Beauty, swapped her for merchant's dead baby in country cottage
    f. Disguised as gypsy, Dream Fairy foretold Beauty's fortune to merchant
    g. Bad Fairy returned to try and seduce prince (12d)
    h. Bad Fairy was sentenced to disgrace
    i. Beauty redeemed Beast (10)
15. Beauty's Fairy Queen/mother's appearance, with story
    a. Imprisoned many years by fairies
    b. Agreed to undergo "ordeal of the serpent" in place of young daughter of Fairy Queen and sage Amadabat
    c. Was released to rejoin family
16. Beauty's step-sisters' and their husbands' arrival from hunt
17. Beauty's merchant/stepfather's arrival
18. Marriage and dispersal to various sovereign duties
19. Stepfamily given work at court

Villeneuve's plot is mechanically ingenious. It must have cost some effort to account for everything so completely. The outline cannot do justice to her obsessive attention to detail. The father's weakness is attributed to the ancient prediction that his daughter would be the means of saving his life and his fortune. The prince's beastly enchantment will not end until "a young and beauteous maiden comes of her own accord to seek [him] out, fully persuaded beforehand that [he is] going to eat her" (p. 79), and conceives a tender affection and proposes to him, without the Beast's ever revealing his identity. Neatly dovetailed into this is Beauty's sentence by the fairies: "Let [the Fairy Queen's] daughter, the shameful fruit of her illicit love, become the bride of a monster, to expiate the folly of a mother who had the frailty to let herself be captivated by the fleeting and contemptible beauty of a mortal" (p. 97).

Although these machinations may become tedious to a modern reader, there is a kind of jigsaw puzzle fascination to them, as well, and considerable humor in effects that must have contained some intentional irony. Perhaps the funniest elaboration of actions is the actual redemption sequence, which, needless to say, is not limited to a simple kiss and transformation. Beauty returns to find the Beast languishing, revives him, goes to bed for another dream meeting with her prince-lover, then finally accepts the Beast's proposal next evening in response to his usual "May I sleep with you tonight" (p. 35), whereupon they pledge their troth and enjoy three hours of fireworks. This is only the beginning.

> However slight was Beauty's impatience to find herself by the side of her most singular mate, she nevertheless got into bed. The lights went out immediately. Beauty could not help fearing that the enormous weight of the Beast's body would crush the bed. She was agreeably astonished to find that the monster placed himself at her side with as much ease and agility as she had herself sprung into bed. Her surprise was even greater still on hearing him begin to snore forthwith; presently his silence convinced her that he was in a profound sleep. (P. 60)

Upon arising, Beauty does indeed discover the Beast has turned into her dream lover, but he is sleeping so soundly that he does not respond to any of her ministrations. She shakes him, checks the sleeping form against her dream-lover's portrait to make sure it is the right prince, and kisses him three times. Still he slumbers. It is not until his *mother* arrives that the prince finally opens his eyes. "He had been awakened by the arrival of his mother and the Fairy, the noise that they made having had more effect upon him than all the efforts of Beauty" (p. 65).

While the story is told by an omniscient third person, the reader is keenly aware of the writer through her style, details, tone, and themes. The elaborate descriptions of theater, opera, art galleries, library, and mirrors reflecting "all that was taking place in the world" (p. 39), of the "avenue of orange trees" and myrtles, attendant monkeys, and conversational parrots project a specific fantasy world belonging more to romantic novels than to fairy tales. There is the illusion of time passing rather than the statement of it, and levels of reality are suggested in a sophisticated layering of fictional mimesis, magic, fantasy, dream, and story within a story (more exactly, a tale of fairies within a fairy tale).

Although there are no asides to the dear reader, the Dream Fairy so repeatedly hammers home her points to the characters that Villeneuve's identification with that character is clear. The deception of appearances and the importance of gratitude are high on a long list of admonitions explicitly attached to the characters' actions. Beauty's central conflict is the reconciliation of love and duty. She proves her honor by recoiling in horror from her beloved dream-prince when he suggests the removal of the Beast who discomfits her. Another typical lesson comes after the prince's condemnation to a beastly form.

> My mother decided to stab herself, and I to fling myself into the adjacent canal. . . . On the way, however, we were met by a lady of majestic mien and form, whose manners inspired profound respect, who stopped us and bade us remember that it was a cowardly thing to succumb to misfortune, and that with time and courage there was no calamity which could not be remedied. (P. 80)

There is even a discreet plug for the monarchy when Beauty and the prince offer to abdicate, stay at the magic castle, and let the Fairy choose new sovereigns while they enjoy life.

> But that wise intelligence represented to them that they were under as great an obligation to fulfill the destiny which had confided to them the government of a nation, as it was the duty of that same nation to preserve for them an eternal respect. (P. 117)

One is relieved to learn, however, that in spite of their noble duties, Beauty and the prince do manage regular retreats back to the castle, during the several centuries of their mortality, in a chariot drawn by twelve white stags with horns and antlers of gold.

The effect of such a multiplicity of fantastic detail is to obscure the actual magic. The ring, for instance, loses its striking significance, the rose fades in the shade of orange trees and myrtles. The magic chests are not as important as their elaborate contents. The mirror is one of many in a labyrinthian palace that reflects Beauty from all sides and mirrors the world as well. Its significance in showing her father's illness diminishes to a minor vision among myriad views.

In stark contrast is Madame Le Prince de Beaumont's seventeen-page version in *Le magazin des enfans* (fig. 3), which appeared in 1756 and was translated in *The Young Misses Magazine* in 1759. From Villeneuve's "Beauty and the Beast," Beaumont cut three major areas which had added greatly to the length but not to the effectiveness of the story. The first was the extensive description of Beauty's entertainments at the magic palace. The second was the dream sequence in which the prince and a fairy appeared to Beauty encouraging her not to be deceived by appearances. The third was the story within a story of Beauty and the Beast's separate backgrounds. The result was the version of "Beauty and the Beast" so widely known and reflected in literature, with the characters important to the elemental plot: the merchant-father, children (three sons, three daughters, of whom only Beauty is named), Beauty (the youngest daughter), the Beast/Prince, the two husbands of the elder daughters, and a helper (the dream fairy).

The characterization is almost archetypal. Beauty is the standard female child protagonist, her inner goodness manifested by outward appearance.

3. Frontispiece and title page of *Le magasin des enfans, ou dialogues entre une sage gouvernante et plusiers de ses élèves de la première distinction,* by Madame Le Prince de Beaumont, 1756. By permission of the E. W. and Faith Collection of Juvenile Literature, Miami University Libraries, Oxford, Ohio.

(In English, we have dropped the first article in "Beauty and the Beast" to turn Beauty into a name, but in French, "La Belle" remains a generic term like "La Bête.") She twice expresses fears of being eaten by the Beast, a creature all the more horrifying for its unspecified nature.[38] Beauty's two older sisters are malevolent, greedy, proud, and jealous. Their punishment is tailored to their crime: they must stand as statues forever witnessing Beauty's success. Beauty's father is ineffectual and her mother is dead.

In the two main characters, however, there is some probing of archetypal surfaces, a shifting of the symbolic to the psychological. The Beast, who is first seen as repulsive, is in the end seen *before any transformation*, as irresistible. He is an ostensible villain who turns out to be vulnerable and even heroic in beastly form. Propp says that villainy "is exceptionally important since, by means of it, the actual movement of the folktale is created."[39] In Beaumont's "Beauty and the Beast," however, the plot initially—and primarily—hinges more on the lack of a hero. Indeed, The search for the lost husband (tale type 425) might better be termed, in 425C, The search for the lacking husband. At best, the hero is an unlikely one in traditional terms. The Beast's task is patience; Beauty's is perception. Beauty, first seen as infinitely desirable, finds herself desiring, and this most loyal daughter turns out to be a promise-breaker, acting in a beastly manner toward a true friend. Before her final choice, one is attracted to the Beast and impatient with Beauty, a development uncharacteristic of folktales or even Villeneuve's version, in which the Dream Prince and Fairy reassure and direct Beauty in her choosing. Both Beauty and the Beast are subject to ambivalence and development that are more characteristic of real life than of fairy tales.

Beaumont's plot is streamlined: the father loses his wealth and moves his family to the country. He subsequently journeys to recover one ship and retrieves the sisters' requested gifts, is lost in a storm, and finds the magic palace. When he takes a rose for Beauty, the Beast demands his life, but Beauty offers hers instead and goes to the palace for three months, where she refuses nightly dinnertime proposals of marriage and requests leave to visit her sick father for one week. When Beauty returns home, her sisters deceive her into overstaying, but she dreams on the tenth night of the Beast's death and returns to declare her love. The Beast is transformed into a Prince and the two are married, while the sisters are punished.

The narrative structure is a simple action sequence of cause and effect. Beaumont's formula is event no. 1 and its effect on the characters, leading to event no. 2 and its effect on the characters. After the first several rounds— loss of wealth, the news of the ship, and the father's picking of a castle rose—

those events and their effects on the characters follow each other inevitably to a climax. In accordance with C. S. Lewis's ideal, the events or plot are the theme here, or in Roger Sale's words, "by saying what happens in the story, one is almost saying what the story means."[40]

The story's happenings, the surprises, come very close to the quality of its "surprisingness," so that it can be read over and over without disappointment.[41] There is repetition in the Beast's proposal and even an obligatory rhyme thrown in, although in no rhythmic pattern. Finally, Beaumont has crowned her events, as d'Aulnoy did not do in her tragic "Ram," with eucatastrophe, the "joy" Tolkien selects "as the mark of the true fairy story (or romance), or as the seal upon it."[42]

The third-person omniscient point of view is complemented by a spare, formal style. The theme of virtue rewarded and envy punished is stated but not overstated. Detail is limited to a few telling embellishments. Although the tone is French court/salon romantic, the tale sticks closely to folk motifs, and the telling maintains a powerful simplicity free from the specific localization that marks later art fairy tales, which often name place, time, and characters. The setting for the Beast's castle is a wild forest, where Beauty's father gets lost during a storm. Beaumont's restraint in presenting such common symbolic elements serves to open Tolkien's "door on Other Time" and allows for that personal imaginative elaboration that "is at once more universal and more poignantly particular."[43] She has also stayed within Tolkien's boundaries of "simple or fundamental things, untouched by Fantasy"[44] in spite of the greater discipline this requires in terms of the story's consistency of logical development. When Beaumont does embroider, it is pithy and very much to the point of plot, as in the case of the sisters' hypocrisy: "Those wicked creatures rubbed their eyes with an onion to force some tears when they parted from their sister. . . . "[45]

Each magic object has a limited but vital role in the story. The rose motivates Beauty's modest request, her father's action, and the Beast's reaction. The chest conveys the Beast's wealth to Beauty's family. The mirror shows Beauty her father's loneliness and tempts her home. And the ring conveys her back to the Beast. While these four objects have a complex symbolism to be discussed later, their symbolic ramifications are not embroidered in the story but are contained to a naive usefulness. With whatever literary and social inventions Beaumont decorated the folk tradition, her version was direct and essential enough to perpetuate the tale in a new kind of modern folk or popular-culture proliferation.

The Beauty and the Monster: A Comedy from the French of the Countesse de Genlis Extracted from the Theatre of Education of Isaiah Thomas, 1785, is a tiny three-by-five-inch pamphlet of thirty-five pages without illustration. It is significant that the story's first century in publication had no graphic depictions in any of the versions, allying it with the oral tradition of leaving the details of appearance to the listeners' imagination. Comtesse de Genlis's comedy in two acts of five scenes each is the first in a succession of plays, poetry, novellas, art, music, and films based on Beaumont's "revised standard version." Genlis's work is not literal but pared down to theme, some episodic variations, and the two main characters, with a commentator.

The characters, Sabina, Phedima (a friend of Sabina's), and Phanor ("a Genius"), are neither developed to the extent of Villeneuve's nor archetypal in the mode of Beaumont's. Sabina represents the figure of Beauty, but her history and situation are quite different. Phedima acts as the chorus, telling the audience what is going on and interceding between Sabina and Phanor, a Beast figure monstrous but sporting a wit and manner not allowed the two earlier Beasts. With both characterization and action limited to exclamatory dialogue, the piece is less a fairy tale than a romantic sit-com, a genre to which "Beauty and the Beast" lends itself several times in the nineteenth and twentieth centuries.

The opening and closing scenes show just how far Sabina has developed. Phanor begs her to stay for a moment's conversation, but after a glance at his face she declares "Oh Heavens!"[46] and runs away. When Phanor appears at the end in his princely form, Phanor says "Ah Sabina! recollect Phanor by the excess of his tenderness," to which Sabina replies, "Oh Heavens!" (p. 36).

However, despite the limitations of her own intelligence, she does have the goodness to respond to Phanor's. As Phedima notes to Phanor, "Sabina has sensibility, a delicate understanding, and a grateful heart: merit and virtue must make deep impressions upon such a temper as hers, and you have every thing to hope from time" (pp. 7–8). Later, to Sabina, Phedima remarks, "But it is your understanding that pleases him, your disposition which has captivated him. If you were ugly, he would still love you" (p. 15), a point never ventured in other versions.

There are two villains of the piece, but neither appears outside explanations to further the plot, as in Phanor's monologue:

Cruel fairy, thou enjoyst the excess of my sorrow: Thy power, superior to mine, has hitherto condemned me to support life under this hideous form;

and I cannot resume my original figure, but by making myself beloved, and in this frightful shape gaining a heart which has been hitherto insensible. (P. 5)

Later, Phedima reveals much about the ideal lover by describing the opposite, Sabina's former betrothed: "The object of her hatred possessed all the charms of the most seducing figure: But he was deficient in understanding and more so in delicacy; he was an ignorant rustick, without one promising quality" (p. 8).

There is almost no action in the play, which proceeds in a series of posed conversations. Sabina encounters Phanor and flees in horror as Phanor laments his evil enchantment. Phedima and Phanor swap notes, including Sabina's background (she was engaged by relatives to a handsome but insensitive suitor when Phanor, overhearing her plight, abducted her to his palace). Phedima and Sabina discuss the palace, a "sacred asylum" with gates forever open "To All The Unhappy." After the three converse on their way to a play, Sabina admits Phanor's attractions of disposition, manner, and wit. Confused, she decides to leave the palace. Phanor gives Sabina a magic ring and then leaves the palace himself so she can stay on protected from the world and unsullied by his ugly presence. Sabina opens the ring box to wish herself wherever Phanor is, finds a suicide note, and declares her love (and her own suicidal intentions), whereupon Phanor reappears in his proper figure.

Just as Phanor's situation is revealed in a rhetorical exclamation to an offstage character, Sabina's emerges through a stilted conversation between Phedima and Phanor: "An orphan, and tyrannized over by cruel and unjust relations, she was about to be sacrificed to their ambition, when fortunately you came and carried us off" (p. 8). Later, Phanor recalls the details of the meadow where he overheard Sabina, retreating from her birthday celebration, confess her unhappiness to Phedima "at the foot of a palm tree" from which Phanor spirits them away. Sabina herself states one of the conditions that every version of "Beauty and the Beast" seems to have in common, an emphasis on the redeemer's choice: "But it must be friendship, and not necessity, that can make me determine to remain here" (p. 24).

When the action is incorporated into direct exchanges, events unfold much more naturally than through dialogue or asides attempting to inform the audience of the story's background. Phanor, for instance, gives Sabina the magic ring, by putting which upon your finger, you will find yourself transported to whatever place you choose; and there, by the power of this same ring, everything you wish will be realized; palace, gardens, containing whatever is most beautiful in art or nature, of which you will be the sole mistress. (P. 31)

Unfortunately, since there is so little action, the play doesn't seem to move past the explanatory stage until the rather touching exit of the three characters to a play (within a play), when Sabina makes her first concession: "Phanor, will you give me your arm?" (p. 21) at the very end of act 1.

The suicide notes are a clever device for capsulizing the Beast's near-fatal decline during Beauty's absence, her declaration of love, and his consequent transformation. "I know that my presence must be disagreeable to you, and I cannot endure life absent from you; I therefore renounce it without reluctance" (p. 33). Sabina responds in kind: "The wretched Sabina will follow you. Yes, Phanor, I loved you; and cannot exist without you" (p. 34). With this the prince appears on a throne of flowers.

Suicide, while it is implied in the folk tale tradition of an animal's grieving and pining (or in some cases, being injured or slain by the beloved), is peculiar to the literary fairy tale in its deliberate, violent forms accompanied with theatrical statements of intention. In d'Aulnoy's "Ram," the heroine even kills herself after the animal dies. Suicide also figures in Villeneuve's portrayal of the Beast/Prince and Queen Mother in their depression over his enchantment. In general, folktales are too concerned about survival for such antics.

While there is no narrative voice here, Phedima has a role similar to Villeneuve's Dream Fairy in her interventions, wise vision, and explication of themes. It is she who softens Sabina's fears: "Learn, however, that this horrid figure which you dare not look on, conceals a feeling, delicate, and faithful heart" (p. 4). She eases Phanor's impatience: "Only think, it is but eight days since you carried us off; and, to speak plain, I must say that more than eight days are necessary to be reconciled to your figure" (p. 7). And it is she who summarizes for readers or listeners the concluding moral: "Ye feeling, virtuous hearts, never complain of your fate; and may this example teach you to know, that goodness and benevolence are the surest means of pleasing, and the only claims to love" (p. 35).

Phedima epitomizes the perspective, good sense, and even humor the author no doubt attributed to herself. Since the characters, action, and objects (only a magic ring) are reduced, with the fairy tale plot structure gone, this version amounts to a thematic struggle over issues of the heart, upon which Phedima/Genlis expounds in an elevated, courtly tone allowing for no mistakes on the part of the audience as to her importance, as well as that of her message.

Villeneuve, Beaumont, and Genlis share a tone of decorous formality, affirm an ideal of courtly love, and emphasize the female protagonist's right to choose. All three were conscious "cultural representatives" bent upon delivering a message, but only Beaumont did not lose the story in doing so. While Villeneuve's "Beauty and the Beast" is entertaining for students of the period, its primary importance is as a gene-carrier from earlier stories, passing on a genetic code responsible for a more important creation. Without Beaumont, "Beauty and the Beast" would not have had memorable impact on the following centuries, but without Villeneuve, "Beauty and the Beast" would not have had memorable impact on Beaumont. Villeneuve's version then, however flawed by tedious abundance of detail, was crucial. By contrast to Villeneuve, Genlis has sacrificed or altered both motif and detail till the story's structure becomes wobbly.

Beaumont maintained basic, sturdy elements that passed on the story's deeper sense, whatever her educational purposes, and yet translated it meaningfully into a modern tradition. "Beauty and the Beast" reflects a transition not only in framework and meaning, but also in audience. It was, in deference to a newly invented "childhood," written explicitly for children; yet it contained concerns of adult life such as sex and marriage that were excluded by the new definition of childhood. During a period when oral and written forms began to overlap as never before, Beaumont took elements of both and melded them into a story of lasting significance, forming a vital link between folk and literary traditions.

More important than her own artistic influence, however, is the noticeable pattern of story elements retained in three such dissimilar eighteenth-century literary versions: the central characters, the simple but symbolic narrative, and certain images which at first seem minor detail but with cumulative appearances begin to acquire metaphoric weight—storm, rose, garden, mirror, ring. The measure of each version's effectiveness is not its cleverness of invention but its fidelity to these core elements.

THREE

The Impact of Bookmaking and Illustration: The Nineteenth Century

As early as 1804, "Beauty and the Beast" began its popular literary proliferation in the form of chapbooks, toy book series, and nursery tale pamphlets.[1] The majority of versions were in brief fairy tale form—Beaumont's own, though she is rarely acknowledged—and were illustrated and intended for children, a new and sturdy book market even if adults were the buyers. The dichotomy between instruction and entertainment as an aim in these books is obviously a conflict for the adult buyers rather than the child consumers. This dichotomy affects the literature of "Beauty and the Beast" from its inception and throughout the nineteenth century as surely as it affects children's books today. An 1843 chapbook has commentary to this effect by Felix Summerly:

> Every age modifies the traditions it receives from its predecessor, and hands them down to succeeding ages in an altered form, rarely with advantage to the traditions themselves. The modern English versions of Beauty and the Beast, adapted "to the manners of the present period," are filled with moralizings on education, marriage, etc.; futile attempts to grind every thing as much as possible into dull logical probability; and the main incidents of the tale are buried among tedious details of Beauty's sisters and their husbands. I have thought it no sin to get rid of all this, without regard to Mrs. Affable, and to attempt to re-write the legend more as a fairy tale than a lecture.[2]

Of course, Mr. Summerly proceeds to develop his own peculiar and forgettable details after lopping off those of his predecessors, but nevertheless he is aware of the problem.

Invariably, the versions that opted for entertainment were the most interesting, memorable, and aesthetically important, and it is those literary versions that passed along the deeper tradition of "Beauty and the Beast" to the twentieth century. The more determined were writers to impress a lesson, the less impressive was their writing. It is the story, with images from the art often accompanying it, that transmits the theme for later, totally divergent, interpretations or lessons. The following five versions, while very different, have proved durable.

The first is *Beauty and the Beast: or a Rough Outside with a Gentle Heart, A Poetical Version of an Ancient Tale,* which is attributed to Charles Lamb. There is some question, debated at length in Andrew Lang's introduction to an 1887 reprint of the 1811 edition, as to whether Charles Lamb actually wrote this version of "Beauty and the Beast." However, the work seems typical enough of several other children's books known to be his that the dispute is irrelevant. "In the style of Charles Lamb" will have to suffice. Graphically, the book is comparable to many other nineteenth-century versions. It is 5" x 6", with 3" x 3" engravings (see frontispiece), and forty-two pages in length (about 12–15 lines per page). But unlike most versions, it is in rhyming couplets of iambic tetrameter. The characters are pared down to a poetic minimum of merchant, three sons and three daughters (unnamed except for Beauty), and the Beast, identified in the conclusion as Prince Orasmyn from Persia.

In addition, there is a "Power" or "heavenly voice," rather than a fairy figure, that takes care of explanations and directions at the end. Much of the development takes place through dialogue between Beauty and the Beast.

> "Am I not hideous to your eyes?"
> "Your temper's sweet," she mild replies,
> "Yes, but I'm ugly, have no sense:"—
> "That's better far than vain pretence"—
> "Try to be happy, and at ease,"
> Sigh'd Beast, "As I will try to please."—
> "Your outward form is scarcely seen
> "Since I arriv'd, so kind you've been."[3]

This passage, an exchange during Beauty and Beast's first meal alone, is quickly followed by a recognition of the relationship's growth during the following three months, "One quarter of the rolling year" (p. 29).

That she her Father's life had sav'd
Upon her heart of hearts was grav'd.
While yet she view'd the Beast with dread,
This was the balm that conscience shed.
But now a second solace grew,
Whose cause e'en conscience scarcely knew.
Here, on a Monster's mercy cast,—
Yet, when her first dire fears were past,
She found that Monster, timid, mild,
Led like the lion by the child.
Custom and kindness banish'd fear;
Beauty oft wish'd that Beast were near. (P. 30)

While the characters maintain a kind of naive objectivity in the spirit of Beaumont's, there is a delicate implication of their growing intimacy quite frequent in the poem. If the appointed hour of nine o'clock passes without the Beast's appearance, "Twas mark'd by Beauty with a sigh" (p. 31). Beauty does a good deal of sighing:

Beauty for fairer evening sigh'd—
Sigh'd for the object once so fear'd,
By worth, by kindness, now endear'd. (P. 36)

And the Beast matches with a bland patience.

Sat humble, or submissive stood,
Or, audience crav'd, respectful spoke,
Nor aim'd at wit or ribbald joke,
But oftener bent the raptur'd ear
Or ravish'd eye, to see or hear. (P. 31)

These two may have been dull company, but they are obviously well-suited, as Beauty finally discovers.

"Ah! fond and faithful Beast," she cried,
"Hast thou for me perfidious died?"

"But no! my grievous fault forgive!
"I feel I can't without thee live."

And, lo! a Prince, with every grace
Of figure, fashion, feature, face,
In whom all charms of Nature meet,
Was kneeling at fair Beauty's feet. (Pp. 37–38)

The protest against any kind of aggression, including wit, is strong throughout the work and coupled with the ideal of dutiful contentment with one's lot. Beauty is called "The Child of Duty," and her song is revealing:

"Ah, no! in days of youth and health,
Nature will smile, tho' Fortune frown:
Be this my song, Content is Wealth,
And duty every toil shall crown." (P. 8)

Here is the first mention of a theme significant in all the nineteenth-century versions and negligible or absent in both the previous and following centuries: a frequent reference to Fate and Fortune, their controlling whims, and the necessity of human adjustment to them.

—Fortune still,
Unkind and niggard, crost his will; (P. 12)

but when eleven
Struck on his ear as mute he sate
It sounded like the knell of Fate. (P. 14)

"That stolen branch has seal'd thy fate." (P. 17)

But no man can his fate controul. (P. 21)

This motif, along with the personification of Nature as an omnipresent other force, is so recurrent in the nineteenth-century versions and so alien to the folk or art fairy tale background of the tale, that it is remarkable how accommodating is the old to the new. Clearly, one reason for the popularity of "Beauty and the Beast" during the first commercial expansion of printed materials was the ease with which the narrative and cast lent itself to popular ideas of the day without sacrifice of the story's basic integrity.

In 1811, cheerful acquiescence equals goodness, not only in virtuous Beauty but also in Beast's behavior. "Fairy-work" and courtly love get barely a nod as affection is otherwise defined in terms of suffering and fidelity.

> "And visit Beast a volunteer
> To suffer for thee, thou mayest live" (P. 18)

> "And O, a thousand deaths I'd prove
> 'To show my father how I love!" (P. 20)

> "Thy vow was giv'n, thy vow was broke!"
> Thus Conscience to her bosom spoke. (P. 35)

Although these themes are explicit, the narrator is not passionate about them but observes a kind of detached commentary not overly burdensome to the narrative. The plot is Beaumont's with some slimming of detail. The comfort dream is eliminated, while the warning dream is compact—"And a sad vision broke her rest!" (p. 35). Equally concise are descriptions of the palace summed up in Beauty's inspection of "Sweet gardens of eternal green; / Mirrors and chandeliers of glass" (p. 25).

Despite the didactic overtones, the pace is brisk and the statements pithy, an effective combination. The sisters who have conspired to destroy Beauty through provoking the Beast's rage at her postponement are meted swift justice: "Transformed to statues you must dwell, / Curs'd with the single power, to feel" (p. 41).

There is no dwelling on magic, either. The mirror is for information, the ring for transport. When the sisters commission their profusion of gifts, Beauty's simplicity is echoed in the narrative style: "Considerately good, she chose, / The emblem of herself,—a Rose" (p. 11). Only once or twice is the poet carried away to extend a few images—perhaps, one feels, to give some antique dignity to the whole, as in the Latin epic-simile.

> Blest times! but soon by clouds o'ercast!
> Sudden as winds that madd'ning sweep
> The foaming surface of the deep,
> Vast treasures, trusted to the wave,
> Were buried in the billowy grave.
> Our merchant, late of boundless store,
> Saw Famine hasting to his door. (P. 5)

The eight delicate engravings precisely balance the text's formal restraint and narrative content. Line work is meticulous and compositions simply focused on the main character, with some architectural structure hinted in backgrounds. Each picture is captioned in meticulous script:

1. "Beauty in her Prosperous State" shows Beauty, attired in Empire gown, reading on her break from clavichord practise as her sisters strut to the rear.
2. "Beauty in a State of Adversity" deposits Beauty before a spinning wheel in a rustic background and homey bonnet.
3. "The Rose Gather'd" portrays a turbaned father clutching his roses in recoil from a snarling bear-like Beast.
4. "Beauty in the Enchanted Palace" has father and daughter clasped in theatrical poses of fear as the now amiable and curious-looking Beast peeks around the dining room doorway as if to see what his own fate has brought.
5. "Beauty Visits her Library" features the heroine's striking Grecian profile as she approaches her book shelves.
6. "Beauty entertained with Invisible Music" approaches the fanciful, with three angelic figures hovering over Beauty's noon repast.
7. "The Absence of Beauty Lamented" shows a grieving Beauty flinging herself toward the moribund Beast, with Ionic garden columns looming behind (frontispiece).
8. "The Enchantment Dissolved" reveals the Prince, garbed in a strange assortment of ruffles, cape, doublet, hose, boots, and feathered turban, kneeling before the Grecian robed figure of Beauty, who stands somewhat startled beside a large urn.

Civility is the hallmark of these illustrations, and the Beast's wildness is kept to an unthreatening minimum; in size, for instance, he is smaller than the humans, or in position lower. The art reflects the same measured care and reassuring certitude as the poem—like Lamb's Beauty and Beast, a perfect match.

The intent of Mr. Lamb and his contemporaries' chapbooks is so serious that it is jolting to step thirty years later into the levity of J. R. Planché's *Beauty and the Beast: A Grand, Comic, Romantic, Operatic, Melo-dramatic, Fairy Extravaganza in Two Acts* (and, it might be added, a *Spoof Royale*). A 6 1/2" x 4" book of twenty-two pages, unillustrated, the drama is written in rhyming couplets of iambic pentameter, with puns, word play, popular tunes, and jibes or in-jokes calculated for a laugh from the adult audience at Covent Garden Theatre on Easter Monday, 12 April 1841.

Most of the character and plot embellishments are more relevant to the times than to the story; yet the entertaining quality is undeniable once a reader becomes accustomed to the sophisticated tenor and unexpected digressions. The dramatis personae are listed on the first page.

> Beauty—Madam Vestris
> The Beast, alias Prince Azor—Mr. W. Harrison
> Sir Aldgate Pump (Beauty's Father)—Mr. J. Bland
> John Quill—Mr. Harley
> Dressalinda—Miss Rainforth
> Marrygolda—Miss Grant
> Queen of Roses—Miss Lee
> Zephyrs—Mr. Gilbert and Master Marshall
> Esprits de Rose—Misses Ballin, Marshall, and Fairbrother
> Members of the Parliament of Roses; Zephyrs (in Waiting);
> Nobles and ladies of court of Prince Azor, etc.

All the characters carry a load of ironic commentary on their own and others' plot functions. The sisters are a prime example of what could be the narrator's feelings in reaction to the fatiguing virtue of earlier Beauties.

> "It makes me mad to hear our sister Beauty
> Say we should be content, and prate of duty,
> And resignation, and that sort of stuff—"[4]

> "That's all she's fit for—with her wax-doll's face." (P. 7)

When the two sniff the merchant's possible windfall, they maneuver him into asking what they want.

> Dress: "Oh, any trifle that falls in your way—
>   A 100 guinea shawl suppose we say.
> Marry: "Oh; sir, I wouldn't think of asking you
>   To buy a shawl for me—that were too rash—
>   I'll take a hundred guineas, sir, in cash."
> Sir Ald: "One's for mere cash, the other for Cashmere." (P. 8)

And when Beauty returns home for the visit with her father, the sisters express characteristic disgust.

> Dress: "Hasn't the Beast then eat you after all?
>   Has he consented back his prey to render?
>   Were you too tough?—or has he been too tender?

Law, Papa, pray don't be so pathetic,
To me such stuff is worse than an emetic." (P. 23)

The Beast himself appears with a song somewhere between folkloric fee-fi-fo-fum and pre-Gilbert and Sullivan chorus.

"Tremble you! Tremble you!
Who dare to pluck my roses,
I'll tear ye limb from limb, and with
    your bones the church-yard strew.
Tremble you! Tremble you!
On turtle soup and punch, rogues,
You've made a hearty lunch rogues,
Now I will lunch on you, lunch on you,
    lunch on you." (P. 12)

Later, he remarks that if Beauty destroys the spell, he will jump out of his skin with joy, and he sings "My love is like a red, red rose." In addressing her, he proposes "Drink to me only with your eyes, /If you object to wine" (p. 19), after reassuring Sir Aldgate that he "wouldn't eat her without her consent." Even Beauty enters into the lively repartee, singing her affection for the Beast to the tune of "Jim along Josey" and answering him tit for tat in their several scenes together. At her most serious, she does declare a theme of sorts, "That I have been the Beast, and he the Beauty!" (p. 28). Most of her comments, however, twist and turn with the others.

Sir Ald: "Accomplished creature!—and, can understand
        What you do read?
                        Affirm that quite, I wouldn't—"
Beauty: "Because, at times, e'en those who write it couldn't!" (P. 8)

The plot itself offers a number of possibilities for diversion, all of them seized on. After a conversation between Zephyr and Roses, the Queen of Roses enters to open the "Parliament of Roses" and present the "Easter Question," with summary facts of the story. This scene fades into one where the two sisters converse about Beauty. Their father enters with good news of a lost ship's arrival and sends "faithful drudge" John Quill after a chaise and four. En route home from the failed vessel, Sir Aldgate and John Q. stumble into the Beast's abode and get quite tipsy at the lunch provided. The Beast enters, Sir Aldgate fetches Beauty, and Beauty and the Beast parry. The Spirits of the Rose and Zephyrs, with the Queen of Roses, appear, dance, and give Beauty sweet dreams. Beauty develops a relationship with the Beast, sees her father in the glass, and requests one day, until sunset, away from the Beast. The sisters administer "poppy juice" to her after the homecoming. Beauty naps past sunset and the Beast laments his false one, while Sir Aldgate and John Q. get tipsy again. Beauty wakes, returns to the palace, and finds the Beast dying. Just as she starts to wish him alive to marry her, the Queen of Roses appears, double-checks Beauty's intentions, and revives the Prince, with court.

The story within a story allows a good deal of political satire, with mention of "foreign flowers" and a "treaty with the King of the Carnations." In fact, an opening speech is directed at the throne:

> Queen of Roses, we'll take care
> To lay before this honorable House the affair:
> If we can get two acts pas'd, without its being nettled,
> The Beast will be *re-formed*, and the Easter question settled;
> No rose, here that blows,
> Will vote against a measure, ma'am, that you propose. (P. 6)

This, after a chorus of "Coal Black Rose," perhaps a reference to the problematic coal mining reform act that was passed four months later in August 1842, against opposition in the House of Lords.

The setting is London, and the talk is of the "Change." The palace gets only a passing glance ("It's a lovely place to live in," p. 17), while the "Bower of Roses *not* by Bendemeer's Stream" and the house called "Pump's Folly," to which the family has fallen from former Lord Mayor Sir Aldgate's previous Mansion House ("from Threadneedle Street to Brixton," p. 6) is vivid. That ubiquitous nineteenth-century figure, Fortune, appears several times as both malicious and sportive. And a magic omnibus ("Time Flies. No Stoppages") with a Zephyr for a driver offers half-hour transport to and from the Beast's abode upon a turn of Beauty's ring ("This beats the railroad out and out, I vow. / This is a way to ring the changes now!" [p. 22]). The extra, John Quill, allows a good deal of badinage about problems with Sir Aldgate Pump's handle and the lack of brains that master and servant attribute to each other.

The Queen of Roses offers Beauty one of the few condolences ever extended for her perpetual disconsolation at losing her Beast.

> Why this surprise?
> 'Tis love hath so improved him in your eyes!
> Where the mind's noble, and the heart sincere,
> Defects of person quickly disappear (P. 28)

If this is meant as a redeeming moral, it is buried in so much raillery that the effect is lost—fortunately, for those Victorians sick of sentiment and searching for a good show. Needless to say, what they allowed themselves and what they allowed their children were two different stories.

Walter Crane's Toy Books, a shilling series published by George Routledge and Sons, were considered by him "as a sideline, essentially belonging to the days of his youth"[5] and all completed before his thirtieth year. They included, besides "Beauty and the Beast," other tales such as "Princess Belle Etoile," "The Yellow Dwarf," and "The Sleeping Beauty," all treated in the same format of twelve pages, 10" x 8 1/2", with full-page illustrations and large print (plate 2).

The striking characteristic of both the text and art for Crane's 1875 "Beauty and the Beast" is heavy outline, apparent in both narrative and design, and probably accounted for by his apprenticeship to a wood engraver to learn the craft of drawing on the wood, a process he continued even after photographic techniques simplified the stages of transferring an original design to the printed page. Always, his preparation included a finished outline drawing, whether on wood or later, card, with color added on black and white proofs from which a printer made separate blocks for each color.

The characters are reduced to the essential merchant/father, three daughters (two unnamed, and Beauty), Beast, and unnumbered sons mentioned in the course of the plot as offering to go in Beauty's stead. There is no fairy, no commentator or chorus, and no comfort or directive dream. The narrative, stripped down and modernized, proceeds at a breathless pace that has a summary quality, well-demonstrated by the tightly packed information of the first paragraph.

> Once upon a time a rich Merchant, meeting with heavy losses, had to retire to a small cottage, with his three daughters. The two elder grumbled at this; but the youngest, named Beauty, tried to comfort her father and make his home happy. Once, when he was going on a journey, to try to mend his fortunes, the girls came to wish him good-bye; the two elder told him to bring them some nice presents on his return, but Beauty merely begged of him to bring

her a rose. When the Merchant was on his way back he saw some fine roses, and thinking of Beauty, plucked the prettiest he could find. He had no sooner taken it than he saw a hideous Beast, armed with a deadly weapon. This fierce-looking creature asked him how he dared to touch his flowers, and talked of putting him to death. (Unpaged)

Here are no ships, no detailing of gifts, no scenes of departure, no forest or storm or discovery and overnight stay in the palace. The magic, when Beauty arrives, is confined to "the doors opened of themselves; sweet music was heard, and they walked into a room where supper was prepared." During her stay at the palace, a sentence is spent on each wonder: birds, monkeys, works of art. Even the recurrent rhyme has lost its poetic form: "Beauty is Queen here; all things will obey her." This is a style neither elaborated in the art fairy tale mode nor distinctive in the folklore tradition, but cold, with more clichés than conventions. The ring and the rose are reduced to utilitarian purpose, and there is no theme or moral represented, even in the ending.

> The moment she had uttered these words [the troth], a dazzling light shone everywhere; the Palace windows glittered with lamps, and music was heard around. To her great wonder, a handsome young Prince stood before her, who said that her words had broken the spell of a magician, by which he had been doomed to wear the form of a Beast, until a beautiful girl should love him in spite of his ugliness. The grateful Prince now claimed Beauty as his wife. The Merchant was soon informed of his daughter's good fortune, and the Prince was married to Beauty on the following day.

The real purpose of this literature is its decoration. Of the twelve pages, half are illustration, with four full-page pictures and one double-page spread. These feature the merchant's confrontation with the Beast, the merchant's return to his family with the rose, Beauty and the Beast conversing on a couch, Beauty followed by elegantly coutured apes, and Beauty administering to the dying Beast. The predominant color is a cheerful red. The solid black lines set off geometrically balanced shapes. There is no white space at all in Crane's illustrations, but a rich detailing of color, pattern, and textural design. Stylized postures and expressions are the rule. This is a Versailles castle garden setting. There is no wildness in either the setting or the Beast, a cloven-booted boar that wears a monocle. The costume is eighteenth-century French court, but Beauty's profiled face minus its feathered hat reveals lines from Greek pottery. Emotion is not absent, but it is held within stylized boundaries, all subjected to elements of design, composition, and ornament.

Crane was sometimes criticized for drawing "from his head" rather than using live models, a practice resulting in some less-than-realistic figures. He lived and worked at the same time as Randolph Caldecott, but modern picture books have gone more in Caldecott's direction of characterizing people and projecting action than of adhering strictly to formal design and ornamentation, which will become apparent in the editions of "Beauty and the Beast" published during the 1970s. Ultimately, Crane's art and story have a bold surface but little depth. They do not exactly stifle an imaginative response; yet, after an initial pleasure in their striking appearance, one feels the lack of subtleties that typify both the text and art of some earlier versions—Lamb's, for instance—subtleties that imply much more than is specified, allowing leeway for individual reaction.

The contrast between Crane's book and Eleanor Vere Boyle's *Beauty and the Beast: An Old Tale New-Told,* published in the same year (1875) by Sampson Low, Marston, Low and Searle, is remarkable. A fifty-seven-page novella of enchantment, Boyle's version is illustrated on almost every 10" x 8" page by delicate black-and-white engravings and ten white-bordered, 5" x 7" color plates (plate 3). The bookmaking is exquisite, with embossed binding, designs bordering the text, well-spaced print, and brilliant reproduction. Both art and story are wrought with detail, but with a timeless sense that expands rather than limits the tale's potential.

The characters are presented descriptively, with minimal dialogue: a merchant, three sons and three daughters (unnamed except for Beauty); the Beast; a dream comforter who also appears in the end as the Beast's queen mother, a "sweet and noble lady"; and the sisters' husbands. Beauty is depicted as saintly as well as lovely—"and she withheld not her small hand from succouring the most ill-favoured of earth's children."[6] In contrast to her tender care of the sick, the forlorn, and even the lowly herbs of the plant world, "the splendour of the merchant's daughters cast a cold shadow" (p. 5) in spite of their appearance: "One, like a dusky night, black-haired and brown-eyed—the other, bright as the morning, with long tresses of red gold" (p. 1). To the merchant, Beauty is "dearer moreover than all else beside, save only his gold." His greatest pride is the "many-oared galleys and full-sailed ships" which come into port laden with precious merchandise.

When the blow falls, the "brothers knit their brows, and spake no word good or bad; only, they laid by in the great painted chest, their swords, and gay clothes of furred mantle and plumed caps, and went to toil in the fields" (p. 9). These same brothers at the end "became most noble knights, and greatly renowned for the destroying of many pagan knights and giants, and of divers fell beasts and griffins of that time" (p. 57), while the sisters "came never near that happy house." Their fates are nearly as bad as metamorphosis into stone:

> The elder had espoused a very proud and learned man, but poor; and by him she was greatly despised. And the younger had for husband a rich man, of very seemly person, who cared nought for other goodliness than his own; and had scorn for his wife, withal she was so fair. (P. 45)

The plot is very little altered from Beaumont's.

1. Days of wealth, proposals, and feasting
2. Ruin and removal to an old seaside fortress remaining to the merchant in a distant fishing village
3. Beauty keeps house and tends goats
4. Rider announces return of ships
5. Beauty's request for a white rose
6. Ship burns at quay as merchant arrives
7. Merchant journeys home, is lost in storm
8. Enters gate, plucks rose, confronts Beast, given one-half year to bring daughter
9. Returns home for six months, then goes back with Beauty
10. Beauty's three years at palace
11. Beauty wanders to a far fountain, sees home tower, deserted, in reflection
12. Requests leave and promises to return in seven days
13. Reunion with father (sisters married, brothers "gone away with many of that land to fight for the Holy Sepulchre")
14. Arrival of envious sisters, who plot Beauty's death
15. Tenth night, Beauty dreams Beast is dying
16. Returns, waits through day, seeks Beast under tree by fountain, calls him her only love
17. Transformation

What distinguishes this version is neither character nor plot, but Gothic style, imagery, and tone. There is a rhythmic quality to the telling, with occasionally a biblical cast.

It was a dark and windy night, the night when they came there, in the season of the year that leaves first turn from green to gold, and barley sheaves stand in the fields, and the vintage is done. (P. 10)

For wit you well, the winter rasure [*sic*] of such like cankers, may not approach the green summer, wherein the flower of true love flourisheth. (P. 57)

The natural world is the predominating presence here; there is an almost pantheistic obsession in the landscapes and descriptions of nature. Wild doves, thrushes, nightingales, "dark cypress spires," fir trees, arbutus trees, fruit trees, acacias, myriad garden flowers, all get sensuous attention with chiaroscuro effects.

Under the shadowy dark-stemmed trees blood-red lilies burnt with a sultry glow. Here and there, in the blackness of some deeper gloom, pure star-like flowers, poised on tall slender stalks, gleamed white and ghostly. (P. 22)

Boyle has, with words, predated many of Cocteau's filmic effects of creating shades of reality via shades of light and dark. White roses, white moths, winter white, an approach to the palace flooded with light/dark contrasts, all lend a dream tone to the story, in which the nature of dream and reality gets specific reference. "Beauty's life passed on dreamfully" (p. 39). Her appearance to her father seems to him a dream, as had his first palace experience and his return to it with Beauty. "A dreamlike brightness seemed to mingle silverly about the dusk of evening" after the transformation (p. 52), "yet was it to her as the fulfillment of some dear dream in old forgotten, long-past days" when the prince holds her (p. 53). Time is suspended during "three twelve months—which in that spell-bound place seemed but one summer long" (p. 39). The season changes from winter to summer as the merchant first passes through the palace gate. It is autumn on the day of Beauty's return to the dying Beast, summer after the transformation that evening.

Fate is another constant presence in Boyle's work:

But fortune is not always kind, and there be many winds both fair and foul; and black days there be, when the Fates send forth a wind, which blows no good to any living soul. (P. 7)

Fortune hid her face, and the world hid hers, for it had come to pass that the rich man, was on a sudden, poor . . . ruin and unhappiness had crept up to the door, and, like a deadly snake, enfolded all her father's house. (P. 9)

Bad luck still clave fast to the ill-starred merchant. (P. 18)

They fared forth together on their fateful way. (P. 30)

And as though constrained by some dreadful fate, he slowly departed. (P. 36)

After a long description of the landscape surrounding the seaside tower where the merchant moves his family after their fall, Beauty calls her sisters to "behold with her this glorious new wonderland where Fate had led them" (p. 11). Even the small engravings reflect Boyle's preoccupation with nature, dream, and fate. They often echo not a literal aspect of the story but a figurative one. A downcast monkey holds a bedraggled peacock feather on the page describing the sisters' bitter disappointment at their father's return without their requested finery. A beetle catches a smaller insect with its pincers on the page where Beauty's six months of life dwindle (or so she supposes) before her sacrifice for her father. A cherub playing a horn to a frog appears on the page describing Beauty's nightly conversation with the Beast (fig. 4). A moth emerges from its chrysalis on the page of the Beast's transformation.

The paintings themselves are, at their best, haunting. There are ten, most captioned from the text. Significantly, the first is the weakest, a sentimentalized visual preface meant to bridge the different realities of the child reader and the story. In this instance, as always, self-conciousness about the nature of childhood seems to mar aesthetic effect.

1. Once, on a cold March day, the little maid ran down to the outer court with her new scarlet cloak, to wrap her friend the old watchdog in!
2. In the king's garden the feast is ready and the minstrels wait.
3. The merchant found a little door in the wall, and he opened it and went into the Beast's garden.
4. Upon the strange prickly leaves some one had curiously carved Beauty's name.
5. At dawn, a lady came to comfort her.

4. *Beauty and the Beast: An Old Tale New-Told*, by Eleanor Vere Boyle, 1875.
By permission of the Newberry Library, Chicago.

6. After supper every night, the Beast asked Beauty to be his wife:
   and every night she said him nay.
7. One sister's husband, like Narcissus of old, worshipped his own
   beauty; but the other was full of learning.
8. Only the ravens in the brake saw the sisters' rage, and heard them
   plot her death.
9. "Ah, dear Beast!" she said; "alas, that my unkindness should thus
   slay thee!" (Plate 3)
10. Love is the magic that makes all things fair.

Boyle's backgrounds are distinctly Italian in landscape, costume, and
architectural detail. Italy was a popular retreat for artists of the day (Crane
spent several years there after his marriage), and Boyle might have traveled
there as well. Hers may be the only sea beast ever used to illustrate the tale, a
sort of walrus/seal figure in black with no human features of face or body.
Several panels of a bedroom scene are decorated with sea creatures, and
deep green is a predominant color throughout, though more specifically in
vegetation than in any ocean scene. Boyle's work echoes the pre-Raphaelite
theme of "Truth to Nature," with the backgrounds for the Beast's appearance
to the father, for the sisters' mortification during the visit, and for Beauty's
declaration to the Beast showing extraordinary attention to details of unusual
foliage. On the other hand, the theatrical poses, centered lighting effects,

Renaissance drapery, and interiors framed with arches and columns all contribute to a sense of the illustrations as stage settings.

What strikes one most forcefully about Boyle's version of "Beauty and the Beast" is her investment in recreating a complete world, both in picture and story, which approaches the conception of a novel without quite leaving the realm of fairy tale. There is a richness here that draws a reader in, an alliance of text and illustration that is stamped with romantic artistry.

*A*ndrew Lang's version of "Beauty and the Beast," which appeared in the *Blue Fairy Book,* 1889, is unquestionably the most widely known in the last decade of the nineteenth century and, next to Beaumont's, the most influential on twentieth-century readers as well. It is therefore intriguing to discover that Andrew Lang only commissioned and polished the adaptation of an obscure writer. As superintendent editor of eleven variously colored fairy tale collections (1889–1910), Lang employed, with special reliance on Mrs. Lang, a bevy of ladies to prepare the texts. In the case of "Beauty and the Beast," "Miss Minnie Wright reduced the novels of the Cabinets des Feés from the original to the proportion of nursery tales."[7] She conscientiously abridged Madame Villeneuve's several-hundred pages to twenty, a task completely subsumed in Lang's name and reputation.

Ironically, Andrew Lang felt his work as a scholar in the Folk-Lore Society might be overshadowed by the famous fairy tale series and wrote "urbane and occasionally patronizing prefaces" that appear "slightly dismissive of the whole enterprise."[8] Whatever his feelings on the subject, however, the series was of enormous importance in rejuvenating an interest in fairy tale reading for children, temporarily obscured by "the child's story of real life."[9] The contemporary *Bookseller* called the *Blue Fairy Book* "amongst the most popular juvenile gifts of the time," and its stories were excerpted for a series of school editions, Longmans' Supplementary Readers, which spurred many imitative collections.[10] Its success immediately generated a commission for further volumes in red, green, yellow, pink, lavender, etc., a packaging gimmick that assured a market among parents looking for the stamp of familiar value and among children who love to collect almost anything.

The wide distribution and popularity of the books did not prevent some detractors from commenting on Lang's editorial style. Tolkien's remarks about Lang are revealing: "I will not accuse Andrew Lang of sniggering, but certainly he smiled to himself, and certainly too often he had an eye on the faces of other clever people over the heads of his child audience."[11] Evidence of this will surface here in the examination of "Beauty and the Beast."

5. "The Enchanted Pig," from the *Red Fairy Book*,
by Andrew Lang, 1890. This edition edited by Brian Alderson and
illustrated by Faith Jacques. Copyright © Faith Jacques, 1976.

Several folk variants of the animal groom tale type appear in the series,
among them "The Black Bull of Norroway" (425A), "East of the Sun and West
of the Moon" (425A), and "Snow White and Rose Red" (426) in the blue
volume and "The Enchanted Pig" (425A) in the red (fig. 5). Lang's long
introduction to the 1887 reprint of Lamb's 1811 edition features considerable
commentary on the story's possible origins and geographical distribution.
His discussion of universal creation (invention) versus transmission (diffusion) reflects one of the major conflicts among folklorists of the time. The fact
that he himself, as a collector, reduced so many folk- and fairy tales to a
similarity of style did not seem to dismay contemporaries who included
Joseph Jacobs and E. S. Hartland.[12]

While the substance is Minnie Wright's, then, the style is Lang's, and the
responsibility for its final form is his, a fact reflected in the following references to him as source in this examination of the text. Villeneuve's elaborate
cast of characters has been reduced to the staple merchant, six sons and six
daughters (unnamed except for Beauty), the Beast, a Dream Prince, a Dream
Lady, and the Prince's queen mother. The merchant is presented as a weak
man: "Being naturally timid, he began to be terrified by the silence"[13] in the

seemingly deserted castle. When the Beast demands one of his daughters, his response is not entirely a clearcut negative. "'Ah!' cried the merchant, 'if I were cruel enough to buy my own life at the expense of one of my children's, what excuse could I invent to bring her here?'" (p. 113). This ostensibly paves the way for the Beast's condition of voluntary sacrifice but in effect ascribes some personality defect as reason for the father's action in handing over Beauty, a slight psychological probe not apparent in any serious earlier versions.

Beauty is being tested primarily for her courage. "See if any of them is courageous enough, and loves you well enough to come and save your life," says the Beast (p. 113), and she proves herself both in her assumption of the punishment ("But as I did the mischief it is only just that I should suffer for it," p. 115) and in her confrontation with the Beast, during which she collects herself, addresses the Beast, and even comforts her trembling father, reassuring him several times with humor or reason. "'The Beast must be very hungry,' said Beauty, trying to laugh, 'if he makes all this rejoicing over the arrival of his prey'" (p. 116).

The dichotomy of weakness and courage is somewhat different from Villeneuve's theme of moral virtue, although remarks on gratitude, honor, and perception have been condensed from her long tirades. "Be as true-hearted as you are beautiful, and we shall have nothing left to wish for," says the Dream Prince (p. 118), who appears to her nightly along with a Lady who warns, "Only do not let yourself be deceived by appearances" (p. 119). Other abbreviations include the exchange between this Dream Fairy and the queen, who has no quibbles over Beauty's mercantile background in the age of the captains of industry.

> "Well, Queen, this is Beauty, who has had the courage to rescue your son from the terrible enchantment. They love one another, and only your consent to their marriage is wanting to make them perfectly happy."

> "I consent with all my heart," cried the Queen. "How can I ever thank you enough for having restored my dear son to his natural form." (P. 128)

Villeneuve's plot, too, has been shortened by the omission of that endless explanation of Beauty and the Beast's family histories, although the dream subplot is still present and some of the palace activities are echoed in brief description. In fact, this version represents a cross between Beaumont's narrative brevity and Villeneuve's enthusiasm for detail.

1. The merchant's house burning down, his ships lost at sea, his clerk's infidelity, all lead to poverty
2. Family retreats to house in desolate place (a "dark forest")
3. News of ship, rose request, merchant's departure
4. Merchant's six month's journey, failure, return in winter
5. Arrival at castle, overnight lodging
6. Plucking of "the fatal rose" (p. 12)
7. Beast appears, condemns merchant (who blames Beauty)
8. Beast gives merchant one month, dinner, and orders him to leave after "you see the sun and hear a golden bell ring" (p. 114) on Beast's horse
9. Merchant returns home, tells story; recriminations; Beauty's decision
10. Father and Beauty ride to palace (she on Beast's horse)
11. The two pack trunks with treasure for family at Beast's invitation
12. Dream Prince consoles her, begs her to find him out
13. Beauty explores palace, finds bracelet with portrait of prince
14. Dinner with Beast and proposal
15. Beauty finds setting of brook with myrtle trees where Dream Prince appeared; wonders if he is prisoner of Beast
16. Beauty enjoys sewing room, aviary (magically removed near her room at her wish), pantomime, and seven other "windows of entertainment"
17. After a "long time," Beauty realizes Beast is gentle, requests visit to father, dreams of prince grieving
18. Wakes up at home, reunion, father recommends following Beast's wishes as interpretation of Dream Prince's requests
19. Beauty two months at home, bored, with no dreams of prince; but puts off departure for father and brothers' sake
20. Dream of dying Beast/stately lady ("See what happens to people who do not keep their promises," p. 126)
22. Beauty returns to palace, waits suppertime, searches for Beast, finds him in a cave ("I was dying because I thought you had forgotten your promise," p. 127)
23. Beast rests up and proposes at dinner; Beauty accepts; fireworks
24. Prince appears
25. Chariot arrives with two ladies, the Dream Fairy and the queen
26. The wedding ("and the marriage was celebrated the very next day with the utmost splendour, and Beauty and the Prince lived happily ever after," p. 129)

Like Villeneuve's, this narrative is strongly flavored with avenues of orange trees, agate steps, unseasonal blooms, skywriting by fireflies ("Long live the Prince and his Bride," p. 128), mirrors, galleries, musical instruments, library books, and wondrous objects—roses in winter, a magically swift horse that "seemed to fly rather than gallop" (p. 115), the infinitely capacious two trunks and later four boxes that move themselves in spite of their impossible weight, the ring that fulfills wishes at its turn on a finger.

As Tolkien observed, Lang lightens the tone with humorous asides—in the merchant's indulging his children, for instance: "As he had, however, six sons and six daughters, he found his money was not too much to let them all have everything they fancied, as they were accustomed to do." Often his philosophical observations relate neither to the story nor to the children reading it. He casts sly little aspersions slightly at odds with a straightforward fairy tale rendering: "The first room she entered was lined with mirrors, and Beauty saw herself reflected on every side, and thought she had never seen such a charming room" (p. 119). The effect of these telling comments is actually a kind of narrator's ironic distance, certainly not unique to this version of "Beauty and the Beast" but striking in relation to Lang's serious involvement with folklore and fairy tales, and influential on the public's conception of a story they considered to be presented in its "authentic form" by a widely published authority.

Lang's version, twenty-two pages of a 5" x 7 1/2" book, is illustrated by H. J. Ford with competent but unremarkable black-and-white pen drawings, one full-page and four half-page. These depict:

1. A bearded father and shepherdess-frocked Beauty in a departing embrace, the sisters enshadowed on the cottage porch.
2. A hairy-faced, enraged beast with elephant trunk and tusks, mule ears, and clawed hands threatening the robed merchant (fig. 6).
3. The dream of Beauty conversing with her prince in a garden.
4. A Victorian-gowned Beauty surrounded by parrots, toucan, etc., greeting her by name.
5. Beauty reviving the Beast with water in a cave.

It is somewhat ironic that the most influential "Beauty and the Beast" to emerge from a publishing field exploding with new technologies is the least attractive of the nineteenth-century storybook versions examined here. (One of the most attractive, Adelaide Doyle's translation, illustrated by Dick Doyle in 1842, was never published but remained in manuscript form for 131 years–figs.) It is also telling that the force behind Lang's best-selling collection was a packaging/distribution scheme that captured the public imagination and pocketbook. Aesthetically, however, nineteenth-century readers had a startling variety and amount of exposure to "Beauty and the Beast."

Several patterns seem to emerge from the five representative versions by Lamb, Planché, Crane, Boyle, and Lang. All but one are by men, in contrast to the women writers of the eighteenth century, and that ratio of four to one

6. "Beauty and the Beast," from the *Blue Fairy Book*, by Andrew
Lang, 1889, illustrated by H. J. Ford. By permission of the
Department of Special Collections, University of Chicago Library.

7. *Beauty and the Beast: A Manuscript by Richard Doyle*, 1842.
By permission of the Pierpont Morgan Library, New York.

seems an approximate reflection of the story's nineteenth-century author-
ship. In most cases, the men have elaborated and personalized their adaptations much less than the women. Although there are hints of the story's
dream/reality dualism, these remain unexplored, as do most of the symbolic
and psychological implications. While somewhat less formal than the eighteenth-century versions, the nineteenth century's nevertheless maintain an
objective distance from characters and reader. The importance of Duty, Fate,
and Nature is a common theme.

Both texts and illustrations often feature an Eastern setting with Moorish
costume representing the period interest in Persian art and philosophy,
which generated the popular translation of Omar Khayyám's *Rubáiyát* in
1859, along with debates on Manichaeanism and Zoroastrianism. The projection of the East as mysterious, exotic, and romantic makes it a more appropriate backdrop for magical tales than industrializing Victorian England. Illustration is certainly the major innovation of the century, and as graphics
become more elaborate in the late 1800s and sometimes the sole reason for a
new edition, one sees reasons for Ruskin's "belief that painting, not poetry,
has greater power to express and move a modern mind."[14]

The nineteenth-century literary versions show a great divergence in
narrative voice. Tone ranges from somber to farcical, detail from elaborate to
nonexistent, style from poetic to brusque. Moral instruction asserts itself, but
so does irony and artistic delicacy. Yet characters and narrative structure vary
little from Beaumont's. Whether the elements of the story are elaborated
visually or textually, they have remained noticeably stable throughout a
century of enormous artistic and technical change. The printed tradition has,
in many ways, reflected the oral. In publication, the story inspires popular
dissemination, and the dissemination further popularizes the tale until, by
the end of the century, it has become a standard reference point in modern
western culture.

FOUR

The Story Internalized: 1900–1950

Five versions of "Beauty and the Beast" spanning the first half of the twentieth century reflect clearly the shock-waves that separated an old era from a new one. A popularized article on the period summarizes:

> The First World War promised to put an end to all wars, but succeeded only in putting an end to Victorian taste, manners, and morals. Sentimentally puritanical novels gave way to mordant, exotic ones; schmaltzy Franz Lehar's melodies bowed to the cynicism of Cole Porter and the syncopation of Gershwin; the soft, undulating curves of art nouveau somehow or other turned into the hard, angular style of art deco; and the notion that duty must take precedence over all other considerations was replaced by a frenetic search for personal fulfillment, regardless of the consequences.[1]

The two twentieth-century versions of "Beauty and the Beast" published prior to World War I (along with several others not discussed here) have a leisurely, entertaining, externalized quality whether child or adult is the intended audience. The one immediately following World War I represents a new kind of separation of the child's world from the adult's, with a segregated literature for the former. The two following World War II incorporate existential, psychological motifs that turn the story inside out, with Cocteau's film also prefiguring the technological complexities that characterize the post-1950 versions. Throughout this historical buffeting, the literary tale thrives, sometimes in its simplest form, sometimes vastly expanded, but always as recognizable as it seems malleable.

In his preface to *Three Gallant Plays*, Fernand Nozière reflects perfectly the relative lightness characterizing prewar versions.

In these dramas there is no discussion of anything except love. There is no dealing with the passion that tortures and kills, but merely the delineation of the delicate intoxication. . . . I maintain that it is permissible to feel enthusiasm for measure and moderation.[2]

Fernand Nozière, born Fernand Weyl and introduced to literary circles through articles and dramatic criticism as André Fagel, thrived on romantic dramatizations of old stories. "Beauty and the Beast" was first performed for guests of Comte Robert de Clermont-Tonnerre at Maisons-Lafitte in 1909, by which time Nozière was a well-established figure in French salons for a score of plays such as the other two in *Three Gallant Plays*—"Byzantine Afternoon" ("set at a time when 'costumes were beautiful and morals were low,'" p. xxv) and "The Slippers of Aphrodite."

The play itself, a "Fantasy in Two acts," is 112 pages long, symmetrically divided into fifty-six pages per act, and set in the oriental palace of Mansour the merchant and in the garden of the Beast. There are nine characters: the Beast, Mansour (rich merchant, seventy), Opal (his oldest daughter, twenty-two), Ruby (his second daughter, twenty), Turquoise (his third daughter, seventeen), the Fairy of Tolerance, Violet (a slave, sixteen), Rock (a young financier, twenty-five), and Yeroum (a young poet, twenty-two). While the characters are representative, they are too vital to be called stereotypical. Each character, to some extent, is made sport of, along with the audience and society at large. The repartee builds up substantial personae. Violet, for instance, the slave who has survived her misfortunes by bartering her beauty, projects her philosophy in a dialogue with the two sisters.

Only the gods are immaculate, and perhaps their reputation is exaggerated. . . . I was thrown suddenly into wretchedness. Such a plunge often breaks one's conscience, which is a luxurious and fragile trifle. (P. 111)

The Fairy of Tolerance establishes herself with lightning remarks. When offered refreshment, she savors the sweets and refuses the black bread: "No, I must keep my figure . . . I am the Fairy of Tolerance, not of Exposure" (p. 119). In disbelieving the freshness of the Beast's six-month-old rose for Beauty, the Fairy declares, "Excuse me, but I always doubt any supernatural thing unless I have caused it myself" (p. 124). This Fairy, as a counterpart to the dream comforters or friendly advisers of earlier versions, rather neatly summarizes that role in relation to Beauty, here called Turquoise, who says to her, "When you are near me, I am with myself. You are neither a relative nor a stranger:—you are my soul" (p. 138).

Yeroum and Opal are an amusing couple tellingly sketched. At one point Yeroum complains, "I shall have to relinquish Opal, for I dare not risk being ridiculous. I am a poet" (p. 144). After a long exchange in which the Beast divines that Opal is an artist but cannot guess whether at painting, sculpture, architecture, or music, she declares, "I vibrate . . . . Before sunsets, in the moonlight . . . . My soul dilates" (pp. 162–163).

The plot itself goes far in casting an aura of inventive frivolity.

Act I
1. Scene between Opal (widowed from a thick, prosaic merchant named Hassan) and Yeroum discussing the night before, in which she received him as a lover but he spouted only poetry.
2. Enter widowed Ruby and sibarite financier Rock discussing the night before, in which she received him as a lover but he only bedecked her with jewels.
3. Discussion between Opal and Ruby on their unsatisfactory lovers.
4. Enter virginal Turquoise, having observed their widower father's arrival after a year's absence, his ships laden.
5. Enter father, rejuvenated by a beautiful slave, Violet.
6. Conversation among Opal, Ruby, and Violet (after Mansour and Turquoise exit), in which the sisters revile Violet and threaten to drive her away.
7. Fairy of Tolerance appears, persuades the two women to reconcile with Violet.
8. Mansour reappears with Turquoise and gifts as Fairy eats sherbets and sweetmeats. After presenting a necklace to Ruby and a vial of hallucinogen to Opal, he gives Turquoise a rose and describes the Beast.
9. The sisters vie to inhale the rose to go in her place to the enchanted garden of the Beast.
10. Exit Mansour with Violet, Ruby, Opal. Turquoise smells the rose and falls asleep, transported to the garden by "Light and the Seven Colors," who dance a "Ballet of Light."

Act II
1. Turquoise, lying near Fairy, awakens in Beast's garden and observes

that a creature's garden reveals his soul; sees Rock and Yeroum and learns that the whole group has sniffed the rose and followed her; seeks solitude in walk with Fairy.

2. Beast appears after her, laments his ugliness, converses with Rock and Yeroum on loving women; agrees to test Ruby's reactions to him.

3. Enter Ruby, who in dialogue with Beast, admits her attraction to him (and his riches).

4. Furious Rock appears to admonish her; she pretends to have seen him spying and played a trick on him with Beast; they reconcile and exit, with Rock excited to slightly more passion.

5. Yeroum and Beast talk till Opal appears, and Yeroum hides to rearrange his imperfect appearance.

6. Opal and Beast talk about "the soul" as she succumbs to his attractions.

7. Yeroum, thunderstruck, comes to reclaim her from such "jesting" with Beast.

8. Enter Mansour, to whom Beast declares his discovery of his own attractions and breaks off engagement with Turquoise, afraid he'll prove a philandering husband.

9. Exit Beast to meditate; enter Violet to converse with Mansour, who reveals (unknowingly) that Turquoise is his only real child, then exits.

10. Enter Beast; Violet shrieks and runs; Turquoise appears and declares her love; the two exit.

11. Fairy appears, hears shriek of Turquoise, distressed at the appearance of an ordinary young Prince Charming after her kiss with Beast; others appear.

12. Enter Prince, who insists she accept his second kiss—as a man.

13. Declarations of all and moral.

This is an ingenious situational takeoff on the "Beauty and the Beast" tradition, satirical but light. The theme of relationships between men and women, with sex as the essential ingredient, is really the same as that of Beaumont's fairy tale, with the Beast's role as a sexual figure and the women's responses to it made explicitly adult. Unlike the ribald banter of Planché, the style here is witty and more archly sophisticated. The dialogue flows naturally and quickly; the location, scene, and character changes are smooth. Mansour's revelation to Violet, for instance, that his first two daughters absorbed, in utero, impressions from their mother's "hearing about" conquests from an officer and refined pleasures from a musician, both "friends of the family" who frequented the house before the girls were born, could have been a distracting aberration from the plot but is so cleverly presented that it contributes to the theme of the play, the naive character of Mansour, and the audience appeal of inclusion into secrets unrevealed to the characters.

There are multiple references to "Beauty and the Beast's" story kin, especially between Turquoise and the Fairy. The wolf "doesn't frighten me," asserts the former. "Little Red Riding Hood was too young to satisfy the wolf's hunger. He wouldn't have eaten me" (p. 135). A moment later, still preparing to meet the Beast, she says "Psyche was sent to meet a furious monster and she met—love. I am like the princess who adores a lion" (p. 136). Vulcan and Venus, Polyphemus and Galatea all get a nod, and the Fairy summarizes for the whole cast of characters at the end:

> To win, you lovers, what you prize
> Use more than speeches, vows, and sighs.
> Zeus who to swan and bull could turn
> Knew very well why women yearn. (P. 186)

There is even a play on the source of the play as well as on the play itself: "And how just one kiss can a man metamorphose / Will be the theme of oceans of verse and bad prose" (p. 186).

Nozière has coupled one of the most profound themes of the fairy tale, the human conflict between body and spirit, with his observations of behavior in his frivolous society and has come up with a telling remark on this new context for an old story. His success in realizing the theme rests on catching the quirks of social behavior. There is never a serious point without its ridiculous counterpoint.

> The Fairy: Little Turquoise, the happiness of humanity is that it is divine in spirit and animal in body. Man is more complete than any god, since he experiences the joys of both intelligence and flesh.
> Violet: Some more sweetmeats? (P. 118)

Later, Turquoise begins to get the drift: "The Beast is approaching. Oh! What Anguish! But how pleasant!" (p. 131). When her kiss transforms the Beast, she is furious.

You should have warned me! Here I was smitten by an exceptional being, and all of a sudden, my fiancé becomes an ordinary distinguished young man. (P. 183)

Funniest of all is a scene in which Opal tries to explain to the Beast that the physical attraction she feels for him is really the tremors of the soul.

> O: Oh, my friend! My friend! You are going to speak of the soul!
> B: Oh! The soul, that's what that—
> O: Why am I so happy at feeling so feeble in your strong hands?
>   The soul!
> B: I understand.
> O: I should flee from you—yet I am happy at being rocked in the arms
>   of the beast.
> B: The soul!
> O: The odor of your fur intoxicates me. It has kept the perfume of the
>   grass where you have slept. A woodland odor—the freshness of
>   thyme and lavender.
> B: The soul!
> O: It seems as though a faun has pursued me across the country.
>   I could hear behind me the increasing sound of his goat feet. I felt
>   his breath upon my neck. I had no strength to flee. Oh, monster!
>   Monster!
> B: My dear soul!
> O: Can you comprehend the beauty of these supernatural superior joys?
> B: It seems to me that I also have a soul! (Pp. 165–166)

Even the magic objects are in for a teasing, the emerald ring more symbolic of the bonds of wealth than the bond of love, and imagery echoed in the girls' names, the merchant's ships of the same colors, and Rock's showy adornment of Ruby with his only sign of affection—jewels. The motif of the rose is rendered humorously transparent in a long group discussion full of not-so-oblique descriptions: "Beautifully white, with a heart as pink as a furtive desire. . . . It looks like some precious tissue. . . . Drops of dew tremble in the mysterious folds of its corolla" (pp. 123–124). Everyone is tremendously drawn to the rose, which is still fresh after six months away from the bush, as it were. Turquoise begs Mansour for a chance to smell it, knowing the perfume will transport her to the Beast's garden.

M: You must not touch it until you know where it comes from.

T: What difference does that make if it charms me!

M: You are my own child. That's exactly what I thought when I first saw Violet. (P. 123)

The sisters vie for a sniff themselves, ostensibly to protect Turquoise and let their "experience meet this assault," and soon everyone is tempted to the Beast's garden ("Then it's a family reunion!" declares Turquoise, p. 137). Sooner or later, as Nozière demonstrates, everyone befriends the Beast.

The year after Nozière's play was first performed, one of the great literary figures of Edwardian times, Sir Arthur Quiller-Couch, adapted "Beauty and the Beast" from Villeneuve's version for a collection to be illustrated by an artist of equal renown, Edmund Dulac. This collaboration produced, with bookmaking of lavish beauty, a classic of long leisurely retellings, including "The Sleeping Beauty," "Blue Beard," and "Cinderella" (the recurrent coupling of "Beauty and the Beast" with Perrault's stories may account for the frequent assumption that he wrote it). It is interesting to note that two years before, in 1908, Ernest Dowson also published a limited edition (three hundred copies) of a complete English translation—one of the few extant—of Villeneuve's version with four voluptuous color plates by Charles Condor. Neither book mentioned Villeneuve.

Quiller-Couch's adaptation, similar to but longer than Lang's, is an elegantly styled, fifty-six-page story reflecting many of Villeneuve's phrases and descriptions but omitting the long account of Beauty and the Beast's backgrounds. Educated at Oxford, a lecturer in classics there and later appointed King Edward VII Professor of English Literature at Cambridge, Quiller-Couch was a celebrated speaker and anthologist (*The Oxford Book of English Verse, 1250–1900*) who was also one of the most popular writers of his time. One biographical note neatly summarizes the literary polish that distingushes his "Beauty and the Beast." "'Q' was essentially a romantic. His chief contribution to letters was his clear and apparently effortless style. It reflects the personality of its author—neat, thorough, colourful, unhurried, hospitable, humorous, and chivalrous."[3] His version was, in many ways, the last of its kind.

The cast has been reduced from Villeneuve's to a core of main characters: the merchant, his six sons and six daughters (the youngest Beauty), the Beast, the Dream Prince, the Dream Lady ("stately," as she is perpetually described) who is the Beast/Prince's mother and a queen. Beauty is a paragon of the three Christian virtues—faith, hope, and love. When her father suspects the Beast of mocking them with gifts too heavy to carry home, his daughter responds with faith.

> "Wait a little," advised Beauty. "That would be a sorry jest, and I cannot help thinking that the Beast is honest; and that since he offered these gifts he will find you also the means to carry them."[4]

Her initial determination to sacrifice herself for her father is coupled with hope.

> "And who knows," said she, forcing a brave smile, "but this fate of mine, which seems so terrible, may cover some extraordinary and happy fortune?" (P. 90)

Her capacity for love mirrors Cordelia's. As her sisters beleaguer the merchant with expensive commissions, Beauty makes the singular request:

> "Dear father," she answered, "I wish for the most precious thing in the world; and that is to see you home again safe and sound." (P. 77)

Most of all, she is a comparison gainer, her bravery contrasting with her father's weakness (as in Lang's version) and her generosity with her sisters' jealousy. The former is especially apparent in her fearful first encounter with the Beast, from which she recovers after clinging for support to her father (who "was too far terrified to find his voice," p. 93), walks alone toward her tormentor, and greets him ("but Beauty controlled hers and answered sweetly," p. 93). Intrinsic to the nature of this courage is her freedom of choice to exercise it, emphasized in a number of passages:

> Whichever you bring must come here of her own free will, or not at all. (P. 84)

> Let her be free to choose whether she will come or no; but tell her that, her course once chosen, there can be no retreat, nor even reflection after you have brought her to me. (P. 85)

> Have you come here of your own free will? (P. 93)

> . . . and since you have come of your own accord, you shall stay. (P. 94)

While none of these heroic characteristics is new to Beauty's depiction, the manner and incidents with which they are developed here seem particularly graceful, as does the Beast's persistent honesty. Similarly, the lucid style and organization of the narrative shed new light on familiar details. The dream sequence, for instance, is presented with more unity of development so as to seem less an intrusion, as it did in Lang, than a nightly visitation in the ancient husk-myth mode, a connection made clear here in the prince's visionary midnight courtship. The duality of animal/man is rendered especially dramatic in a climactic dream where the prince meets Beast and threatens to kill him for the love of Beauty, who stays his dagger in a test of her love, loyalty, and perception.

Without clutter, Quiller-Couch has also retained some of Villeneuve's palatial elaborations in an orderly but unlabored array. The music room, library, self-lighting candles, garden, sewing room, aviary, and monkey house form a self-contained fantasy world crowned with the "window room," in which each window reveals a new surprise: theatre, opera, fair, promenade, gaming room, royal reception/water picnic/ball, and finally a television-like glimpse of the "whole world."

> State embassies, royal weddings, coronations, pageants, armies, revolutions, sieges, pitched battles—she could sit at her ease and watch them all, which was far more amusing than it is to read about them in a newspaper. (P. 113)

The themes slip through the story with barely a ripple. The father voices his share in Beauty's incapacity to leave home after he euphorically welcomes her return ("as though she had sprung from another world," p. 120).

> "As for you, my dearest child," said the merchant, "when your sisters are married, you shall keep house for your brothers and me, and so my old age will be happy." (P. 121)

Yet he finally advises her to acquiesce to "these phantoms of your dreams," urging her not to be deceived by appearances, to accept with gratitude the Beast's good heart and marriage proposal. The beginning of Beauty's separation from home comes later in the visit with a phrase neatly unifying the symbolic and concrete: "For one thing distressed her and spoilt all her happiness—she never dreamed at all now" (p. 123). The different levels of reality and fantasy and the nature of magic flash in telling moments, as when Beauty rushes back to the palace only to find herself bored when the Beast does not appear.

The shows were there as before; but opera and comedy, fête and pageant, held no meaning for her: the players were listless, the music was dull, the processions passed before her eyes but had lost their power to amuse. (P. 125)

There is no magic without love. Neither agate staircases with balusters of carved gold, on the one hand, nor the glow of obligations satisfied, on the other, can account for the joy Beauty feels when she revives her dying Beast. Still, Quiller-Couch cannot resist the opportunity of a moral in rhyme, and two concluding verses recommend maidens to the happiness that repays duty and the satisfactions of helping the wretched.

For the most part, Quiller-Couch's imprint on "Beauty and the Beast" has not been made through character or plot variations but through stylization and emphasis. A few telltale flourishes are a direct inheritance from Villeneuve: "Dinner does not take very long when you are all by yourself" (p. 99, and also in Lang, p.119). But many are his own: "Could the horse have felt the weight on the good man's mind, it had never made such a pace" (p. 87). The rose appears with the constancy of a real character, not only with a central role in the request, gift/theft, and penance but also in repeated references that give it palpable presence.

Quiller-Couch's descriptions are simple, swift, and slightly tilted toward the humorous: "The Beast's face turned pale—which, for such a face, was no easy matter" (p. 116). Edmund Dulac's six color plates, 5 1/4" x 6 1/2", bordered and framed in the 8 1/2" x 11" pages, pronounce that humor graphically but maintain, at the same time, a serious integrity of craft—a balance similar to that of the text.

Each of the illustrations is captioned with a sentence from the story.

1. He had been fasting for more than twenty-four hours, and lost no time in falling to.
2. The good merchant let drop the rose and flung himself on his knees.
3. Soon they caught sight of the castle in the distance.
4. She found herself face to face with a stately and beautiful lady.
5. These [parrots] no sooner saw Beauty than they began to scream and chatter.
6. Ah! What a fright you have given me! she murmured (plate 4).

The elaborate costumes and settings are Moorish, echoing a Victorian graphic trend of fairy tale illustration previously noted and giving this the flavor of an Arabian Nights tale not hinted at in Quiller-Couch's text. The Beast, a human disfigured with animal ears and claws, shows a sense of the grotesque common in Dulac's work. The father's small, rotund figure and foolish expressions not only reduce his dignity in almost every scene but also serve to satirize the other, more romantic effects of the art. While Dulac's watercolor and gouache paintings are often sensual, he has kept the content remarkably discreet for this story, given its implications. Beauty and the Dream Fairy are both as mannered as they are bejeweled. There is a static quality to all the figures belying the action of several dramatic compositions, even the amusing attitude of Beauty holding her ears in defense against an assault by a flamboyant array of parrots.

The influence of Japanese painting on Dulac's landscapes, especially the trees bordering the castle grounds on Beauty's arrival and framing her head as she kneels over the dying Beast, is striking. Suffused colors, made by an overlay production process whereby red, yellow, and blue are used in full strength over each other, produce a soft line that is never truly black.[5] The light, too, is subdued, and the foreground and background are flattened out on a plane. Although Dulac was not born until after Crane and Boyle had illustrated "Beauty and the Beast," his work bears a kinship with them that marks it, like Quiller-Couch's, as the last of a kind. While published for children, Dulac's illustrations are an adult art form, and the jump to Margaret Tarrant's pictures just ten years later unveils a whole new concept of illustrating for children.

The stage was actually set for condescension by a version of "Beauty and the Beast" that came out the year after the Quiller-Couch/Dulac collection. In 1911, Anna Alice Chapin published *The Now-A-Days Fairy Book*, which was illustrated by Jessie Willcox Smith (plate 5). Their sentimental story entitled "Beauty and the Beast" bears remote resemblance to the fairy tale. A little girl named Saidie, after purposely losing her toy monkey because it is ugly, feels remorseful enough to rescue it from the hands of some dirty ragamuffins tearing it apart. In the process, her Lady of Colonial Days doll (Mistress Louisa Geraldine Frances Valentina Goodman) is lost, only to reappear magically at a birthday party where it wins first prize in the Doll's Competition of Beauty. The author frequently patronizes children's speech patterns: "'Saidee!' gasped Charming. 'Ve Beast, he does look eggsackly like you!'"[6] Chapin is also the most blatantly stereotypical in defining the female: "Like a great many little girls, she had a few airs and graces, silly ways of tossing her head, and fiddling with her fingers" (p. 68). It is Smith's art, however, that is most revealing of the step down to an artifically separated set of emotions reserved

8. *Beauty and the Beast: An Entertainment for Young People, the First of the Series of Little Plays for Little People*, by Julia Corner, illustrated by Alfred Crowquill, 1854. By permission of the Department of Special Collections, University of Chicago Library.

9. *Beauty and the Beast*, by Albert Smith, illustrated by Alfred Crowquill, 1853. By permission of the Department of Special Collections, University of Chicago Library.

for childhood. Her illustration of a little girl's tea party with a demure toy under an idyllic rose-covered trellis in a picket-fenced yard completely defuses the power of the tale. It becomes a coy occasion for play—or an adult's nostalgic view of play—and a visual trendsetter for artists such as Margaret Tarrant, who stick closer to the story but inherit Smith's graphic taste for sweetened juvenile iconography.

Some earlier versions were certainly child conscious. The "Little Plays for Little People" series by Miss Julia Corner and Alfred Crowquill (1854) overdoes rhyming couplets and doll-like figures in its didactic, multi-fairied presentations of "Beauty and the Beast." (Figures 8 and 9 show Crowquill's illustrations for two graphically contrasting versions of "Beauty and the Beast," one naively childlike, the other sophisticatedly satirical.) Aunt Mary's 1856 version (fig. 10) revises Madame de Beaumont's eighteenth-century

10. *Beauty and the Beast*, from Aunt Mary's Series, 1856. By permission of the Department of Special Collections, University of Chicago Library.

stone statue punishment of Beauty's siblings for the benefit of penitent young readers:

> Her sisters, after continuing in their mortifying situation several years, were restored by the good fairy to their original shape, and by their conduct fully atoned for their past follies.[7]

Laura E. Richards's retelling, illustrated by Gordon Browne in 1886, is cute and condescending, with Beauty harassed by sisters Gracilia and Superba. A tree narrates the story ("Long, long ago, before there were railways or radishes, and when the moon was still made of green cheese, there lived in the Kingdom of Rigdom Funnidos a rich merchant who had three fair daughters")[8] and is interrupted constantly by some children asking questions. Captain Edric Vredenburg's retelling (fig. 11) of "Beauty and the Beast" rivals the Chapin/Smith version for saccharinity and stereotyping. He eliminates any element of surprise by beginning the story "Once upon a time, a long while ago, there was a Beast" and assuring readers, before the tale gets under way, that "something very wonderful happened to the Beast and to somebody else."[9] Beauty herself sounds like a housekeeping robot: "Dear me, it was awful, the way those two sisters grumbled, but Beauty, oh dear no, she was all smiles, for her heart was as sunny as ever, as she rolled up the sleeves of her print frock, and cooked the dinner, and scrubbed the floors, and made herself useful, here, there, and everywhere" (p. 64). Of course, "the two sisters turned over a new leaf and were less selfish, and they were happy, so this is a very happy ending to the story" (p. 66). E. Nesbit (fig. 12), while outdoing both Chapin and Vredenberg's sexism ("Beauty, for her part, kept the house clean and pretty, washed, starched, ironed, baked, brewed, and sewed")[10] hews more to a respectfully "adult" tone, in spite of—or per-haps because of—her stature as a children's book writer.

12. E. Nesbit, *The Old Nursery Stories*, 1908. By permission of the de Grummond Children's Literature Research Collection, University of Southern Mississippi.

Despite the existence of patronizing precedents and of the historical tension between the aesthetic and the didactic in literature for children, the decade of 1910–20 marked a distinct difference, a shift toward increased compartmentalization of the juvenile (see Price's art, fig. 13). During the period between the wars, Margaret Tarrant was a children's illustrator especially noted for her pictured nursery rhymes and for *Fairy Tales* (1920), a "collection of the most popular tales by Perrault and the Brothers Grimm"— of which two out of six are by neither. (The public seems determined to give these men a corner on the market.) It is significant that while Crane, Boyle, and Dulac were considered general illustrators who also turned their hands to various art work besides books for children, Tarrant did little else.

Her twenty-page adaptation of "Beauty and the Beast" is based on Beaumont's, with the complete elimination of the dreams and a reduced cast consisting of the Merchant, three sons and three daughters (including Beauty), and the Beast. First readings of this version seem smooth and straightforward, but a number of touches have subtly reshaped it. The images, tone, and even plot seem in a new way, tamed, even curbed. The textual and graphic evidence for this change is startling.

There is, for instance, just before the merchant loses his way and enters the Beast's castle, a careful reassurance that everything will be all right: "On his return he met with a wonderful adventure, which was to have some strange results."[11] The merchant is portrayed not only as loving "his sons and

13. "Beauty and the Beast," from *Once Upon a Time: A Book of Old-Time Fairy Tales*, by Katherine Lee Bates, illustrated by Margaret Evans Price. Illustrations copyright © 1921, 1949 Checkerboard Press, a division of Macmillan, Inc. Used by permission. All rights reserved.

daughters better than his wealth" (p. 69), but also as strong "for, being an upright and honourable man, he had no thought of breaking a promise made even to a Beast" (p. 76). A paragraph is devoted to his feeling that the Beast is more generous than murderous and that Beauty can manage anyone (pp. 77–78). The Beast is by turn respectful and pitiful. The term "poor Beast" appears often, at least three times on one page (p. 85). When Beauty cannot revive him by calling and moistening his temples, she pours the whole bowl of water on his head, with instant results.

Beauty, on the other hand, is ingenuous but determined. At the first marriage proposal, which previous Beauties found intimidating at the least, Beauty is undaunted.

> "No, beast," she replied at once in a very decided way; whereupon her suitor gave a great sigh which nearly blew out the candles, and retired, looking very doleful. (P. 81)

The only time she falters, at their first meeting ("he had *such* a mouth, and two such ugly teeth came right over his lower jaw!"), Beauty is immediately reassured: "You are a good girl. I am much obliged to you" (p. 79).

There is no dream comforter/adviser/chorus here because none is needed. A last-minute fairy appears at the wedding to still the sisters' spiteful remarks by turning them into statues. "For all we know they are there still, for they were certainly *very* disagreeable people" (p. 88).

Even the details of setting are toned down to a limited scale, the castle grounds reduced to a well-manicured lawn:

> In the garden also everything was in first-rate order. The flower-beds were full of beautiful plants, the walks clean and hard, the grass-plots soft and smooth as velvet carpets. (P. 74)

In fact, when Beauty and her father approached,

> the two travellers could not help feeling a little comforted by the beauty of the scene; and the nearer they came to the Beast's palace, the fresher became the greenery, and the thicker the throng of chirping birds. (p. 78)

Even Beauty's suite is telescoped to modest proportions.

> She timidly opened the door and found herself in a large room, beautifully furnished, with bookcases, sofas, pictures, and a guitar and other musical instruments. (P. 80)

The word comforted or comforting appears twice in the paragraphs following this description and frequently on other pages. Throughout, the expository prose maintains a comfortable, matter-of-fact tone as neat as the lawn.

> By working hard, morning, noon, and night, the merchant and his sons were fortunate to earn enough to keep them from want. In fact, in one respect the merchant was better off, for whereas, during the time of his prosperity, he had often been kept awake at night by anxious thoughts for the safety of his ships, his warehouses, and his stores of gold and silver, such thoughts now never entered his mind, and he slept soundly and peacefully until morning. Also his conscience was clear, for he had always been honourable in his dealings, and, though everyone knew of his misfortunes, he was still respected by all whose respect was worth having. (P. 70)

Later, the magic mirror does show him pining for Beauty, but the very explanation of grief or apprehension in any character seems to moderate the emotion: "So, you see, the merchant was rather dull and lonely" (p. 83).

Tarrant's three full-page illustrations also modify the images from powerful to charming (plate 6). The Beast has lost his strength and become a toy of the nursery room; perhaps a lovely toy, but not as meaningful. He is more pitiable and cuddly than ugly or terrifying. The first scene, in which he appears to the merchant, shows light-weight cartooned caricatures with "play-pretend" medieval costumes and castle. The colors run to pink, blue, lavender, and pale green.

The second picture shows a composition similar to Boyle's dinner scene, but here the Beast is more ludicrous than anything else. In contrast to the sad dignity of that earlier jet black sea creature's head, its tiny animal eyes, and its long curving tusks, Tarrant's monster needs only its bangs trimmed to be the perfect pet. Beauty has acquired the good looks of her creator's society, a kind of sunshine-apricot-advertisement wholesomeness that appears even more pronounced against the frame of intense blue, which adds some depth to the background.

The touches of Art Deco in the last scene of Beauty lamenting the prostrate Beast are striking. The costume and the composition are more elegantly designed than in the first two scenes. But still, the figure crumpled on the ground is more pathetic than tragic, with its hand covering its face in the gesture of a child hiding. Beauty's pose itself is more ladylike than distraught. Beauty's one genuine cry of anguish after the handsome young prince appears to say "'Thank you, Beauty' and . . . all sorts of sweet and tender things" (p. 87) might be applied to Tarrant's own gentling transformation of the tale for the protection of children: "But where is Beast? I do not know you. I want my beast, my lovely Beast!" (p. 87).

Whereas Tarrant's work confines the images of the story to a juvenile realm, John Heath-Stubbs' poetry, published in a collection entitled *Beauty and the Beast* in 1943, abstracts the images beyond children's reach. With few exceptions, the versions following this period are created by writers and artists who produce for either children or adults, but not both. In spite of the ideal of a continuum of quality, based on the theory that every age group finds a level of satisfaction in well-wrought art, the specialization of the artist in one age group has an effect on his or her work. While earlier versions of "Beauty and the Beast" may have been clearly aimed at one audience or another, the fact that their creators did work in both areas seems to have enriched them with a kind of crossover awareness of the balance between simplicity and sophistication.

Heath-Stubbs' fifty-eight-line unrhymed lyric poem in eight stanzas extracts the tone and images of the story in order to beam an existential spotlight on the two main characters. The setting is the Beast's garden, with the inevitable implications of the primal biblical drama enacted between animal, woman, and man. There is no action or even dialogue, but four alternate monologues: her two comprising three short stanzas to each section; his two, one long verse per section. The metric variations of rhythm and line length distinguish their voices: hers, clipped and clear; his, un-curbed and blusterous.

Beauty and the Beast

Beauty

1   My silver flesh is sifted out
2   For one red rose
3   And my gay beauty sold—perhaps—
4   For a beast to play with, for
5   A crump pad-paw;

6   Not for dromedaries sweating
7   Under fiery stones,
8   Or the white mules bunched with bales of stuff-silk—
9   Only the petals plucked, the powdered anthers'
10   Upward curving.

11   Here in this garden

12 The birds are singing
13 For pride.
14 I walk at noon
15 Between the roses
16 Of this close garden.
17 I am learning.

The Beast
18 O soul thrust through the thick flesh, spirit whelmed
19 In black-blood tides! O sharp spark all but quenched
20 In soft numb sponginess of a beast's brain!
21 My shagg'd sides torn in the thickets, hands made clumsy
22 And blunt with earthnut-grubbing; yellow teeth
23 That have known red flesh! These uninhabited
24 Grounds and gardens, once my pleasant places,
25 Have heard through the long nights my baffled bellow,
26 My wet mouth coughing and snorting to the moon!
27 I am the evil hermit of this fastness,
28 Lurking for travellers among the trees;
29 By force and fraud now have I captured Beauty;
30 Not to rend, but bend to pity
31 I am learning.

Beauty
32 Here in this garden
33 I am learning
34 The rose encloses
35 A sharp secret.

36 I have a fishing line
37 That will not break—
38 A smooth skein of silk,
39 And a steel chain:
40 I will drag out the drowned image
41 From the troubled water of your eyes.

42 Groped I for a rose
43 And grasped a thorn?
44 I have found a fire
45 Asleep in the ashes;

46   I will teach the flame

47   To make clay hard and brittle.

The Beast

48   I am learning to turn from the wet mistiness

49   Of Spring, among the fallen leaves, and the roots

50   Of rough-barked trees, where I howled to the cold

51   Full moon, a hairy female flank wanting;

52   I am haunting in secret the paths of this closed garden;

53   Heavy with roses, shrill with incessant bird-song,

54   Where she walks, with her white foot hardly stirring

55   The live green grass. My flesh is twisted and tortured

56   With sharp writhings of my awakening spirit—

57   O soul like a stream of lava, cleaving through

58   The uncouthness of clay, assoil the soiled flesh![12]

In the first section, Beauty laments she has been sold as a creature's plaything, not for the high price of precious goods but for one rose. Secluded in a garden, humbled even before birds, she is learning. In the second section, the Beast discovers a soul awakening in his body; he, too, is learning. In the third, Beauty learns that the rose is more than it appears; she will save the Beast's soul and civilize the flesh. In the last, the Beast begins to learn of a soul absolved, the flesh set free. The common bond, "I am learning," unites them, but Beauty learns of a natural force, the rose's sharp secret, sexual flowering; the Beast learns feeling within physicality. Their different reflections of the same garden are especially telling in parallel lines 11–16 and 52–53. She walks at noon, with birds singing for pride, between roses, in a *close*, or intimate space. He haunts at night the secret paths of a *closed*, or shut, space, feels the roses as heavy, the incessant birdsong shrill. They learn by reaction to each other.

A consideration of Heath-Stubbs' diction benefits from historical references cited in the Oxford English Dictionary. The simple opening verb "sift," for example, not only means sieved to separate the coarse from the fine—something Beauty thinks has been applied to her but ironically finds she will apply to the Beast—but echoes with older meanings of measurement, putting a person on trial, scrutinizing narrowly to find out the truth by close inquiry. The word "crump" in line 5 not only means crooked or deformed, but also, in its verb form, to bend (echoed in line 30) and, amazingly, to eat with a dull sound. "Assoil" is a term with religious, political, and physical overtones: to absolve from sin, pardon, forgive, or even set free from excommunication; to discharge, release, acquit, clear of criminal charge; to deliver, set free, purge; to atone, expiate. A gloss of the poem reveals antique touches in word choice that project the scenario back in time and underscores the story's symbolism.

The imagery is resonant with color, but in addition to the obvious contrast of silver flesh, white mules, and white foot with reds of rose, blood, spark, flesh, fire, and lava, there is also a strong textural play. *Tides, quenched, sponginess, wet mouth, smooth skein of silk, drowned, water, mistiness,* and *stream* all find a foil in the *anther's upward curving, sharp spark, sharp secret, line, steel chain, thorn, clay hard and brittle, rough-barked.* The firing of clay (into pottery, a mark of civilization) signifies the transformation of animality, the duality resolved and working. Stripped of narrative devices, this telling is nonetheless powerful. While reducing the story to its simplest point, Heath-Stubbs retains important images and projects elemental voices.

Not only has the story's kernel been exposed, but also its characters' internal conflicts and motivations. The characters speak directly, for themselves, and introspectively, of themselves. The growing prevalence of psychological interpretation during the first half of the twentieth century has affected the story's recreators, who explicitly explore in art forms the fairy tale motifs which their scientific colleagues analyse.

The final version of this period demonstrates most clearly how the story turns inward. About Jean Cocteau's "Beauty and the Beast," released just three years after Heath-Stubbs' poem, Jean Decock wrote, "The preoccupation of the film with an abundance of signs and objects draws our attention to the unconscious."[13] Not only do the film footage and two-hundred-page shooting script extend the possibilities for probing beneath the story's surface, but Cocteau's diary of the filming probes into his own experience of recreating the story.

This elaborate artistic display and documentation could have overwhelmed the story even more than Heath-Stubbs's abbreviation risked hollowing it, but Cocteau forged an intense inner vision that he protected fiercely from banal effects. The defense of his purity against technical problems—post-war black-outs, lack of photographic equipment and supplies, health problems of the cast, four-hour makeup jobs per scene, airplanes buzzing the set, impossible weather conditions, uncooperative chickens, and more—adds yet another level of reality to the storytelling.

Cocteau's film has now become a classic, shown often in fine arts theatres and rerun regularly on public television. At the time it came out, however, it shocked a population devastated by World War II with its focus on what seemed of slight importance—a fairy tale—compared to the harsh realities of survival. Yet Cocteau was dealing with survival—even revival—of the spirit, and his rendition of "Beauty and the Beast" as a movie explored new possibilities both for the story and for the medium he used to tell it.

In the tradition of fantasists from E. T. A. Hoffmann to Jorge Luis Borges, Cocteau is obsessed with levels of reality, labyrinths, mirrors, dreams, surrealistic images, all of which blend naturally with and extend easily beyond the traditional story of "Beauty and the Beast." Time and space take unexpected turns in the film; light and dark, surfaces and depths play on one another. Yet throughout, Cocteau emphasizes the importance of the ordinary to the sphere of the extraordinary. He exacts of narrative and photography the "clean sculptured line" of true poetry,[14] which he contrasts with popular contemporary "diffuse lighting and the use of gauzes" for fuzzy, sentimental effects (p. 65). At one point, he compliments his cameraman for achieving "a supernatural quality within the limits of realism. It is the reality of childhood. Fairyland without fairies. Fairyland in the kitchen" (p. 97). Writing the script with "only a short sentence or a few lines" to every shot (p. 27), he encouraged the actors to follow the narrative thread as simply as possible, "stripped of complicated gesticulation and clutter" (p. 32) for an overall "slow rhythm without real drama" (p. 120).

Several times, the film became "too beautiful . . . too artistic" (p. 55), a direction Cocteau tempered with harsher contrasts. He avoided moving the camera, kept to still shots, reduced the picturesque, sharpened precision (pp. 14, 19, 31).

> We recorded the sound of the arrows. As always the real sound was false. We had to translate it, invent a sound more exact than the sound itself. (P. 31)

He awakens from a nap after an exhausting morning take: "I had been dreaming and jumping with both feet into a reality that is more real than my dream" (p. 31). He cites the work of Vermeer and Gustav Doré as his inspiration, refers often to Perrault, reflects on the nature of myth and his translation of it.

> fantasy has its own laws which are like those of perspective. You may not bring what is distant into the foreground, or render fuzzily what is near. The vanishing lines are impeccable and the orchestration so delicate that the slightest false note jars. (Pp. 5–6)

Several passages reveal the extent of Cocteau's identification with "Beauty and the Beast" as it personifies his own beliefs.

I chose that particular fable because it corresponded to my personal mythology. (P. viii)

Gradually I am coaxing my myths and childhood memories back again. (P. 60)

The movie screen is the true mirror reflecting the flesh and blood of my dreams. (P. 69)

My work is that of an archeologist. The film exists (pre-exists). I have to unearth it from the shadow where it sleeps, with a pick and shovel. Sometimes I spoil it by being too hasty. But the fragments left intact shine with the beauty of marble. (P. 57).

The film itself is so well integrated that its visual and verbal dimensions constantly extend each other. The first time we catch sight of the sisters, for instance, one is admiring herself in a hand mirror while Beauty kneels away from the camera to tie the vain girl's shoe. In the first close-up of Beauty—scrubbing on her knees—"we see her face appear as a reflection in the floor."[15] In the Beast's palace, Beauty's mirror speaks to her: "I am your mirror, Beauty. Reflect for me. I will reflect for you" (p. 134). When the sisters look into the same mirror, one sees herself grown old and ugly, the other sees a monkey. When the first asks the second what she has seen, the monkey mouths, "Nothing" (p. 332). (Monkeys appear in illustrations by Crane and Boyle, too, as "aping" the vanity of appearances.) Later, the sisters hurl the mirror at Beauty with the accusation, "It will show you what a Beauty will become in order to please a Beast" (p. 334). Beauty must learn to believe not what she sees, but what she feels. The Beast must learn to bear her seeing. Over and over he admonishes her not to look at him. Her looking first frightens but finally saves him.

The theme of deceptive appearances gets frequent comment in the script as well. The least perceptive of the characters says, "I don't believe in magic powers. The monster lulls Beauty to sleep and makes her see what he pleases" (p. 282). One sister remarks enviously on Beauty's prospect of marrying a wealthy suitor, even a beastly one, "There are a lot of other husbands that have beards and horns" (p. 276). In an exchange between Beauty and the Beast, he confesses, "Aside from being ugly, I have no wit," which Beauty inverts: "You have the wit to be aware of this" (p. 150). Beauty's revelation at the end—"I was the monster, my Beast"—climaxes the many reversals explored in both picture and dialogue.

Of course the ultimate contradiction is the appearance of the prince. "The Beast is no more. I was he" (p. 372). But there are more playful reminders of the contradictions of human behavior. When the prince asks her if his looks displease her, she replies "Yes . . . No" (p. 376). Later he asks "You're happy?" to which Beauty responds, "I'll have to get used to this" (p. 378). As he prepares to fly away with her, she says "I like to be afraid . . . with you" (p. 380). Beauty's brother at one point says, "I'm not afraid. I'm thinking," to which his friend replies "That's the same thing" (p. 354). And to the ironies of the traditional plot, Cocteau adds his own twists. The sisters whom Beauty dresses in the film "will carry the train" of her dress (p. 383). The suitor who shoots an arrow in the opening scene is shot with an arrow in the conclusion.

The characters have been increased by one important addition, Avenant, a friend of Beauty's brother and a would-be suitor. Representing man's bestial nature in contrast to the Beast's natural bestiality, the human Avenant extends the duality of Beast and prince to a trinity. The prince, of course, supersedes both the other characters but is played by the same actor, clarifying the roles as three aspects of one personality. Others in the cast are named but maintain a fine balance between archetypal anonymity and convincing human traits.

Beast, Avenant, Prince	Jean Marais
Beauty	Josette Day
Merchant	Marcel André
Adélaïde (1st sister)	Mila Parely
Félicie (2nd sister)	Nane Germon
Ludovic (brother)	Michel Auclair
Magnifique (the horse)	

The action adheres surprisingly to the traditional plot, given a film's dependence on action and dialogue and Cocteau's conscious limitations on the latter. Although unafraid of pauses in pacing for a timeless quality, he has insisted on a strong narrative line, often editing out distractions included in the original filming, such as scenes of Ludovic and Avenant in their gambling excesses and the deception of a draper to whom they attempt to marry one of their sisters (for a modest fee). The narrative suits Cocteau's determination to experiment with ideas through classical techniques and structure as a means of reducing distractions for the audience considering those ideas. One entry in the diary substantiates this.

> In the rest of the film (to be done at the studio) I will supply the movement and detail—but I suspect that the rhythm of the film resides in me more than in the mobility of the camera or of the protagonists. Perhaps I won't be able to do very much in the face of a mechanism which will only come to realization in the cutting-room. The main thing is to add one fact to another, to interest the spectator instead of distracting him. (*Diary*, p. 33)

The story unfolds basically in two settings, a provincial farm at Roche-corbon, which Cocteau found just before concluding he would have to build a set; and a chateau with outdoor scenes in several parks.

1. Quarrel between sisters and boys (crossbow scene)
2. Encounter between Avenant and Beauty (scrubbing floor on sisters' orders)
3. Merchant enters with good news of a cargo ship returned
4. Humiliation of sisters on a visit to duchess, spite on return home, family dissension
5. Merchant leaves, Beauty's request for rose
6. Ludovic petitions money-lender
7. Lawyer turns father out at night after creditors claim ship
8. Merchant lost in storm, arrives at chateau
9. Drinks and sleeps, finds horse missing and dead deer, picks rose
10. Beast appears, condemns him to die in quarter hour—or bring daughter in his place within three days
11. Gives horse (Magnifique) for transport
12. Roses presented to Beauty with father's story; quarreling among children
13. Beauty sneaks away to palace
14. Finds room, mirror; panics, tries to flee, meets Beast, faints
15. Beast carries her to bed, speaks
16. Dining scene, with conversation and proposal
17. Night fear: Beauty hears animal cry, hides; Beast comes into her room, she orders him out
18. Morning, she sees Beast drinking; evening, walks with him as he struggles not to chase deer

14. *Beauty and the Beast,* by Jean Cocteau, 1946. By permission
of Hammond Filmscript Archives, Fales Library, New York University.

19. Another walk, she lets him drink from her hands
20. He comes to her room, bloody, after a hunt; Beauty confronts and closes him out (fig. 14)
21. Removal of merchant's furniture as Avenant and Ludovic play chess
22. Beauty begs leave to go home for a week, Beast flees in anguish
23. Scenes of Avenant and Ludovic's excesses and deception of draper (mostly cut)
24. Beauty sees father in mirror, becomes ill; Beast makes her swear to return in one week
25. Beauty leaves, Beast faints on her bed
26. Father/Beauty reunion
27. Sisters and boys quarrel as they hang out sheets, see Beauty in gown and father recovered
28. Beauty's pearls turn to burned rope when she tries to give them away
29. Discussion about Beast between father and Beauty
30. Sisters plot; brother and friend wheedle Beast's secret
31. Tavern scene when brother and friend plot; sisters rub eyes with onion
32. Father/Beauty discuss on last day; sisters beg and persuade her to stay; steal key
33. Sisters torment her, Avenant presses her, father is dismayed
34. Beast despairs
35. Sisters and boys meet to conspire at night in stable; horse appears with sack containing mirror
36. Boys leave on horse; Adélaïde sees herself as old woman in mirror, Félicie as monkey; they take mirror to Beauty
37. She sees Beast weeping, puts on glove to get back to castle; returns home for key; mirror breaks; she returns to castle
38. Beauty searches for Beast; finds him dying
39. Avenant and Ludovic break into Diana's lodge
40. Beauty cries over Beast, promises to be his wife; declares love
41. Statue shoots Avenant, turns to Beast; Ludovic falls to his death
42. Prince Ardent takes her away in magic cloak to kingdom

Because Cocteau took such care with the mundane details of sheets flapping in the wind or chickens clucking from the coach house, the marvelous objects he multiplies do not seem overwhelming. The mirror, the key to the pavilion, the glove that transports Beauty back and forth, the pearl necklace burning Felicie's hand, Beauty's tear turned diamond, the statue of Diana shooting Avenant, the flight in the cloak, and the statues following every human move with their knowing eyes and waving their arms to light the way with torches simply document the story's straightforward progress. The rose itself, the most powerful of the symbols, remains a rose, juxtaposed most dramatically in one long shot with a burning candle, the two signs of passion.

As memorable as any of the actual pictorial content is the varied quality of light in the film. At times it gleams "like a piece of old silver which has been polished till it shines like new" (*Diary*, p. 21). For some sequences, Cocteau waited for the sky to become overcast with clouds—"they give the light the elegance of pearl" (*Diary*, p. 35). What he has done in black and white makes later technicolor efforts seem dull. His was a deliberate attempt to cast new light, literally and figuratively, on an old story. His success in commanding new techniques to reveal timeless truths and in choreographing technicians affecting camera work, music, set and costume design, properties, production management, wardrobe, makeup, editing, sound engineering, script continuity, lighting, sets, production, business management, and special sound effects (a crew of secondary storytellers who could make or break his vision of the film) assures his *Beauty and the Beast* a transition of integrity into an age of technology and sets a standard for new versions of the future.

The period of 1900–1950 represents a transition into ever more, and more varied, versions of "Beauty and the Beast." A representative list such as the one in appendix 4 of nineteenth-century editions would run to meaningless pages and become simply a quantitative analysis. Each version here must stand for many others that are like it but less impressive: the 1910 Quiller-Couch/Dulac collection, for instance, is echoed in the early 1920s *Classic Fairy Tales* illustrated by W. Heath Robinson and in the early 1930s *Arthur Rackham Fairy Book* (fig. 15) both well-known, traditional, and less distinguished in text and illustration of "Beauty and the Beast" than Quiller-Couch/Dulac's. Tarrant's 1920 book typifies any number of cozied-up versions, including the 1942 *Tenggren Tell-It-Again Book*, with its pitiful, cuddly troll Beast (fig. 16).

Along with the number of editions must be considered the impact of each type. Popular collections, for instance, have widespread influence on a large audience of children, though perhaps not the eventual power of one film classic such as Cocteau's. Nozière's and Heath-Stubbs' works, however, are a better barometer of the tale's cultural and artistic standing: They affect a small circle of people but reflect how deeply entrenched is the tale as a basis for development of certain images and motifs, which leads to great aesthetic diversity.

Whereas in earlier centuries, the unconventional version was an aberration, in the 1900s the story becomes multi-traditional. The variety in these five examples is only a beginning. Although innovative figures such as Cocteau may respect tradition, they nevertheless play with characterization and action, project new patterns of narrative voice, and experiment with graphic media. What becomes more and more apparent amidst these individualistic

15. "Beauty and the Beast," from *The Arthur Rackham Fairy Book: A Book of Old Favourites with New Illustrations,* 1933. By permission of J. B. Lippincott.

16. "Beauty and the Beast," from *The Tenggren Tell-It-Again Book*,
illustrated by Gustaf Tenggren with text edited and adapted by
Katharine Gibson, 1942. Western Publishers and Little, Brown, and Co.

literary and visual elaborations is the stability of the central archetypes, narrative structure, and images, objects, and symbols—the still, small voice of the story that seems to outstay shifts in dramatic action and personae.

Notably absent from even conventional versions of the 1900–1950 period is a heavy emphasis on moralizing. Nozière spoofed it, Heath-Stubbs and Cocteau spurned it, Tarrant neglected it, and Quiller-Couch tacked it on in what seemed an effort to recapture the fashion of the old days. Quiller-Couch's is also the only instructive fairy godmother figure. It is nevertheless clear that Nozière, Heath-Stubbs, and Cocteau are abstracting messages from art and entertainment, whether or not those messages are didactic. Their overt preoccupation with meaning, balanced as it may be with a sense of aesthetic conventions, is a new stage in the development of "Beauty and the Beast."

The deception of appearances becomes not a homily but an existential recognition. Perception replaces obedience, and understanding supersedes advice as an ideal in the maturation process. The transition away from didacticism to thematic interpretation during this time is slightly different from the later psychological investigation of the story. These writers and artists, mostly male as in the nineteenth century, dwell not so much on the Oedipal triangle or archetypal patterns of a collective subconscious as on the struggle of the individual to achieve a balance within him- or herself and with another, or by extension of the other, with a larger framework of family and society. The story represents personal dualities of light and dark, reality and fantasy, animal and spiritual, male and female, alienation and reconciliation.

This search for and awareness of meaning unfortunately deepens the split between adult and child audiences. As writers and artists specialize and invest in a separate world of childhood and children's books, their treatment of the tale often assumes an artificial veneer intolerable to adults. At the same time, the adult exploration of paradox, mazes, mirror images, and other sophisticated elements suggested by the story signifies little to children. It has probably captured their attention no more than did earlier expositions on morality. What is most important to the story's internalization is its external clarity; those who perceive its intrinsic metaphorical strength have achieved the greatest understanding of it.

FIVE

Mass Markets and Media: 1950–1985

From 1950 to 1985, the publications and media productions of "Beauty and the Beast" multiplied dramatically but ephemerally. Of the many picture book versions published during that thirty-five-year period, only a dozen were in print in 1985. Eight were of mediocre quality and published by small houses that could not sustain backlists long; the other four were fine editions but still threatened by an economy that forces books out of print as soon as immediate postpublication sales drop. Mass media productions, by their very nature, are often limited to one airing. The one-act opera by Vittorio Giannini, with a moving libretto ("Beauty was a girl who lived in dreams")[1] by Robert Simon was broadcast on the radio in 1951; the recording is inaccessible if it exists at all, and the score almost impossible to find. An elaborate television production viewed by millions in 1977 has never been rerun.

As the analysis of previous periods has suggested, the effect of so many printed versions of such varied quality seems to duplicate oral dissemination. Both children and adults are exposed to the story periodically and ubiquitously, with a constant action of divergence and convergence around certain motifs despite the seeming permanence or authority of printed words and celluloid images. The pattern of adaptations available to any given individual must be random when a comprehensive search over several years has found so many versions, even those mass marketed at production, difficult to attain. The adaptations examined here represent those most likely to exert the most steady impression on the most people. Yet it is probable that similar conclusions would emerge from other examples—and awesome to think of this and future generations exposed to entries in the standard Library of Congress computerized holdings printout, at present more than seven feet long, summarizing over and over,

Through her great capacity to love, a kind and beautiful maid releases a handsome prince from the spell which has made him an ugly beast. READY FOR NEW COMMAND[2]

The impact of one adapter, such as Andrew Lang in the late nineteenth century, or one illustrator, such as Edmund Dulac in the early twentieth, on public awareness has been reduced not only by plurality but also by mediocrity. A substantial percentage of the versions available suffer from trivialization of images, both written and pictured. A work of essentially poetic nature is often caricatured for light comic effect or reduced to its lowest common denominator for a consumer perceived to be substandard. In 1951, for instance, *Beauty and the Beast: A Play for Children* sported a heroine named Jane, the merchant Mr. Clement with his nephew Mikey, and Hodge the Wizard, with everything explained (including the prince's spell) in a carefully modernized, conversational tone. Of course, condescension to a juvenile audience is not limited to contemporary versions, as was noted in the chapter 4 discussion of versions by Chapin/Smith et al.

Still, in extent of distribution, most nineteenth- and early twentieth-century versions were not dime-, drug-, or grocery-store items. They were not marketed as supplements to public school curricula, nor were they sold as activity books in airport convenience shops. Irene Lenkoff's *Beauty and the Beast: Yes & Know Invisible Ink Fairy Tale Storybook* (1980) suggests, at the end of the story, that readers "use your Magic Pen to mark the blanks beside each right answer. . . . The merchant passed by a —rose garden — peanut field —corn field —duck pond." A brochure advertising the 1979 film of "Beauty and the Beast" (a 19-minute, color, 16 mm. production featuring doll-faced marionettes) announced to attendees of an educational conference that "THE BEAST will be at the Coronet booth . . . to meet you, sign autographs, and have his picture taken with you." "Remember," advises a companion leaflet, "Beauty and the Beast can also be ordered on approval; after evaluation it may be returned if for any reason you are not enchanted by it, and your billing [$350] will magically disappear."[3]

One publishing company that customarily aims at educational and school library markets offers a common sample of "Beauty and the Beast" with Disney-like, slapstick illustrations calculated to grab restless readers' attention and a "dumbed-down" style calculated to ease reluctant readers to the end of the book. The sisters on the first page, one thin, the other fat, are sticking their tongues out at each other. Later, they cackle hideously while scheming against Beauty (fig. 17).

They were not as lovely as Beauty. They were not as generous and kind as Beauty. They were too busy thinking of themselves to be thoughtful of anyone else.[4]

This is not, in fact, a particularly bad book. There are others less competent and more boring, with the minimal feeling and individualization evident here drained out of them. The most frequent offender in the versions of the period is not poor crafting but slick blandness, making it difficult to explain to consumers what distinguishes a "bad book" from a good one. In the absence of an opportunity to experience the story at full strength, a

17. *Beauty and the Beast,* illustrated by Karen Milone. Copyright 1981 by Troll Associates, Mahwah, New Jersey.

weakened version may seem adequate. Even critics and reviewers are often unaware of the story's background or careless in evaluating new versions.

In 1983, consumers spent $404.7 million on hardcover juvenile books, according to the Book Industry Study Group, a trade research organization; by 1987, the figure had jumped to $731.9 million. Fairy tales are a big part of this industry, particularly as the market has shown an increasing shift, since the 1970s, from library to trade-store consumption. Lavishly illustrated editions of "classic" stories are easier to sell than newly written, less familiar children's literature, and publishers do not have to pay for texts that are in the public domain. As a result, folk and fairy tales have proliferated in both single-edition picture books and collections of variable quality.[5] Fortunately, "Beauty and the Beast" has survived its frequent dilution and found expression through a number of re-creations with staying power. This discussion focuses on several picture books (the story's most common vehicle for several decades), one selection from an anthology, a young adult novel, and two adult short stories appearing in science fiction and fantasy collections.

Beauty and the Beast, retold by Philippa Pearce and illustrated by Alan Barrett in 1972, has minimized details in both text and art with forceful results. Based on Beaumont's plot and characters, the story presented here reduces the number of children to three girls—"all that the story really needs," as Pearce notes in an afterword.[6] Only the last dream, the appearance of the dying Beast necessary to the climax, remains. The merchant does not return with Beauty to the castle; she sneaks off alone one night, thereby dispersing any doubts as to the merchant's strength of character. Fathers do not give away their daughters but sometimes let them slip away when they are truly determined.

The style itself is spare (where Cocteau's mirror said "Reflect for me. I will reflect for you," Pearce's says "Show-Show"). The telling is not ungraceful, however, and Pearce has supplied some imaginative specifics of her own. The roses, for instance, first evade the merchant's grasp, setting up an element of suspense before the Beast's appearance. (The rose bled in an oral version collected in Delarue—see appendix 3.) Beauty's knife and fork spring into her hand, and the palace offers storybooks, toys, Persian cats, and Spaniels; this is the first version to mention what a girl-child rather than a woman might consider treasures. But overall, the narrative relies on action, with relatively little description or dialogue, to carry the themes, and graphically Barrett has mirrored Pearce's concentrated tone in his gouache paintings.

The opening and closing cameo frames, for instance, telescope a distance of time and place—the aging father, the obedient daughter. The mottled pages and rough textures give an appearance of antiquity. The subdued colors set a foreboding tone. As the scenes progress, they remain isolated in round cameos of other place and time, but they enlarge, with colors growing more intense; still very impressionistic, the work indulges in few details. The strong focus of white on a horse and on the snow-streaked wind slanting down at it, reveals the father small and helpless in the storm, with neither face nor forest outlined at all. In the full vista following it, the story world takes over, with the small introductory cameos left behind as doorways. The blue gives a powerful, brooding sense of magic as it does with Mercer Mayer's 1978 book (picture-book scenes of magic are often dominated by the color blue). Shapes are implied rather than elaborated.

The Beast revealed is a real and frightening horror of the imagination, a fragment of nightmares, his eyes, nostrils, and fangs magnified to fill the page, yet dragged downward in lines that imply pain as well as the capacity to inflict it. In only one picture does Barrett's diminutive Beauty appear with the Beast, and there the composition of the two figures shows them powerfully pulled as in a tug of war, the Beast one way and Beauty another. Barrett does not show their growth toward friendship and acceptance. He deals, as Pearce does in her written work, with only a few basic developments, but with tremendous force.

Like the first powerful portrait of the Beast, the last reflects white glints across his face to create a terrifying ghostly pallor (matching the merchant's first terror under white-smudged roses and white-smeared sky), with a midnight blue consuming him as he lies dying in his coliseum-like surrounding. The prince who replaces him appears in a burst of soft orange sparks again created by an impressionistic texture that leaves out details in favor of central impact (plate 7). At the end, the characters are put back in their frames of remote time and place, but this prince retains an animal power and roughness in his face that none of the other fairy tale princes have, and it makes for a stronger conclusion. Beauty has changed position from a submissive bowed head to a decisive, straightforward gaze. Sheered to minimal appearances, the two main characters are nevertheless rendered distinctive by Barrett's strong, stark visual suggestions.

Diane Goode's 1978 art work could not offer a more startling contrast to Barrett's. Her close translation of Beaumont's story is smooth, with full-page paintings exuding an elegant, French-court flavor. Fleurs-de-lis decorate the endpapers, and the miniature reflection of a distant land in the "O" of "Once" represents not so much an archaic time as a conventional fairyland, with green tendrils curling out of the mist into the present of a new telling. Where Barrett's colors are muted and brooding, Goode's are almost gay, sometimes affecting or even contradicting the mood of tension in a serious scene but adding luster where they are well integrated. The skillful line work is most evident in occasional black-and-white pictures, but there is careful attention to drafting throughout, with a complex maze of arches framing several compositions and other architectural features forming a prominent focus. The play of lines and space, light and shadow is subtle when it is not overwhelmed with lavish patterns of turquoise, purple, or gold in costumes and settings (plate 8).

Despite the strong drawing, the lion never looks truly fearsome. In fact, he appears, in his magnificent robes, as worried as Beauty and her father. The sisters, on the other hand, show a genuine petulance, and the small, rouged tautness of Beauty's face is affecting. This is a formal, almost flowery portrayal of the story much in accord with Beaumont's elevated sentiments and poles away from another picturebook version published the same year.

Mercer and Marianna Mayer's re-creation is a dramatic blend of adaptation and illustration that has immediate appeal. The plot structure is closer to Lang's Villeneuve-based version than to Beaumont's, with the dream sequence included and the sisters' punishment curtailed from their turning into stone statues to their simply envying Beauty's happiness. Dialogue is a mainstay, with each character explaining instead of explained, as in Beauty's reassurance after the merchant's business collapse:

> Don't worry, Father. You'll see—it will be a new life for us. I will love to live
> in the country. It will be as though we were having a vacation all year long.[7]

The sisters vociferously protest their fate and weasel out of chores. And to Beauty's persistent questions about his day, the Beast retorts angrily,

> I hunt. I prowl the woods for prey. I am an animal after all, my lady! I must kill
> for my meat. Unlike you I cannot eat gracefully. (P. 25)

Although their development stays on a symbolically abbreviated plane, Mayer's characters nevertheless assume more reality than stock types, and their relationships quicken accordingly beyond a statement of roles. In their evenings together, Beast emerges as something of a magician as well as a vivid storyteller, justifying Beauty's growing rapport with him. She herself is attached to a tiny red bird with whose loyal affection she identifies: "Often she would take the little bird from its cage, letting it fly free. Though the windows were open wide, it would never leave the tower" (p. 23).

Both the conflicts and the commentaries are direct. The Beast's confrontation with the merchant explicitly defines each.

> "I would never allow my daughter to take my place!' protested the merchant. 'Kill me if you must." But the Beast refused.

> "It must be your daughter's choice. If she will not come, then at least go to your family and say good-bye. If you do not return I will come and find you." (P. 15)

Later, the old woman of her dreams admonishes Beauty, "Your prince cannot return to you . . . . Since he has failed to make you his wife, you must not really love him" (p. 31). The Beast himself explains his enchantment.

> When I was a boy I was very vain and quite proud. My palace was filled with servants and everyone honored me and did my bidding. One day an old hag came begging at my palace gate. I showed her no pity, she was so ugly. The sight of her did not move me and I sent her away without food or money. As she left she warned that I would spend the rest of my life wandering in my fine palace without a friend till someone could find beauty in me. I laughed at her; but when I returned to my palace, I found it empty. I have been alone ever since. (P. 29)

Although the text is relatively long for a picture book, it moves quickly and is faced on every page with an absorbing depiction. Mercer Mayer's story-art has almost a filmic effect, its series of images presenting the tale independently from (though in this case harmoniously with) the words. Details both define the action and heighten the symbolism. In a striking example of the latter, the Beast is connected to ancient cultures through numerous Egyptian figures of animistic worship appearing as statuary in his palace: Ba, a bird-symbol for the soul; Anubis, the god of the dead; Wadjit, the cobra goddess. Peering from the back of Beauty's room is Isis, goddess with cow's horns who brought the dead fertility god, Osiris, back to life and doubled as mother/life-giver and enchantress with powers to cure the sick—obviously a parallel to "Beauty and the Beast" in Mayer's iconography. (Apuleius, author of "Cupid and Psyche," was initiated into the cult of Isis, a fact noted by von

Franz in her introduction to *A Psychological Interpretation of the Golden Ass of Apuleius*, p. 8.)

One scarab joins Beauty's cloak while another decorates the statue of a lion that resembles those guarding certain pyramids. The bridle of the Beast's horse is also decorated with a scarab. In the first glimpse of Beauty's house, a crucifix hangs on the wall; in her first glimpse of the Beast's palace, an ankh holds the same position over her head. These symbols blend sufficiently into background shadows or graphic details of the story to elaborate without intruding.

There is a propelling movement to the pictures. The drama of emotion mounts urgently with the Beast's appearance. The first pictures show a peculiar foreshortening of figures, a caricaturing of faces. The dominant color in the earlier spreads is brown. But with the Beast comes a dominance of deep blue, first introduced in the approach to the castle and running through most of the scenes with a magical setting. Here Mayer deepens the mood and realizes his characters more completely. There's great suspense in seeing the Beast's clawed figure, its face left to the imagination, leaning over the vulnerably sleeping father.

The Beast's face is no disappointment—a lionish visage of fury, with glowing eyes and unrelenting snarl. There's no trace of cuteness, but real anger. In comparison, the father's down-turned mouth and rolled-up eyes seem almost farcical. The flow of feeling in the illustrations is as marked as the pace of action. The foreboding in Beauty's backward glance against the wind is justified in the next scene pressing her confrontation with the Beast. Tension is built by somber colors and the Egyptian funeral symbols already mentioned. The Beast is calmer but has lost none of his threatening stature. By contrast, the next striking composition shows Beauty at her most vulnerable, stressing her tearful payment of her life for a rose.

Mayer's invention of "whatever Beauty wants" stresses her loneliness within the wealth, with only one bird to talk to—a pronounced contrast to the raucous parrots of past versions. The castle has many Gothic elaborations, which, although they usually focus on the main characters and on their relationships, occasionally overwhelm them. Mayer's dream sequences are appropriately static, interrupting the dramatic development that resumes with Beauty's urgent journey home to her sick father.

The sequence of the Beast's impending death is a study in sorrow. From blown roses to surrendered paws, he lies entwined by wintry vines and gnarled roots. Beauty for the first time sees the Beast vulnerable as he weeps into the mirror, and in one of the most poignant and intimate of all the various artists' reconciliation scenes, she puts her face on his for the acceptance kiss (plate 9). Because the scene is so powerful, it is hard to follow. Indeed, it is impossible. The prince pales by contrast. The Beast had been dearly accepted on his own terms and one wishes a bit of him, at least, were left.

The lion visage seems dominant in Beasts of this period, and Michael Hague's illustrations for *Beauty and the Beast*, which appeared first in a calendar and small press (Green Tiger) book accompanying a retelling by Deborah Apy but which were widely distributed in a 1983 hardcover edition, are no exception. However, where Mayer was preoccupied with Egyptian religious creatures half animal, half human, Hague elaborates his scenes with motifs in a Hellenic/Christian dichotomy. Greek statuary adorns the Beast's palace. The ram horns (reminiscent of d'Aulnoy's "Le Mouton") thrusting through the Beast's leonine mane parallel the horns atop a bust of Pan, the figure central to the Beast's secret garden, which also shelters an antlered deer and horned goats. The unicorn featured in this version seems a sentimental addition, though theoretically it bridges classical nature worship and Christian tradition. Christ raised the horn of salvation and dwelt in the womb of the Virgin Mary. Beauty, whose lap the unicorn seeks out, is a virgin offering salvation to a soul incarnated in a beastly form shed at death. Although never explicitly spelled out, the allegory of purification and resurrection is clear through associations.

The unicorn is only one of the inventions that Apy has injected into a sixty-four-page version combining features of Jean Cocteau's 1946 film with the traditional Beaumont structures. The sisters are decorated with names, Jeanette and Adelle. They discuss at length the virtues of peacock feathers and the drawbacks of a simple sister. Dialogue of a much more elaborate nature than Mayer's stretches the story here, punctuated by an occasional marvel such as the butterflies (Psyche is the Greek word for butterfly as well as soul) that burst from the trunk appearing on the merchant's return with the rose and the bad news.

> "It is magic, Father. It must have something to do with the Beast. . . . Here, Father, is all that my sisters asked for," said Beauty. . . . "It must mean that things are as they should be, even if we don't understand them. Don't you see, Father, this is a sign that things will be well."[8]

In the dreams appear the usual fine lady and the prince, apparently drawn from the Villeneuve/Lang version, and a small unicorn that grows in the course of the story to maturity and appears in carvings on a chest and on Beauty's bed. The aviary and palatial entertainments also find their way here, along with a balcony scene in which Beauty's physical attraction to the Beast becomes tangible as they dance. Several passages seem directly lifted from Cocteau: "At the top of the glass were written the words 'Reflect for Me,' and, at the bottom, the word 'I Will Reflect for You'" (p. 29). Later, the Beast enters Beauty's sleeping chamber with blood on his hands from a kill (p. 39), and Beauty's description of him to her father echoes the filmscript almost word for word.

> Sometimes he's funny and makes me laugh. Other times, though, he seems so very sad that I must turn away from him so as not to cry myself. (Apy, p. 56)

> But now he makes me want to burst out laughing, sometimes; and then I see his eyes and they are so sad that I turn my own away so as not to cry. (Cocteau, p. 252)

The sentence Beauty speaks next is the same in both versions, "Certain forces obey him, other forces command him" (Apy, p. 56; Cocteau, p. 252). Whether Apy is unconsciously drawing on a literary tradition established by Cocteau or simply plagiarizing is open to debate.

Hague's paintings, too, reflect the influence of other children's book illustrators: Rackham-like woods-creatures in the forested maze where the merchant is lost and Beauty later rides; a dream fairy figure strikingly akin to Dulac's, in a similar pose before a tent-like canopy around Beauty's bed—both supported by clouds. Cocteau's death-scene swans appear in Hague's as well (fig. 18). Hague incorporates nice touches of his own, however: Beauty is surrounded by a flock of humdrum geese in her noon-day barnyard; two of the same birds, ethereal in night flight, wing over her head as she dances with the Beast. Hague's scenes are predominantly dark, almost Gothic, with intense flashes of color and refined texturing of drapery, foliage, marble, wood, stone, feathers, fur, and other contrasting surfaces. Striking compositions centralize the main characters in an artful variety of postures more memorable than the faces.

Less romantic than Hague, Mayer, or Goode's interpretation, is a 1985 picture book by British artist Warwick Hutton. The text is a dignified retelling of Beaumont's version, as well distributed from page to page for reading aloud as Marianna Mayer's, with less modern dialogue. Hutton is a master of

18. From *Beauty and the Beast*, retold by Deborah Apy,
illustrated by Michael Hague. Copyright © 1980 and 1983 by Michael Hague.
Reprinted by permission of Henry Holt, and Company, Inc.

lighted landscape and light-filtered interiors, striking examples of which appear in each painting. He builds the father's ride into an ominous situation with boulder-black clouds, one fork of white lightning extended in the wind against the horse's white tail, white bones of another horse (or perhaps the Beast's prey) on the left and the eerie green-under-gray of a coming storm. All this is heightened by a too-distant rift in the clouds behind and in the deep shadow ahead. The serpent on the ground could only be deadly.

Hutton's restraint in color, even in showing the garden, and in line, even in showing the father's emotional expression, is marked in contrast to Mayer's depiction, which is so exaggerated. This Beast is a darkly vague hulk. His few frontal closeups suggest features of a gorilla (plate 10), an animal close in evolutionary development to humans. In his first appearance, the lighting effect comes straight from a circled sun, and the shadows thrown make a brilliant composition. The Beast is thrice threatening for his back's being turned; and the peacocks, along with their towering-hedge replicas, make a kind of play on reality, pointing at the kneeling victim. They are an inventive contrast to Dulac's parrots and Mayer's one red bird.

The palace features a patterned mosaic of Eastern splendor, cool in the shadows and well lit by the sun; but for all the wealth, it is fine-lined, carefully shaped, and never cluttered or overstated. Hutton shows with clarity and grace what it is like to be alone. Beauty's isolated figure, dwarfed by the palatial grounds over which she looks with her back to the viewer, projects a total silence and stillness. The Prince's amazed expression at being transformed offers a contrasting hint of humor. Hutton has walked a fine line between distance and involvement, keeping the tone of personal romance subsumed in formal patterns.

The 1983 collection of eleven Perrault and two Beaumont stories translated by Angela Carter and illustrated by Michael Foreman cast "Beauty and the Beast" into a half-medieval, half-futuristic mode, with castle and costumes out of the Middle Ages and a one-eyed monster that suggests a mutation from science fiction. A newt and frogs gather at his dying moment, and there is not a rose in sight. Brownish purples and dark blues dominate the three full-color paintings bleeding off 8" x 11" pages. A skull supports the candlestick whose flickering lights cast a shadow of the Beast in a sketch above the opening paragraph. The castle looms with an ominous face of window-slits and a toothy gate. The goblet and dainties set before the viewer, who is forced into a frontal view of the Beast from Beauty's perspective, are noticeably missing from the Beast's place. He sits at the table

19. (above) From *Beauty and the Beast,* by Rosemary Harris. Illustration by Errol Le Cain. Illustration copy-right © 1979 by Errol Le Cain. Reprinted by permission of Doubleday, a division of Bantam, Doubleday, Dell Publishing Group, Inc., and by Faber and Faber, Ltd.

20. "Stages," an illustration by Maurice Sendak, 1978, from *The Art of the Broadway Poster*, by Michael Patrick Hearn, 1980. Reprinted with permission of Maurice Sendak, courtesy of Ballantine Books, a Division of Random House, Inc.

with nothing before him but his reptilian hands (plate 11). Yet his decline below moonlit topiary is still poignant.

Beauty and the merchant are almost unnoticeable in these pictures, as is the inch-high prince sitting up in the illustrated strip bordering the story's end. It is ironic that this most grotesque of Beasts should accompany a demure translation of Beaumont's story. And it is interesting that Carter has included a related Beaumont story, "Sweetheart," which overtly moralizes about a prince turned beast until he can learn to be good, do what he is told, and find a mate with the same virtues.

Many noted children's book illustrators, including Roger Duvoisin (in Virginia Haviland's *Favorite Fairy Tales Told in France*, 1959), Hilary Knight (in *Beauty and the Beast*, 1963), Alice and Martin Provensen (in *The Provensen Book of Fairy Tales*, 1971), Errol Le Cain (in Rosemary Harris's *Beauty and the Beast*, 1980—see figure 19), and Francesca Crespi (in *Little Box of Fairy Tales*, adapted by Olive Jones,1983) have undertaken picture-book or anthologized versions of "Beauty and the Beast." Even Maurice Sendak has offered a swashbuckling vision of the Beast in a poster (fig. 20) for a Broadway production of Stuart Ostrow's experimental play, *Stages*, which played for only one night in 1978.

Etienne Delessert's 1984 picture book, which in the first edition mistakenly attributes the story to Madame d'Aulnoy, is accompanied by sophisticated, surrealistic paintings that will challenge junior high school students to plumb both art and story. Illustration, book design, and format are coordinated to lead perceptive viewers through the symbolic overtones. Single- or double-page spreads focus on dramatic highpoints featuring a griffin hideous one moment and vulnerable the next (plate 12); at times, he peeks in miniature form over or at the framed text. Natural elements such as a storm, night, or flower are personified with human faces, while social acquaintances rejecting the family after its loss of wealth appear with serpents' heads. Implications of resurrection surface in a phoenix figure. The drama of color and action coupled with subtleties of humor and sadness invite close involvement.

Every picturebook version has its followers:

> I liked the story because it showed that things that may seem mean and furoshoise [*sic*] outside can still be loving, efectionet [*sic*] and caring just on the inside as a human. (David Ward, third grade, Forest Glen Elementary School)[9]

. . . or its detractors:

> I didn't like it becouse [*sic*] it was boring. I lost my attanchon [*sic*] to the story.
> By the time it was done I was picking my shoe. (Anonymous third grader,
> Forest Glen Elementary School).

Three-year-olds have been absorbed by the emotional drama of Mercer
Mayer's adaptation. Primary graders and older elementary school children
respond to increasingly complex versions. And since 1978, adolescents have
been captivated by Robin McKinley's novel *Beauty*.

The creation of a contemporary, first-person, young adult novel from a
fairy tale could raise a host of technical problems for the novelist and objec-
tions from devotees of traditional lore. *Beauty, A Retelling of the Story of
Beauty and the Beast* was included by American Library Association commit-
tees in both the Notable Children's Books and the Best Books for Young
Adults lists for 1978. It was Robin McKinley's first novel, written in the throes
of a negative reaction to the television adaptation starring George C. Scott, in
which McKinley felt that the point had been missed and the aesthetic
thinned. The story, she maintains, is about honor. Honour is her heroine's
real name, given to match her two older sisters', Grace and Hope, by a
mother who does not survive the birth of baby Mercy, who also dies. In the
tradition of the story from its origins, Beauty is a nickname, but one bestowed
here, ironically, on a five-year-old who cannot comprehend the concept of
Honour and requests Beauty instead, an appellation retained into a gawky
adolescence.

For a 247-page novel, the cast is compact, with secondary characters
introduced and developed naturally within the context of the traditional plot.
Grace, Hope, and Honour (called Beauty) Huston are the sisters. Their father, Roderick Huston, is a shipwright/merchant and carpenter. Robert
Tucker is a sailor and fiancé of Grace; Gervain Woodhouse, an ironworker/
blacksmith who marries Hope. Greatheart, a horse given to Beauty by a
family friend, leads her to the palace of the Beast and keeps her company
there. Lydia and Bessie are two breezes who attend Beauty in the palace.

A few minor characters make brief appearances essential to McKinley's
revisions: Ferdy, whose first kiss repels Beauty in a reaction that presages her
resistance to admitting love for the Beast; Pat Lawry, who courts Grace in
Robbie's absence; Mercy and Richard, twins born to Hope and Gervain;
Melinda Honeybourne, Gervain's widowed aunt, manager of the Red Griffin
and Roderick Huston's eventual wife; and Orpheus the canary, who cheers

the company throughout their resettlement in the country. All but Orpheus further the theme of male/female relationships, and the canary serves as a link with the birds Beauty later coaxes to her palace window—a sign that her involvement is weakening the Beast's enchantment.

There are no villains here. And where fairy-tale brevity benefits from the Beast's initial and terrible impression to lend tension to Beauty's dilemma, it is McKinley's task to maintain that tension through a longer work in which the Beast's essential nobility quickly becomes apparent. The conflict, of course, is shifted to an internal level with Beauty's rite of passage. It seems ultimately fitting that modern teenage fiction should emerge from an old tale of the journey into maturation.

To sharpen this focus, McKinley has altered the father's weakness and the sisters' villainy (those faults shifted the onus of responsibility away from Beauty's self-determined choices), in much the same way that Villeneuve either omitted or explained away the family flaws. All three are paragons of integrity, as are the girls' suitors, their virtue fortunately relieved by practical, down-to-earth humor and genuine affection. Beauty herself is strong-willed to obstinate, plain and thin, a tomboy passionate only about animals and books. She is a smart, adolescent ugly duckling, with everyone else's assurance that she will eventually turn into a swan. True to life, Beauty believes only her own critical assessment. She is as deprecatory of her physical appearance and as apprehensive of mirrors as the Beast (there are none in her room at home nor in the palace of the Beast).

The narrative, covering Beauty's fifteenth to eighteenth years, is structured into three parts. The first establishes the family background and situation, the courtship of the older girls, the loss of the ships (and with them, Grace's fiancé), the auction of goods, the removal to Gervain's childhood home in the north country, his marriage to Hope and prohibition not to enter the reputedly enchanted forest behind their home, the birth of their twins, and the father's trip to the city to recover one ship, from which he returns with a rose. In section two, the father tells his story of finding the Beast's castle and picking the fateful flower, after which his saddle-bags are opened to reveal rich gifts. Beauty determines to go back in his stead after the month's reprieve and dreams twice of the castle as she prepares to depart.

The third and last part comprises more than half of the book, beginning with the farewell of father and daughter at the castle gate and ending with her declaration of love for the Beast and the celebration. With unexpected holding power, McKinley amplifies descriptions of Beauty's settlement into life at the palace, the development of her relationship with the Beast, her homesickness and desperation to tell Grace of Robbie's return (seen through a magic glass, or nephrite plate, belonging to the Beast) before another suitor proposes, and the visit home, which convinces Beauty of her love for the Beast and delays her return till almost too late. The reader knows that Beauty must finally accept her own physicality and release the Beast, but the questions of how and when raise anticipation and even anxiety during Beauty's last ride, when the Beast's magic weakens and she must find him on the strength of her own love.

Sustaining the plot are the book's compatibly blended point of view, pace, style, tone, and theme. The first-person narrative lends immediacy, fosters a reader's identification with the protagonist, and allows a candid look at Beauty's internal journey. The Beast shows mature perceptions, developed during his two hundred years of brooding alone in the palace, on their first meeting, when he tells her he would only have sent her father home unharmed had she decided not to come to the palace herself.

> "You *would?*" I said; it was half a shriek. "You mean that I came here for nothing?"
>
> A shadowy movement like the shaking of a great shaggy head. "No. Not what you would count as nothing. He would have returned to you, and you would have been glad, but you also would have been ashamed, because you had sent him, as you thought, to his death. Your shame would have grown until you came to hate the sight of your father, because he reminded you of a deed you hated, and hated yourself for. In time it would have ruined your peace and happiness, and at last your mind and heart."[10]

But Beauty's knowledge, limited to an honest if impetuous intuition at the book's beginning, develops through her solitude at the palace and her experiences with the Beast, as evidenced in self-examinations that slowly raise her to the Beast's level of awareness.

> I had avoided touching him, or letting him touch me. At first I had eluded him from fear; but when fear departed, elusiveness remained, and developed into habit. Habit bulwarked by something else; I could not say what. The obvious answer, because he was a Beast, didn't seem to be the right one. I considered this. (P. 170)

Without becoming too confessional, these insights bond the reader to Beauty as she progresses through nightly more difficult denials of the Beast's proposal to taking his arm and finally realizing her feelings in face of the family's animosity toward the Beast.

> I knew now what it was that had happened. I couldn't tell them that here, at home with them again, I had learned what I had successfully ignored these last weeks at the castle; that I had come to love him. They were no less dear to me, but he was dearer yet. (P. 215)

The frequency of vivid scenes keeps Beauty's development from dwindling into a diary. A confrontation she forces between her horse Greatheart and the Beast, whom all creatures fear, is gripping. Beauty's discovery, in the library, of future books that have not yet been written and her attempts to understand Robert Browning or to envision modern inventions referred to in other works is quite funny, as are the struggles of the two attendant breezes to outfit her like a lady. Her encounters with the Beast are natural, as often light as moving.

> "It's raining," I said, but he understood the question, because he answered:
> "Yes, even here it rains sometimes . . . . I've found that it doesn't do to tinker with weather too much. . . . Usually it rains after nightfall," he added apologetically. (Pp. 141–142)

The occasion on which she feeds him her favorite dessert, however, proceeds from a touching note to a powerful confrontation—the last barrier she throws up against him before her vision (literally, in this case) begins to clear for a new sensual awareness.

A deceptively simple style blends drama with detail. Part of the book's appeal is certainly its descriptions of a life anyone might long for—leisure spiced with high cuisine and horseback riding, with learning for learning's sake thrown in at will. These descriptions are by turn specific and suggestive, allowing readers to luxuriate in a wish-fulfilling existence but leaving room for them to grow their own fantasies. The marvels of palace life are quite explicit.

> I returned my gaze to the table. I saw now that it was crowded with covered dishes, silver and gold. Bottles of wine stood in buckets full of gleaming crushed ice; a bowl big enough to be a hip bath stood on a pedestal two feet tall, in the shape of Atlas bearing the world on his shoulders; and the hollow globe was full of shining fresh fruit. A hundred delightful odours assailed me.

At the head of the table, near the door I had entered by, stood a huge wooden chair, carved and gilded and lined with chestnut-brown brocade over straw-coloured satin. The garnet-set peak was as tall as a schooner's mast. It could have been a throne. As I looked, it slid away slightly from the table and turned itself towards me, as another chair had beckoned my father. I noticed for the first time that it was the only chair at that great table, and there was only one place laid, although the table gleamed to its farther end with the curved backs of plate covers, and with goblets and tureens and tall jeweled pitchers. (Pp. 107–108)

Other passages leave a strategic amount of information to the reader's imagination. During Beauty's first conversation with the Beast, she sees only his "massive shadow" (p. 113), heightening a dread that peaks when he finally stands to reveal himself. Even then, only his body is delineated; the specifics of his face are implied by Beauty's reaction.

"Oh no," I cried, and covered my own face with my hands. But when I heard him take a step towards me, I leaped back in alarm like a deer at the crack of a branch nearby, turning my eyes away from him. . . . What made his gaze so awful was that his eyes were human. (P. 116)

Bit by bit, through references to long white teeth and tangy fur, readers can construct an image of the Beast, but it is largely their own.

There are twists of humor throughout dialogue and description that balance the darkest hours of both Beauty and the Beast for a tone alternately sweet and bitter, ingenuous and sophisticated. Underlying all the various shades of emotion, however, is a sense of inevitable destiny, the fairy-tale security that all will be well in spite of threats and confusions. The roses Beauty plants in winter bloom to comfort her before she leaves home. A griffin on the ring (and later necklace) given her by the Beast looks powerful but not predatory. In spite of Beauty's association of the Beast with the Minotaur when Gervain first tells her of the rumored enchantment, the mazes she encounters at the castle simply mirror her own internal loss of direction.

I dreamed of the castle that Father had told us about. I seemed to walk quickly down halls with high ceilings. I was looking for something, anxious that I could not find it. I seemed to know the castle very well; I did not hesitate as I turned corners, went up stairs, down stairs, opened doors. (P. 82)

I found myself in the castle again, walking through dozens of handsome, magnificently furnished rooms, looking for something. I had a stronger sense of sorrow and of urgency this time; and also a sense of some other—presence; I could describe it no more clearly. I found myself crying as I walked, flinging doors open and looking inside eagerly, then hurrying on as they were each empty of what I sought. (Pp. 91–92)

I walked across more corridors, up and down more stairs, and in and out of more rooms than I cared to count. . . . I soon lost my sense of direction, and then most of my sense of purpose, but I kept walking. . . . After a while, perhaps hours, I came to a door at the end of a corridor, just around a corner. (Pp. 109–110)

Nearly every day we found ourselves traveling over unfamiliar ground, even when I thought I was deliberately choosing a route we had previously traced; even when I thought I recognized a particular group of trees or flower-strewn meadow, I could not be sure of it. I didn't know whether this was caused by the fact that my sense of direction was worse than I'd realized, which was certainly possible, or whether the paths and fields really changed from day to day—which I thought was also possible. (Pp. 137–138)

"I can't seem to keep the corridors straight in my head somehow, and as soon as I'm hopelessly lost, I turn a corner and there's my room again. So I never learn anything. I don't mean to complain," I added hastily. "It's just that I get lost so very quickly that I don't have the chance to see very much before they—er—send me home again." (P. 142)

It is Beauty's inner pressure and the Beast's need that tell time; there are no clocks in the palace. Like Cocteau, McKinley is intrigued with different dimensions of reality. The space, time, and logic of the primary world are suspended in the secondary world. Beauty's bridging both requires some adjustment.

You look at this world—my world, here, as you looked at your old world, your family's world. This is to be expected; it was the only world, the only way of seeing, that you knew. Well; it's different here. Some things go by different rules. (P. 177)

It was slowly being borne in on me that my stories about the castle and my life there had little reality for my family. They listened with interest to what I told—or tried to tell—them, but it was for my sake, not for the sake of the tale. I could not say if this was my fault or theirs, or the fault of the worlds we lived in. (P. 210–211)

And as Cocteau admonishes, only true believers can know a world other than the mundane. Beauty's sisters are too pragmatic even to receive a message from the Beast. Her father accepts the dreams sent to comfort him by the Beast, and Gervain believes in the rumored enchantment of the forest and in Beauty's fate after she has drunk from the forest stream. Beauty herself develops her already strong instincts into a sixth sense so sharpened that she can not only see, hear, and smell the ordinary more keenly but also divine the invisible: envision the Beast in his palace from her country house without a magic glass (p. 211); understand her attendant breezes' gossip.

As the mysterious becomes familiar, it is less awesome. One reviewer accused McKinley of fettering archetypes with concrete realization, of reducing the larger-than-life to normal. Another critic countered this charge with a defense of the book's fairy-tale facets, quoting Tolkien on the creation of a secondary world.

> Fantasy is a natural human activity. It certainly does not destroy or even insult Reason; and it does not either blunt the appetite for, nor obscure the perception of, scientific verity. On the contrary. The keener and the clearer is the reason, the better fantasy will it make.[11]

Making enchantment "believable on its own terms and by realistic standards"[12] is perhaps simply making the jump from fairy tale to fantasy. Fairy tales assume belief, on either a literal or symbolic plane. Fantasies assume only a suspension of disbelief; the rest is a matter of persuasion. It was McKinley's determination to make the story immediate to contemporary readers, to keep the fantastical effects to a minimum and thus obey the rules of convincing fantasy.[13]

The next version also falls into the realm more of fantasy than of faerie. Angela Carter's thirteen-page story, "The Courtship of Mr. Lyon," published in 1979 in a collection called *The Bloody Chamber*, has a modern setting of English country manor and London hotel suite. The characters are only four: Beauty, her father, the Beast (Mr. Lyon), and a liver-and-white King Charles spaniel that figures strategically in the plot (an interesting addition in light of the British variant of 425A, "The Small-Tooth Dog"). The narrative, covering midwinter to early spring, begins with Beauty waiting for her father, but his car is stuck in a snowstorm. Entering the wrought-iron gates of "a miniature, perfect, Palladian house that seemed to hide itself shyly behind snow-laden skirts of an antique cypress,"[14] the father shelters within to find himself welcomed by the spaniel with whiskey, roast-beef (thick-sliced and rare) sandwiches, and a telephone placed at his disposal. On his way out, he sees one last perfect white rose clinging to a wintry bush and steals it. "At that, every window of the house blazed with furious light and a fugal baying, as of a pride of lions, introduced his host" (p. 124).

Beauty's father pleads his case and shows the Beast a photograph of Beauty, whereupon father and daughter are commanded to come to dinner. At dinner it is suggested that her father's business problems will be reversed with the help of the Beast's lawyers if Beauty accepts country hospitality while her father proceeds to London. Forcing a smile, she agrees and spends the winter in luxury. Her growing companionship with the Beast terminates abruptly with her father's summons to London high society, to which his success has restored him. Beauty remembers the Beast but abnegates her promise to return until one day the bedraggled spaniel appears and urgently shepherds her back to the dying Beast, whom she kisses, transforms, and marries.

Carter has grafted the old onto the new here with some brilliant writing and subtle structural maneuvers that render her abbreviated account effective. There is even space for a few telling descriptions, as in the opening forecast.

> Outside her kitchen window, the hedgerow glistened as if the snow possessed a light of its own; when the sky darkened towards evening, an unearthly, reflected pallor remained behind upon the winter's landscape, while still the soft flakes floated down. This lovely girl, whose skin possesses that same inner light so you would have thought she, too, was made all of snow, pauses in her chores in the mean kitchen to look out at the country road. Nothing has passed that way all day; the road is white and unmarked as a spilled bolt of bridal satin. (P. 121)

Later passages are trimmed but synchronized for maximum impact, especially in the repetition of rose and lion images.

The aura of timelessness, underscored by these changes from past to present and vice versa, imbues, even overwhelms, present-day trivia: "He knew by the pervasive atmosphere of a suspension of reality that he had entered a place of privilege where all the laws of the world he knew need not necessarily apply" (p. 122). The lion's-head knocker is made not of brass, as he first thinks, but of gold, with agate eyes. The spaniel waits for him on a Kelim runner. The Beast himself appears as a "leonine apparition" in a step back from the action, literally a double-spaced break in the text.

There is always a dignity about great bulk, an assertiveness, a quality of being more *there* than most of us are. The being who now confronted Beauty's father seemed to him, in his confusion, vaster than the house he owned, ponderous yet swift, and the moonlight glittered on his great, mazy head of hair, on the eyes green as agate, on the golden hairs of the great paws that grasped his shoulders so that their claws pierced the sheepskin as he shook him like an angry child shakes a doll. (P. 124)

Beauty, later caught up in a swirl of London activities, is "so far away from the timeless spell of his house it seemed to possess the radiant and finite quality of dream and the Beast himself, so monstrous, so benign, [seemed to be] some kind of spirit" (p. 130). Beauty herself at first possesses the timeless quality.

The camera has captured a certain look she had sometimes, of absolute sweetness and absolute gravity, as if her eyes might pierce appearance and see your soul. (P. 125)

The reader is aware only of this inner beauty until she begins to be corrupted by empty society and sees in the mirror a "lacquer of prettiness"—accompanied by Carter's first real physical description of her. It is a far cry from her reflection in the Beast's eyes, when "she saw her face repeated twice, as small as if it were in bud" (p. 128).

She perceives early on that "her visit to the Beast must be, on some magically reciprocal scale, the price of her father's good fortune" and refers to herself once as "Miss Lamb." She is also aware that this "restful time"—with its dinners of grilled veal, the rosewood revolving bookcases well stocked with French fairy tales, the glass bed and fleecy towels, the "pastel-colored idleness"—is more than a holiday. For after their surprisingly easy conversations each night, he helplessly declares himself.

As she was about to rise, he flung himself at her feet and buried his head in her lap. She stayed stock-still, transfixed; she felt his hot breath on her fingers, the stiff bristles of his muzzle grazing her skin, the rough lapping of his tongue, and then, with a flood of compassion, understood: All he is doing is kissing my hands. (P. 128)

Always, she flinches from his touch, and even in tears at their parting, cannot drop upon his shaggy mane the kiss to which she feels moved. Her subsequent freedom fills her both with relief and a "desolating emptiness,"

1. *Beauty and the Beast*, from Aunt Mavor's Toy Books no. 18, ca. 1867.
By permission of the Trustees of the British Library.

2. *Beauty and the Beast,* by Walter Crane, 1875. By permission
of the Department of Special Collections, University of Chicago Library.

3. *Beauty and the Beast,* by Eleanor Vere Boyle, 1875.
By permission of the Newberry Library, Chicago.

4. "Beauty and the Beast," from *The Sleeping Beauty and
Other Tales from the Old French,* illustrated by Edmund Dulac, 1910.
By permission of the Library of Congress.

5. "Beauty and the Beast," from *The Now-A-Days Fairy Book*, by Anna Alice
Chapin, illustrated by Jessie Willcox Smith, 1911. By permission of the de Grummond
Children's Literature Research Collection, University of Southern Mississippi.

6. "Beauty and the Beast," from *Fairy Tales*, by Margaret Tarrant, 1920.
By permission of Thomas Y. Crowell Co.

7. *Beauty and the Beast*, by Philippa Pearce,
illustrated by Alan Barrett, 1972.
By permission of Thomas Y. Crowell Co.

8. From *Beauty and the Beast,* adapted from the tale of
Madame Le Prince de Beaumont and illustrated by Diane Goode. Bradbury Press,
1978. Reproduced by permission of Macmillan Publishing Company.

9. From *Beauty and the Beast,* by Marianna Mayer.
Illustration by Mercer Mayer. Copyright © 1978 by Mercer Mayer.
Reproduced by permission of Four Winds Press, an Imprint
of Macmillan Publishing Company.

10. From *Beauty and the Beast*, adapted and illustrated by
Warwick Hutton. A Margaret K. McElderry Book, 1985.
Reproduced by permission of Macmillan Publishing Company.

11. "Beauty and the Beast," from *Sleeping Beauty and
Other Favourite Fairy Tales*, by Angela Carter, illustrated by Michael Foreman, 1982.
Reprinted by permission of Michael Foreman and Victor Gollancz.

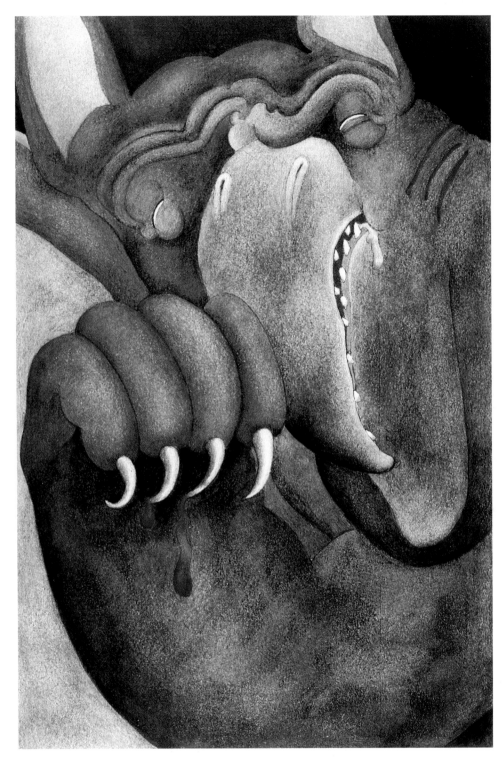

12. *Beauty and the Beast,* illustrated by Etienne Delessert, 1984.
By permission of Creative Education, Inc.

which she rushes to fill with, ironically, flowers and furs. Yet there is no hesitation when the spaniel comes. The magic is almost dead in her heart as well as in the spring garden she finds unblooming, the desolate house.

The care taken with the last scene makes it one of the few transformations consistent in power with earlier portions of the story. Beauty flings herself on the dying Beast.

> When her lips touched the meat-hook claws, they drew back into their pads and she saw how he had always kept his fists clenched but now, painfully, tentatively, at last began to stretch his fingers. Her tears fell on his face like snow and, under their soft transformation, the bones showed through the pelt, the flesh through the wide, tawny brow. And then it was no longer a lion in her arms but a man, a man with an unkempt mane of hair and, how strange, a broken nose, such as the noses of retired boxers, that gave him a distant, heroic resemblance to the handsomest of all the beasts. (P. 133)

From the first "dawning of surmise" on his face when the Beast sees Beauty's photograph to the understated triumph in his concluding request for breakfast, his gentleness and power are well tempered. The "happily ever after" statement, too, offers a perfectly contained telescopic view: "Mr. and Mrs. Lyon walk in the garden; the old spaniel drowses on the grass, in a drift of fallen petals" (p. 133).

Carter's success in updating the story without losing its timeless quality is carried one step farther by Tanith Lee in her futuristic "Beauty," a forty-page selection from a collection called *Red As Blood, or Tales from the Sisters Grimmer* that was included in the American Library Association's 1983 list of Best Books for Young Adults. This version features one essential difference, however, in addition to the science fiction elaboration of setting. The focal transformation is clearly and overtly Beauty's, never the Beast's, and is completely inner. The Beast's physical form is a matter of revelation and permanent acceptance.

The characters include Mercator Levin, his three daughters—Lyra, Joya, and Estár—and a nameless alien residing on Earth. The narrative is sectioned into four parts, starting with Levin on his way home from a successful space voyage. Upon docking his cargo, he receives the dreaded green rose, a summons rarely but irrevocably handed to earth families by powerful resident aliens for a son or daughter of the household. The homecoming party (it is Levin's 151st birthday) becomes an occasion for selecting which child will go, but the decision is quick. Lyra is a precocious musician committed to career and lover. Joya is four months pregnant. Estár, the restless spirit never at home in her own family or society, fills all the omens; she had even asked her father to bring her a rose from his travels. There follows the background story of the aliens' mysterious requests and their victims' apparent freedom, contradicted by the increasing sadness of these select young people on home visits that eventually cease altogether.

In the second section, Estár is fetched from home by a mysterious vehicle. Confused and enraged, she settles into an alien's estate and, after a month of refusing to see him, finally invites a confrontation. He is completely covered, in deference to humans' reaction to his kind's reputedly hideous form, but Estár discovers a telepathic rapport with him unlike anything she has known. Over the course of conversations, dinners, and walks in the garden, she grows to love him.

The third section sees her back home for a visit, during which she feels isolated from her family and finally anxious to get back to the alien. Deeply disturbed by her own and her family's uncertainty about the alien's ultimate motives—specifically whether he will become her lover—she asks him to reveal himself, something Joya has urged to relieve Estár's anxious state of limbo. When he does, she returns to her family—at the beginning of the last section—in speechless shock, which they and the reader attribute to the horror of the alien's appearance. Nevertheless, she is drawn back, and only at the conclusion does the reader learn the Beast is so strangely beautiful that Estár cannot hope to be loved in return.

Then he reveals to her the story of her own birth and the real reason behind the aliens' residence and summons. Their perfection, it seems, had led to sterility until a method of embryo implantation, secretly done in women who miscarried and awoke from a drugged state believing them-selves lucky enough to have retained their babies, resulted in children with physical attributes of the host body but souls of their alien parents. Eventually these children grew into a restless maturity that signalled, via the aura of a rose planted at their birth, the time they should return to their real culture and a companion with whom they could bear, because of their physical alterations, children that would survive. The restless Estár has found her rightful home and perfectly compatible mate.

The environmental adornments distract very little from the essential themes of the story. Household robots, ultimately equipped transports, weather control, the manmade mountain and dwelling of the alien are all more scene-setting than interfering, to the author's credit. Tapes, consoles, and serving mechanisms echo libraries and palatial conveniences of past versions. A voice-bead hovers "in the air like a tame bird"[15] or comes "to perch on her fingers, . . . a silly affectionate ruse. . . that it was somehow creaturally alive" (p. 196) in reflection of consoling creature-companions in Beauty's previous isolations.

The garden receives its symbolic emphasis, with a twist, in descriptions of illuminated flowers from another planet "mutating gently among the strands of terrestrial vegetation" (p. 183).

> Three feet high, a flower like an iris with petals like dark blue flames allowed the moon to climb its stem out of the valley below. (P. 183)

> Alien roses, very tall, the colors of water and sky, not the blood and blush, parchment, pallor and shadow shades of Earth. She walked through a wheatfield of roses." (P. 194)

The summons rose itself, "slender as a tulip, its petals a pale and singing green" has "no thorns, or rather only one and that metaphysical, if quite unbearably penetrating" (p. 170).

It is not so much the details of the story that create its self-conscious tone, but a jigaw puzzle effect manipulating readers toward the protagonist's "raison d'Estár" (p. 178). The pieces of the puzzle, however—both the story-within-a-story subplots and the build-up of suspense—are cleverly fitted. Through Levin's foreboding, through the apprehension engendered by the alien's suggested hideousness, and through Estár's reactions themselves, one is prepared for but still intrigued by her fate, a quality of the earlier fairy tale.

Levin's foreboding begins immediately on the first page with his consideration of Estár, "ill-named for a distant planet, meaning the same as the Greek word *psyche*" (p. 168). He worries about her inability to express or fulfill herself, in sharp contrast with his other two daughters. "She did not reach to kiss him as the others did, restrained, perhaps inhibited" (p. 172). Her life seems as uncertain as her birth—she was nearly aborted. Her preferences in dress, decoration, and reading run to the archaic.

Aware that she is a misfit, she is not yet prepared to be sacrificed to the unknown. The reader suffers her anxiety through artfully planted disclosures. It is rumored that the aliens

> covered their ugliness with elegant garments, gloves, masking draperies, hoods and visors. Yet . . . there were those things which now and then must

be revealed, some inches of pelted hairy skin, the gauntleted over-fingered hands, the brilliant eyes empty of white, lensed by their yellow conjuctiva. (P. 176)

When the alien finally appears to Estár, "Not a centimeter of body surface showed," leaving her to speculate the worst. At dinner, "the blank shining mask" (p. 184) rearranges itself disconcertingly as he eats, the visor "constructed of separable atoms and molecules" (p. 183). Even his voice is distorted by some mechanism to avoid its offending her kind.

The reactions of Estár herself to an unknown threat range through stages of self-knowledge: confusion, fear, control, honesty, and understanding. At first she defines the issue as one of power: she is angry that there is no choice. But then it appears she is "not a slave, not a pet. She was free as air" (p. 181). When she tells the alien she wants to return home forever, he senses instantly it is a lie to herself. She does not even want to leave the table. The fear of the sexuality to which her love would inevitably lead causes her to let it go unrecognized. She plays hide-and-seek games to elude him, but he simply does not appear. Her plans to escape become daydreams in which he finds her. She dreams of him before his uncovering and after. She experiences the strangeness of her own home, where she has become the alien. There, her face takes on the pain common to other victims.

> The expression of the children of Earth sacrificed to monsters or monstrous gods, given in their earthly perfection to dwell with beasts. That dreadful demoralizing sadness, that devouring fading in the face of the irreparable. (P. 200)

But of course, she is really coming into her own and "unable to reveal her secret. . . . They would not realize her sadness was all for them" (p. 208).

Sexuality is acknowledged overtly as a key issue by her father's and sisters' direct inquiries, her own conflicts, and the minute description of the alien unmasked.

> The hirsute pelt which covered his kind was a reality misinterpreted, misexplained. It was most nearly like the fur of a short-haired cat yet in actuality resembled nothing so much as the nap of velvet. He was black, like her sister Joya, yet the close black nap of fur must be tipped, each single hair, with amber; his color had changed second to second, as the light or dark found him, even as he breathed, from deepest black to sheerest gold. His wellmade body was modeled from these two extremes of color, his fine

musculature, like that of a statue, inked with ebony shadows, and high-lighted by gilding. Where the velvet sheathing faded into pure skin, at the lips, nostrils, eyelids, genitals, the soles of the feet, palms of the hands, the flesh itself was a mingling of the two shades, a somber cinnamon, couth and subtle, sensual in its difference, but not shocking in any visual or aesthetic sense. The inside of his mouth, which he had also contrived to let her see, was a dark golden cave in which conversely the humanness of the white teeth was in fact itself a shock. While at his loins the velvet flowed into a bearded blackness, long hair like unraveled silk; the same process occurred on the skull, a raying mane of hair, very black, very silken, its edges burning out through amber, ochre, into blondness—the sunburst of a black sun. The nails on his six long fingers, the six toes of his long and arched feet, were the tint of new dark bronze, translucent, bright as flames. His facial features were large and of a contrasting fineness, their sculptured quality at first obscured, save in profile, by the sequential ebb and flare of gold and black, and the domination of the extraordinary eyes. The long cinnamon lids, the thick lashes that were not black but startingly [sic] flaxen—the color of the edges of the occipital hair—these might be mistaken for human. But the eyes themselves could have been made from two highly polished citrines, clear saffron, darkening around the outer lens, almost to the cinnamon shade of the lids, and at the center by curiously blended charcoal stages to the ultimate black of the pupil. Analogously, they were like the eyes of a lion, and perhaps all of him lionlike, maybe, the powerful body, its skin unlike a man's, flawless as a beast's skin so often was, the pale-fire edged mane. (Pp. 201–202)

Here, too, is a religious aspect that appears strongly throughout the story to the last page (along with the sensuousness of the acceptance kiss). Estar loves the alien "spontaneously, but without any choice" (p. 208), in exact parallel with the Protestant theological explanation of predestination. Those without grace—the family and friends of the saved—do not understand.

And when she no longer moved among them, they would regret her, and mourn for her as if she had died. Disbelieving or forgetting that in any form of death, the soul—Psyche, Estár (well-named)—refinds a freedom and a beauty lost with birth. (P. 208)

Estár's death, referred to repeatedly ("she felt as if some part of her had died," p. 196; a drugged sleep "aping the release of death," p. 198; etc.), ends in resurrection. Her redemption comes through confirmation of her Other-ness.[16]

The determined, humorless intensity of the vision is especially marked in contrast to light incorporations of the story in mass-market versions mentioned earlier or teenage romances that arbitrarily use the story's themes at a superficial level. Halfyard and Rose's *Kristin and Boone* (1983), for example, centers on a television production of "Beauty and the Beast" in which adolescent actors become involved with each other and their physically deformed director. Barbara Cohen's 1984 *Roses* plumbs the story somewhat more deeply in a modern parallel of the father-daughter-suitor triangle, with the suitor role divided into two characters. The Beast is a hideously deformed middle-aged florist who hires beautiful young Isabel in seeking redemption for a death he once caused an actress resembling her. High school senior Rob understands Isabel's fear of physical closeness to be a result of her mother's early death, seeks to overcome it with loving patience, and wins his suit.

Certainly the metaphors for self-acceptance and reconciliation with the Other that appear in "Beauty and the Beast" are commonly borrowed. In 1982, millions of children around the United States caught their breaths in hushed sorrow as a small boy cried over the dying form of his ugly, extra-terrestial friend. The same children clapped and cheered with released tension as the beast's heart, dead by all measurement of medical machinery, relit suddenly into a bright throbbing red at the boy's words, "I love you." The terrifying unknown had been transformed into the affectionate familiar. In the film *E.T.*, the motif of "Beauty and the Beast" rose like a phoenix and captured the imagination of yet another generation.

Scores of picturebooks, including the Caldecott Award–winning *Girl Who Loved Wild Horses* (Paul Goble, 1978—see fig. 21) and *Buffalo Woman* (Goble, 1984)—both illustrated native American legends about the human adapting to the animal—reveal intriguing parallels with "Beauty and the Beast." The very problem of spiritual versus materialistic values—a theme central to the story—is enough to turn the art forms of a computerized world that seemingly threatens literary tradition back to the fairy tale for plot, characters, and motifs.

The archaic force of Barrett's illustrations, the nostalgic fairyland of Goode's, the Egyptian symbolism in Mayer's, the classical/Christian iconography in Hague's, the medieval setting for Foreman's, the Persian splendor of Hutton's are all efforts to reach into the past for better understanding of the present in terms of story. There are indeed stronger religious overtones in the versions of this period, notably Mayer's, Hague's, and Lee's, than in any other. Love as the only possible resurrecting force is a theme of unequaled importance in a nuclear age.

21. Illustration by Paul Goble. Copyright © 1978 by Paul Goble.
From *The Girl Who Loved Wild Horses.* Reproduced by permission
of Bradbury Press, an Affiliate of Macmillan, Inc.

22. Madame Le Prince de Beaumont, based on a
portrait by Delatour, from *Beauty and the Beast*, by Anne Carter.
Illustrations © Binette Schroeder. First published
in the U.K. by Walker Books, Limited, 1986.

The three women—McKinley, Carter, and Lee—who have extended the
tale into fantasy and science fiction have focused more than any other writers
on the kinship between Beauty and the Beast. Their concept of the relationship is not so much the romantic courtship of old, as a deeper connection out
of loneliness for both characters. Since the Beast is obviously an alien to
society already, it is Beauty on whom they concentrate, a person who seems
to have been tailored for social fitness but in fact feels alienated or isolated
(although both McKinley and Lee's sister figures are supportive and never
ostracize Beauty). Lee's Estár (like Gabrielle Villeneuve's Beauty in the eighteenth century) is not even the merchant's real daughter, and it is her version
that most radically projects the alienation theme to a conclusion of Beauty's

23. From *Beauty and the Beast,* by Mary Pope Osborne. Illustrations copyright © 1987 by Winslow Pinney Pels. Reprinted by permission of Scholastic, Inc.

permanent separation from family and Earth environment for her coupling with an untransformed alien.

This is a curious update of Cocteau's identification with the alienated Beast and one resolved quite differently. Where his ending whisked the two away in glamorous flight, Carter and McKinley show a settled couple who have reached an accord with equal measures of sympathy and humor. One couple walks in the garden with their old dog; the other prepares for a marriage that graces the long hard testing of having lived together and squabbled as well as dined elegantly at nine.

In all three extended versions, the exercise of maturation for Beauty seems less a release from oedipal involvement than an adventure in self-discovery that goes beyond traditional self-acceptance. Honour Huston, the future Mrs. Lyon, and Estár Levin are all strong protagonists who deal with fate willfully in spite of their vulnerability. The eighteenth century's liberation of Beauty from Psyche's physical captivity and emotional bondage in "Cupid and Psyche" is paralleled here with greater force.

Each writer varies characters, events, viewpoints, and details of the Beast's habitat with imaginative relish but cleaves to the central characters, narrative structure, and images: the leading cast of Beauty, Beast, and father, the rose, the seasonal cycle, the city/country foil, the garden of confrontation and knowledge, the journey of maturation, the magical tides of time, space, and dreams. Each has tried to retain fairy tale within fantasy.

The question arises, with increasing variations on the story, of when a remodeled version is no longer the same tale. Whether the variations are textual, with realistic or fantastical elaboration, or visual, as in the contemporary plethora of picture books, the eighteenth-century literary tale of "Beauty and the Beast" is still identifiable by its motifs, much like its folk counterparts. Each year adds more versions. Anne Carter's 1986 retelling of "Beauty and the Beast," illustrated by Binette Schroeder (fig. 22), was published simultaneously in Germany, France, and the United States. Mary Pope Osborne's 1987 adaptation, handsomely illustrated by Winslow Pinney Pels (fig. 23), ends anticlimactically "and everyone had a wonderful time—even her grouchy older sisters." A popular CBS television series about a deformed misfit who lives in underground New York and loves a beautiful woman lawyer was widely reviewed in 1987 and 1988.[17] The list (and the study) could go on. However, the period primarily in focus here, 1740 to 1985, should serve to allow some conclusions about the elements that have remained stable among widely varied printed versions.

SIX

The Enduring Elements

A three-century inventory shows that the story of "Beauty and the Beast" thrives on a range of diverse literary treatments. Yet some are obviously more effective than others. From a summary perspective, it is clear which versions are most successful and why. There is also evidence for concluding what central aspects most literary versions retain and which of these constants are most important. Finally—and remarkably—the most effective *literary* versions prove to share the same motifs that have been retained in *oral* variants, a pattern that suggests significant continuity of creative process between the two traditions.

Of the three eighteenth-century versions examined, Beaumont's is undoubtedly the best and most lasting. Villeneuve's is overwrought with subplots and Genlis's is reduced to a thematic flirtation. Among nineteenth-century versions, Lang's adaptation of Villeneuve's story stands out and influences many readers in the twentieth century. Boyle's book—though in some ways a masterpiece—is overdescriptive, Crane's elegant but somewhat superficial, Planché's funny but confined by political or social references of the day, and Lamb's heartfelt but heavily moralistic. In the first half of the twentieth century, both the Quiller-Couch/Dulac and Cocteau versions are memorable, with Nozière's play cleverly contrived but also trivialized, Tarrant's sweet but sometimes weakened by that very quality, and Heath-Stubbs's powerful but abstract. Between 1950 and 1985, the Pearce/Barrett, Mayer, and Hutton picturebooks, along with McKinley's novel, dominate a crowded field. Goode's version vacillates between strong and pretty, the Apy/Hague version introduces some meaningful but ultimately distracting new elements, Foreman's illustrations are somewhat heavy for Carter's light translation. Carter's short story is economically crafted but leans toward the Gothic, while Lee's is sometimes forced.

Although each of these versions has been considered earlier in detail, it is possible at this point to note what qualities characterize the most successful: the versions by Beaumont, Lang, Quiller-Couch/Dulac, Cocteau, Pearce/Barrett, the Mayers, Hutton, and McKinley. These versions vary greatly in length, medium, and cultural context, none of which seems to be a quality-determining factor. What they do have in common is a strong sense of story, a balanced development of character, plot, style, tone, and motif—sometimes amplified by graphics (or to allay purists' criticisms, by visual suggestion). Pertinent to this observation is A. K. Ramanujan's introduction to a perceptive essay called "Hanchi: A Kannada Cinderella."

> Though the typical structures are common, the realized tale means different things in different cultures, times, and media. It is regarded here not merely as the variant of a tale-type, a cultural object, a psychological witness (or symptom), etc., but primarily as an *aesthetic* work. I believe that, in such tales, the aesthetic is the first and experienced dimension, through which ethos and world view are recreated, and carried, by the primary, experiential aesthetic forms and meanings.[1]

The story's effectiveness as a literary/artistic whole steadies it through myriad historical changes. In a sense, the most powerful elements of the story shake off all reformers to assume a singular, distinctive shape over and over again despite vagaries of aesthetic invention and moral intention. In discussing traditional formulas, Lévi-Strauss cites their "lowest truth-value. . . . what gives the myth an operative value is that the specific pattern described is everlasting; it explains the present and the past as well as the future,"[2] an observation that clearly applies to other types of tales as well.

At the same time, the formula cannot be reduced from simple to simplistic. The power of the pattern is metaphorical. The implications, ambiguities, dualities, and paradoxes suggested by the story defy compression in other than symbolic terms. Cleanth Brooks warns against generalization and "the heresy of paraphrase" in critical interpretation and cites Wilbur Urban on symbolic meaning: "Poetry says what it means but it does not say *all* that it means; . . . the so-called blunt truth has a way of be-coming an untruth."[3]

Before focusing on the pattern of symbolic elements central to "Beauty and the Beast," it is worth noting that many recreators widely separated by time, place, and culture have duplicated some small implication of the story without any possibility, in several cases, of knowing each other's work. The authors of the two romantic novels discussed here, for instance, are two hundred years and an ocean apart, and McKinley has never read Villeneuve.[4] Yet both develop scenes in which Beauty releases the Beast from an obligation to marry her just because she has released him from his enchantment. Both portray Beauty as, primarily, honor. But to express this idea, to instruct the young, to analyse the psyche, are all purposes second-ary to telling the story.

There is, in every storyteller who deals with "Beauty and the Beast," a dialectic between the force of the material and the will to shape it. In each case, the images have dominated the intent. This leads to the question of what patterns have emerged through many storytellers' varied development of character, narrative structure, narrative voice, and image/object/symbol— the groups of elements originally identified by structural function.

Images, Objects, and Symbols

In discussing images, it is important to consider range of meaning rather than narrow definition. Northrop Frye warns,

> The allegorization of myth is hampered by the assumption that the explanation "is" what the myth "means." A myth being a centripetal structure of meaning, it can be made to mean an indefinite number of things, and it is more fruitful to study what in fact myths have been made to mean.[5]

In terms of Frye's own construct, "Beauty and the Beast" would probably straddle the closely allied categories of myth (a term he does not use folkloristically) and romance, with cyclical and apocalyptic imagery characteristic of both.

The seasonal cycle is either signified or fully developed in every version of "Beauty and the Beast." The merchant sets out in reasonable weather, but his trip carries him into winter—the winter of his old age and to some extent, defeat. He is unable to recoup his losses or satisfy Beauty's request for a summer rose. Lost in a snow-storm, he finds the Beast's palace surrounded by summer, the proper age for courtship. Before Beauty makes her decision to return to the Beast's palace, the Beast's world begins to die with him and turn to winter. McKinley develops both the natural seasons and their magical reversals in a pattern similar to Cocteau's day/night and light/dark polarities (these latter are important to Beauty's dreams and transport between worlds). The imaginary world is often portrayed as the opposite of the ordinary, but both worlds usually come together with the metamorphosis in spring, as in Carter's story (Lee does some amusing twists with weather control in her science fiction piece).

The change from city to country, from country to hidden forest/garden is also crucial to each version. Beauty's movement from civilized society to a secret retreat parallels her progression from the outer public realm to the inner personal one. To balance her fully developed psyche, her educated sensibilities, she needs to explore her animal nature. The garden and moonlit landscapes characteristic of many versions (along with the castle mazes and magic chests that enlarge with wealth contained within) summon strong images of female sexuality. Beauty must fully accept her innermost nature before she can love fully.

Signifying this love is the rose that Beauty requests and that her father takes from the hidden garden. In both classical and Christian traditions, the rose is a symbol of love and the suffering born of love. It has been associated with Venus/Aphrodite, the Virgin Mary, and the blood and suffering of Christ, hence resurrection and immortality. Thomas Mintz sees the rose as representing both the Beast's masculinity and Beauty's femininity, the thorns signifying the former and the seeds and color of menses/defloration the latter.[6] The rose was preferred by alchemists in attempting transformations and was eaten, according to Apuleius, to restore to human form a man changed into an ass. There is an intriguing note, in *Funk and Wagnalls Standard Dictionary of Folklore, Mythology, and Legend*, that relates directly to the Beast's disproportionate outrage at the theft of his rose. "Throughout the Teutonic area the rose belongs to the dwarfs or fairies and is under their protection. In many places it is customary to ask permission of their king lest one lose a hand or foot."[7] Or a daughter. The Beast will give away his material possessions generously enough but vent full rage on anyone stealing the emblem of his suffering, love, and redemption. That emblem must be a sign to the sole virgin who suffers, loves, and redeems him. In popular terms, the rose has come to represent romance, fantasy, the paradox of innocent passion.

The Beast's garden has biblical overtones of the meeting between Adam and Eve, and the Beast himself suggests the introduction to carnal knowledge. Whether understated or elaborated, the garden figures as an important backdrop in every version of "Beauty and the Beast," as the natural setting for fertility and growth. Secondary animal helpers—the horse, birds, monkeys, etc.—also signify Beauty's rapport with nature, her underlying sympathy with the Beast.

Magic actually figures very little in "Beauty and the Beast." Magic cannot solve the central problem; only human love and perception, upon which the final transformation is conditional, can do that. It is interesting that the magic device of the ring, certainly an ancient pledge but a man-made one, appears less frequently than the many nature symbols. Even the climactic fireworks seem to be a civilized translation of fire itself, one of the four elements and of course an age-old accompaniment for rites of sacrifice, purification, transformation, celebration, communion, and thanks. Here it is hard to resist applying Frye's theory on the "point of epiphany" (the connection made between "an apocalyptic world above and a cyclical world below"[8] by smoke rising or visions appearing in a burning tree or flash of light, etc.) to the soaring fireworks and flashes that invariably light up the Beast's transformation after Beauty's declaration of love. (In Cocteau's case, her "burning look" performs the alchemy.)

Completing the representation of the four elements—fire symbols, the garden imagery of earth, the appearance of winds and zephyrs representing air—is the Beast's frequent revival beside or with water, from Beaumont's eighteenth-century "canal" to the assorted streams, lakes, or fountains of newer versions. The Beast is thirsting for love. Dying, he goes to the water (and is often pictured lying in it), but only Beauty can help him drink or, by sprinkling him with it, help him to renewed life—i.e., wash away his past so he is born again. The religious implications are intriguing. In fact, there are several funny near-baptismal scenes in some of the stories, and one cannot help remembering Cocteau's trouble with the recalcitrant swans that tried to drive the dying Beast from their native pond.[9]

Each of these motifs, objects, and symbols is elemental but, paradoxically, expansible. A rose is a rose is a rose; yet every narrator's is unique, as the immense variation in narrative voice, the next function to consider, makes clear.

Narrative Voice

In point of view, style, detail, tone, and theme, there is much less identifiable consistency than among the basic motifs common to "Beauty and the Beast." The narrative voice, while constant as a function, is the most diverse in form and thus the weakest of all the elements in surviving changes of time or culture. Tonal variations fluctuate from erotic to moralistic, literal to introspective. On the whole, there are more serious than humorous versions, though an ironic mix is not uncommon. Detail can be starkly or elaborately effective, more the former than the latter in these twenty-two representative versions. As evidenced by the previous chapters, style is almost too diverse to categorize; a rough division of the versions on a range from simple (more traditional) to sophisticated (less traditional) shows that about half tend to be simpler, half more sophisticated.

Although Beauty's is the most frequent point of view, the Beast is often the most sympathetic character; this shift between them is strategic to the reader's absorption of the underlying themes. Identificaton with all that is good, beautiful, and vulnerable on the surface grows into a perception of what is good, beautiful, and vulnerable beneath it.

Narratives in the omniscient third person are most typical, but those in the first person also prove successful. Because of the structural simplicity of fairy tales, the narrative voice is usually that of the writer or adapter who relates the story, although the writer also commonly asserts commentary through chorus figures. (In cases of first-person narrative or versions in the form of novel or novella, the narrative voice is more complex.) Since the narrative voice includes not only the tone established by authorial style and detail but also the themes represented through authorial or choral comment, the choral figure belongs more to a discussion of narrative voice than of character.

Half of the versions examined—all those more traditional in tone— include an adviser or comforter who also serves somewhat instrumentally in the plot, usually in the dream sequence, the rewarding of hero and heroine, and the punishment of the sisters. The figure is always female, beautiful in a wisely aging way ("stately"), magical as well as sensible—a fairy who is the voice of conscience, and often the voice of the writer. Villeneuve's original fairy is Beauty's aunt (her mother's sister), who, in addition to moralizing throughout the story, functions importantly in narrating the prince's and Beauty's long background stories and engineers their fates by manipulating people, situations, and dreams. While Beaumont tones down the fairy's importance, her comments are still didactic and her role crucial. It is she who makes sure readers understand the deception of appearances and turns the sisters to stone. She is echoed in form and function by Boyle, Lang, Quiller- Couch, Tarrant, Pearce, Goode, Mayer, and Apy, with variations. Tarrant, for instance, who reduces her to "a fairy who was present" at the end, prefers to moralize overtly through authorial comment. No comforter is needed be- cause the reader is reassured relentlessly through description and prescrip- tion.

Less traditional forms of the story incorporate the fairy godmother figure into assorted different characters. Genlis projects the role through Phedima, friend and adviser to Sabina. Planché works through the Queen of Roses and her zephyrs-in-waiting. Nozière spoofs the figure with his Fairy of Tolerance, as does McKinley with her two attendant breezes, Lydia and Bessie. Lee assigns the role to one of Estár's older sisters, while Carter at least partially employs a devoted spaniel to nudge Beauty's awareness.

Only Lamb, Crane, and Cocteau (all male!) feature no fairy godmother figures, Lamb because he substitutes a "heavenly voice," Crane because he strips the story bare, and Cocteau because he makes the camera his commentator. While in "Cupid and Psyche" the mother-in-law figure, Venus, offers vengeance instead of direction, several versions of "Beauty and the Beast" cast the dream comforter/adviser as the queen mother of the prince— Beauty's future mother-in-law. Appearing as frequently as she does, however, whether flippant or serious, the fairy godmother persona is more voice of experience than deus ex machina, despite her powers of enchantment. She is an important element of socialization and internalization. Beauty must listen and learn in order to redeem herself and the Beast, as, by implication, must readers.

Whereas the themes stated by the choral figures are generally homiletic, the underlying themes that various writers stress unconsciously or consciously are much deeper and more complex: the relation of human to animal, intellectual to sexual, girl to woman, woman to man, marriage to family, individual to partnership, loyalty to freedom of choice, compliance to power, honesty to social amenities, reality to appearance. There seems to be room for all of these thematic tensions projected through myriad variations of detail. Whatever the play of narrative voice, from adages to agate stairs, the force of the other elements gives an extraordinary consistency of underlying impact. While narrative voice in fact represents an individual author's primary aesthetic contribution, this individualizing voice is ultimately less important to a powerful, lasting version of the story than faithfulness to and skill in manipulating the other elements of the story—symbolic objects and settings, characters and their relationships, and narrative structures.

Narrative Structure

The narrative structure allows significant variations without weakening the story; the plot is basically the comings and goings of a family. There is no physical adventure, quest, or danger. Journey is the framework of the story.

The family journeys from city to country, the father journeys to recover the family's fortunes, Beauty and her father journey to the Beast's palace, Beauty journeys home and back to the Beast, the family journeys to the wedding. ("Cupid and Psyche" features Psyche's additional journey to prove herself by a series of tasks to recover Cupid.)

What makes such simplicity durable is the plot's perfect metaphorical carriage of the theme. The outer journeys serve as vehicles for the inner journeys. The statements of action and perception are not always parallel but sometimes converge or diverge. The configuration is more a journey within a journey, the two occasionally touching in developments of event and meaning. This mutual movement figures in the story's adaptability for illustration and especially film, which picks up naturally on the tension between motion and pause.

Beauty's sojourn at the Beast's palace and her visit home are clearly inner journeys. The conflicts of leaving home and growing into a mature relationship build the real movement under the surface action. The two levels come together in certain key events, dramatic highpoints in most written and illustrated versions. The father's encounter with the Beast is pivotal, as is Beauty's meeting with him, her family reunion that breaks the taboo of "staying too long at home" (see chapter 2, p. 10), her finding the Beast near death, and the transformation.

At other points in the story, the two levels (of action and subsurface movement) are divergent. The loss of wealth that at first seems an important calamity simply signals change. The request for the rose, which supposedly shows Beauty's contentment with her lot (she is embarrassed by her sisters' clamor for wealth and asks for the simplest gift under pressure from her father or a reluctance to show them up as greedy) signals a deep need that cannot be satisfied without breaking the family circle. Her steady refusals of the Beast's proposal mask a growing affection for him.

The elemental events in both the Villeneuve and Beaumont stories, which form the basis for the majority of others, vary little. Versions based on Villeneuve's all eliminate the complex backgrounds of Beauty and the Beast but include pared-down activities at the palace and developments in the dream sequence. Those based on Beaumont's add the punishment of the sisters. The few plots that deviate from the two original eighteenth-century versions focus on the transition between family setting and Beast setting or, in extreme cases, the Beast setting alone, with references to the past. All the action in Genlis's play, for instance, takes place at the palace, but there is a conversational flashback to Sabina's life before Phanor abducted her to save her from loveless marriage. Heath-Stubbs too, in distilling the themes from the plot, focuses on the palace garden situation. But Planché, Nozière, Carter, and Lee, while digressing from the elemental plot, all shift from family world to Beast world to new world according to the journey structure, whether the vehicle be magic omnibus, rose perfume, automobile, or automatic transport. In statement of the inner journey, the plot lends itself to—in fact, demands at certain points—dialogue, which is richly mined for purposes of characterization in plays and novellas.

Characters and Characterization

Depending on how many characters are introduced, "Beauty and the Beast" can be a social drama, family drama, triangle, courtship, or lonely struggle for individual fulfullment. Beauty and the Beast are clearly essential, but at least one version, Heath-Stubbs's, avoids their actual encounter by means of alternate monologues, stressing the rounding of each personality through implied contact with the other. Almost as important as Beauty and the Beast in most versions is the role of the family—Beauty's father and sisters—to which is often added the dream comforter or choral/adviser/mother figure previously discussed. The brothers and animal helpers are variable in both number and role.

All of the characters have a capacity for both symbolism and development, role function and relationship, which lends their appearances great flexibility. The father has been presented as weak or strong, with varying shades of complexity between. The siblings have been portrayed as anything from good to ungracious to villainous, Beauty from vacuous to determined, the chorus from sanctimonious to witty to wise, the animal helpers from mechanical to sympathetic. Whatever the degree of development, their symbolic nature is clear; yet without any development at all, their archetypal patterns are still satisfying.

These patterns include the father-daughter relationship, sibling rivalry, courtship, the father-daughter-suitor triangle, and the chorus-protagonist-(reader) affiliation.[10] In only three versions does the father have a relationship with anyone other than Beauty: Planché's sidekick, John Quill; Nozière's concubine, Violet; and McKinley's widow/fiancé, Melinda Honeybourne. In none does Beauty have other contacts outside the family, chorus, and Beast. Her only friends are animal helpers, variously horses, birds, or dogs. The three main characters (Beauty, the Beast, and the father) who develop in the course of almost all versions, reflect, in their growth, the same kind of rhythmic movement apparent in the plot: alienation, isolation, reconciliation. This is identifiable as a basic pattern of internal growth by anyone faced with disrupting change. The father, alienated from his family after Beauty leaves, retreats into the isolation of illness before he can accept Beauty's coming of age and reconcile himself to old age.

Beauty herself clearly follows this pattern. Her visit home only clarifies an alienation she has long experienced. She is marked by difference; and more, she is changing. Her isolation at the palace is a vision quest, removed from time, a realization of maturing sexuality and spiritual growth. As Joseph Campbell has declared of Psyche,[11] Beauty is the hero of the tale. This is even more true in Beauty's case than in Psyche's because Beauty is not thrown to her fate but chooses it, however reluctantly. Reluctance characterizes many of the heroes cited by Campbell—it is perhaps a sign of intelligence, given what lies ahead. Yet the hero must venture forth or live forever unfulfilled.

Beauty's is the journey to the underworld, to existence beneath surface appearances. Along the way, she faces the danger all heroes encounter, a monster representing—perhaps created by—her own fear. Beauty's triumph is a strength of perception that leads to reconciliation with self, mate, family, and society. Her good looks become irrelevant, an ironic context for her previous failure to see. As her inner vision clears, she refocuses the old adage: beauty is in the *eye* of the beholder. Beauty is not what one sees but how one looks at it, not passively, artificially, but actively, probingly. Her vision becomes a "burning gaze." Beauty, like the Beast, is an inner force. In dissipating her fears, she dissipates the fearsome aspects of the Beast.

Because he is the catalyst for change, tension, and conclusion; pivotal to beginning, middle, and end; and the concentric focus in relationships with each and all the other characters, the Beast is the center of the story. Of the whole cast, it is the Beast who provides the unique and most compelling element of the tale, who offers both writers and illustrators the most imaginative possibilities for interpretation. This figure is presented with dimensions unusual to fairy tale males. Although one can point to plenty of handsome princes or even precedents for good-hearted blockheads who can make a princess laugh (surely a sensible prerequisite for marriage), those are barely outlined heroic or comic figures, while the Beast is fully sensitive and potentially tragic. He is, in short, capable of love, an emotion of little importance in the development of many fairy tales except as a convenient denouement. The Beast's courtship is never assumed or forced. At the beginning, he lures Beauty through her bonds of affection for her father but soon works to transfer them to himself. When she refuses his nightly proposals, he sadly retreats and tries again the next day. His redemption from loneliness depends, not on strength or valor, but on another's love and consent.

The Beast is neither a comic *dummling* nor a clever adventurer, and of course he is not handsome. He uses none of the traditional male accoutrements of power and daring; what he does is set a good table and wait. In fact, he shows traditionally female attributes of delicate respect for Beauty's feelings, nurturance, comfort, gentleness, and patience, all of which he has learned through a humbling experience. He has learned the hard way that life without undeceived affection is rather a thorny paradise, even fenced with roses; Beauty must learn the same. To expose the true heart, Beast has been stripped of his beauty and wit, as Beauty loses her wealth, status, and family. By dint of such exposure and by the intimacy established between the characters and the reader, one is suddenly looking not only at another fairy tale time but also very close to home.

The moment when Beauty faces the Beast is psychologically familiar and offers a barely concealed point of identification for the modern reader (it is precarious to speculate about earlier states of consciousness). Each person knows a moment of fear in beholding the beast in others or him/herself. On a deeper level, each knows the slow growth of loving and accepting the unacceptable, whereupon, miraculously, disparate parts become integrated. The fear of being unacceptable lies deep within child or adult reader. The bestial part may be hidden, yet is always present, tempting exposure, either by welling up from within (as portrayed in Cocteau's Beast hunting his prey at night) or by responding to the charisma of it in others. "Beauty and the Beast" offers the promise that for all our human ugliness and brutality, we can be acceptable, even lovable, to another human being.

The continuing relevance of "Beauty and the Beast" as a modern theme stems from this fearful knowledge that we are each beastly, juxtaposed with the hopeful knowledge that we are each beautiful. Moreover, whatever the imbalance of our inner beauty and beast, we seek to balance with others who have complementary imbalances. The story is a fundamental recognition and definition of what is "good and bad" in each individual and each relationship. The complexity of that good and bad includes but goes beyond the Freudian sexual interpretation commonly articulated in explanation of the story. Certainly the tale is sexual. Beauty's relationship with the Beast is, after all, a journey from fearful revulsion through platonic affection to the acceptance of a sexual mate, a husband. Her attachment to her father is devoted, almost erotic as described in their reunion, during which her father, responding to the maid's shriek at finding Beauty back home in bed, "held her fast locked in his arms above a quarter of an hour. As soon as the first transports were over, Beauty began to think of rising, and was afraid she had no clothes to put on. . . ."[12]

Beauty learns to appreciate and finally takes the consummate mate. Yet outlining the transference of a child's oedipal attachment to acceptance of mature sexual love, while accurate, seems to disregard some other important aspects and leaves little room for the human variables of time and place that the story seems to encompass.[13] That the "marriage of Beauty and the Beast is the humanization and socialization of the id by the superego,"[14] may very well be what Beaumont, in terms of her own society, intended by that final ecstatic transformation. Yet a reader's common response to the story is actual sympathy for, identification with, and attraction to the Beast, a brute force harnessed by need. The id seems to supersede the ego as the story's prime focus.

The transformed or tamed (read "humanized") prince is not nearly so memorable as the Beast, a figure of power and vulnerability combined. That is a rich combination of natures. It is the Beast as beast who rivets attention and burns the story into one's mind. It is the Beast on whom storytellers, writers, and artists focus their imaginations. The climax of the story is Beauty's love of the Beast himself, not the transformation and marriage, which is anticlimactic if pleasant. Therein lies the great disappointment of many graphic and literary conclusions of "Beauty and the Beast." The prince seems bland in contrast to the powerful reconciled beast; he is in fact anticlimactic to the forceful struggle of balancing beauty and beast. The final product must be not a handsome saint but a whole human being. The Beast has our sympathy already, and his is a hard act to follow.

Beaumont may have tried to tame the Beast by placing him in the mannered framework of an ordered world. But whether by accident or design, she succeeded rather in combining what Jung polarized in his theory of visionary (primordial) versus psychological (personal) creations. "We are reminded of nothing in everyday life, but rather of dreams, night-time fears, and the dark, uncanny recesses of the human mind."[15] The Beast as a beast is still the dominating power of the story, and Beauty must come to terms with it. The Beast makes the story one of Jung's "primordial experiences" that "rend from top to bottom the curtain upon which is painted the picture of an ordered world, and allow a glimpse into the unfathomable abyss of the unborn and of things yet to be."[16] It is the Beast that makes "the undisguised personal love-episode not only connected with the weightier visionary experience but actually subordinated to it." He is a "true symbol—that is, an expression of something real but unknown."[17] It is the Beast who seems to propel the story so powerfully from the eighteenth century through the twentieth.

Aesthetic Perspectives

The Beast's representation over two hundred years demonstrates a distinct shift from formal symbol to personal identity. This shift comes with the same noticeable movement from an eighteenth/nineteenth-century emphasis on narrative surface to a twentieth-century stress on internal theme. After 1900, both the story and its main character are turned inside out. In most twentieth-century versions, the stress clearly has shifted from a statement of virtue rewarded to a question of psychological complexity. Jean Cocteau's film, for example, adds an important character, Beauty's swain Avenant; Avenant and the Beast are counterparts who die simultaneously, their faces superimposed at the moment of the appearance of the prince, who has the same face as both of them without the Beast's animality.

The change is most concisely illustrated by two of the poetic versions. Charles Lamb's portrayal, like all descriptions of the Beast before 1900, is entirely from Beauty's point of view. John Heath-Stubbs's modern poem, on the other hand, allows the Beast, alternating with Beauty, to speak vividly for himself. Lamb's Beast suffers in silence broken by few lines. "Am I not hideous in your eyes?"[18] The suffering and "Black-blood tides" of Heath-Stubbs's Beast call to mind scenes and sounds in Cocteau's film where the Beast is tormented by his bloodlust and, when he satiates it, by the very blood of the deer he has slain. "Excuse me," he murmurs softly to Beauty, "for being an animal. Forgive me. . . ."[19]

The Beast is unacceptable to humanity, an outcast from society, the antithesis of culture. His genuine efforts to resolve the conflict between animal sexuality and civilized restraint also make him a foil for false culture, an antihero. He sees through appearances. He sees what he really is, accepts it, and reshapes it, unlike "men of society" whom appearances deceive. Using the Beast as a lens, writers from Beaumont to Cocteau have been critical of their societies' values.

> Yes, yes, said the Beast, my heart is good, but still I am a Monster. Among mankind, says Beauty, there are many that deserve that name more than you, and I prefer you, just as you are, to those, who, under human form, hide a treacherous, corrupt, and ungrateful heart.

The eldest (sister) had married a gentleman, extremely handsome indeed, but so fond of his own person, that he was full of nothing but his own dear self, and neglected his wife. The second had married a man of wit, but he only made use of it to plague and torment everybody, and his wife most of all.[20]

Cocteau's merchant family is sharply satirized, with dissension, deceit, snobbery, and false appearances making the Beast look sweet indeed. The merchants, lawyers, and creditors are vulturous. Friends of the family cruelly turn away as soon as the merchant loses his wealth. The sisters wear false faces for social climbing and rub onions on their eyes to affect tears. The Beast, by contrast, is true to his nature, if torn.

Merchant: You mean . . . this monster has a *soul*?

Beauty: He suffers, Father. One half of him is struggling against the other. He must be more ruthless to himself than to others.

Merchant: Beauty, I've seen him. He has a dreadful face.

Beauty: At first, he is awfully frightening, Father. But now he makes me want to burst out laughing, sometimes; and then I see his eyes and they are so sad that I turn my own away so as not to cry.

Merchant: . . . don't tell me you consent to live with this monster.

Beauty: I must, Father. Certain forces obey him, other forces command him. . . . He appears to me only at those times when his cruelty is not to be feared. Sometimes he has a regal bearing and sometimes he limps and seems the victim of some infirmity.[21]

While commenting on the vices of society through the Beast's alienated struggles, writers nevertheless find his socialization necessary. He must, sadly enough, die and rise again tamed. Every culture has found the Beast both vital and doomed. Heath-Stubbs points to the paradox in Beauty's decision "to teach the flame / To make clay hard and brittle"—the civilized shaping of passion. We are forced to pin our hopes on an untried prince who may combine the best aspects of creature and created.

Though all versions recognize the Beast's alienation from himself and society, each varies in the subtlety with which his conflicts are revealed. Earlier Beasts confine themselves to a civil nightly proposal of marriage, accompanied in almost all versions by a sigh upon Beauty's refusal; modern Beasts struggle openly with their natures. Beaumont's Beast exhibits a gentlemanly restraint by disappearing after the ritual meal; Cocteau's haunts Beauty's bedroom door and once bursts in at night before she sends him away. Cocteau clarifies the Beast's passionate nature through recurring graphic images of plucked roses, torch flames, hunting impulses, blood-stains, and physical magnetism.

Earlier writers are content to leave the Beast's meaning to suggestion. The eighteenth/nineteenth-century story's formal treatment may imply not superficiality but subtlety on the part of its adapters. The Beast's twentieth-century angst may reflect obsession as well as imagination on the part of modern adapters. Victorians may not have been afraid to explore the Beast too deeply or to confront him too directly so much as they were content to let the tip of an iceberg express an underwater continent.

In terms of effect, it is questionable whether an explicit exploration of the Beast's conflict between animality and humanity makes him a more power-ful figure. Cocteau's personalizing a human counterpart does not neces-sarily strengthen the conflict suggested so starkly, in folktale tradition, by Beaumont's elemental Beast, nor does it necessarily enrich a reader's imagi-nation. Cocteau's inquiry into the question of what is real and what is not is stimulating but diverting: statues move; the worlds of magic and reality are reflected in a dreamlike cinematic chiaroscuro. "My night is not yours. It is night in my domain; morning in yours."[22]

It is interesting to note that the latest historical development in the recreation of the tale—children's picture books of the 1970s and 1980s—has seen a nineteenth-century adherence to the minimal narrative but has shown, pictorially, the twentieth-century trend toward intimate detail. Illu-strators have always had the problem of containing (and thereby weakening) the mysterious Beast within a specific image; some of the most powerful portraits are the most mysterious and undefined.

Most early engravings and copperplates, like those in the edition of Charles Lamb's book (1811), show formal restraint in conceptualizing the Beast. Walter Crane's boar (1875) is more decorative than wild. Eleanor Vere Boyle's walrus (1875) has a dignity inspiring compassion. Edmund Dulac's monster (1910) moves toward a troubling combination of human and animal that reaches a climax in Jean Cocteau's conflicted Beast (1946). Jessie Willcox Smith (1911) and Margaret Tarrant's toylike tone (1920) diffuses the power of the image, while Alan Barrett's nightmare quality (1972) heightens it. Diane Goode's prettified lion (1978) is almost farcically elegant, while Mercer Mayer's lion (1978) promises more and delivers it with emotional force. His casting of the Beast as a lioness and Beauty as almost a twin of the prince suggests that the artist is extending the theme of male/female relationships to a Jungian male/female duality within the individual. Foreman's Beast

(1982) is a futuristic mutant, and Delessert's (1984) a surrealistic collage of symbols assembled into a visage. Warwick Hutton's primitive apelike beast (1985) is strong, albeit even more effective with his face hidden but suggested from behind by a looming stance.

The Beast is what Jung would call "one of the figures that people the night-world," something the artist tries to summon without diminishing. "Whoever speaks in primordial images speaks with a thousand voices."[23] Each individual imagines his own Beast most vividly, whatever the verbal or graphic versions to which he has been exposed. Cocteau acknowledges the indefinable nature of the Beast by having him shrink from Beauty's open "burning gaze." "Beauty, you must never look straight into my eyes . . . your eyes are burning me. I can't bear your eyes."[24] Yet it is her "look of love" (Regard d'amour") that finally transforms the Beast. He must be seen and loved for what he is. As he thunders to the terrified merchant during their initial encounter, "We don't say 'My lord' we say 'Beast.' I don't like compliments."[25] In Cocteau's film, the Beast's pavilion, to which he gives Beauty a key, has been interpreted as housing the collective unconscious.[26] There is evidence that earlier writers were well aware of fairy tale characters' erotic and mimetic potentialities. Discussing a different beast born at the end of the seventeenth century, one commentator gives a clear example of this awareness in noting how Perrault seemed "to read 'Little Red Ridinghood' as an allegory of sexual awakening, an interpretation that twentieth-century Freudian critics thought they were newly discovering."[27]

Moral
Here you see that little children,
    Especially little girls
    Who are beautiful, well built, and pretty,
Do very badly by listening to all sorts of people,
    And it's not surprising
    That the wolf eats so many of them.
I say *the* wolf because all wolves
    Are not the same.
There's one kind that's mild-mannered,
    Without bluster, without spite, without fury,
    Who cozily, amiably, and gently
    Follows young ladies
Into their houses, into their boudoirs,
And alas! they don't realize that these gentle wolves
Are the most dangerous wolves of all.[28]

Of course, the wolf is a villain indeed, exactly the kind of villain expects on first encounter with the Beast. But the Beast is neither archenemy nor traditional hero. He is a much more poignant and affecting figure than the prince who succeeds him because he is in conflict with himself, while the Prince is perfect. The Beast combines a forceful nature with a gentle naiveté, brute strength with painful yearning. The Beast wants a relationship with Beauty; he will lure her but will not force her into it. Instead of trying to eat Beauty, he feeds her. He is powerful, yet vulnerably at the mercy of his unrequited passion. He is terrifying and also magnetic. In one century he can be saved by the offer of a hand in marriage; in another, by a look of love. The Beast offers didactic French governesses, moralistic Victorian storytellers, and worried post-Freudian artists a metaphor for sexuality adapting to society. They have all, in turn, adapted the metaphor to their differing cultures or ideals.

SEVEN

Into the Future

The aesthetic survival of a strong story follows similar patterns in the oral and literary traditions. Tracing "Beauty and the Beast" through many years of publication and many printed or pictured versions exposes a clear distinction between the central and the peripheral aspects of the story. At its center, certain elements are constant.

1. Characters and characterization: Beauty, Beast, family (father, sisters)
2. Narrative structure: journeys of action and maturation
3. Images, objects, symbols: rose motif, seasonal cycle, city/country setting, garden of confrontation and knowledge, magical modes of time, space, dreams

Narrative voice is the great variable in the story's perpetuation. Variations of style, tone, theme, detail, and point of view, as well as medium, format, and illustration encircle the constant elements. The narrative voice is, after all, the storyteller. Character, narrative structure, images, and symbols constitute the story. Ultimately, the artist is not as important as the story. An elemental story will survive almost any telling. An enduring story will reveal a nucleus of elements that can withstand centrifugal variation by tellers and interpreters. Certain versions will last longer than others; a few will become historical landmarks. The marriage of abiding story with abiding craft is ideal, but the story is primal, the craft optional. Over time, storytellers come and go, but the strong story stays.

In the final analysis, story goes beyond personal artistry to include basic elements that survive social/historical fluctuation and artistic/intellectual interpretation. The elemental story is not fragile, but neither is it static. In a kind of Darwinian scheme of literature, the story that has the capacity to bear different meanings in different times and cultures will survive. Moreover, as a strong story is defined by its core of elements, the strong storyteller is defined by respect for that core. Although "Beauty and the Beast" was coded from folkloric genes, its strongest codifier was literary, and its survival has implications for the contemporary children's literature that it has joined.

Although not originally intended for an exclusively young audience, fairy tales have become, primarily and perhaps irrevocably, provender for children. Storytellers—both creators and recreators—today enter the domain of juvenile trade publishing or other media to be heard (see chapter 5 covering the years 1950–85). A great many of the approximately three thousand juvenile trade books published every year[1] include, incorporate, adapt, adopt, or extend fairy tales and folklore. Yet children's literature is not always acknowledged or welcomed as the heir of fairy tales. Today, as in the past, literature for children is frequently dismissed as slight. Some of it is. Like folklore that has *not* survived, many contemporary children's books do fade quickly. Those that endure will contain the qualities that make good folk or fairy tales (which are not good by definition) powerful and adaptable.

Like "Beauty and the Beast," a successful children's book is a metaphor for strong emotions and at the same time a structure for sound story elements. One without the other will not qualify the story for lasting impact. The shortcut of imbuing a story with more symbolic weight than its elements can carry is common, as is the crafting of a story without emotional significance or metaphorical resonance. Like "Beauty and the Beast," the children's book is a literary miniature, with levels of meaning for all ages. It has much in common with the narrative or even lyric poem: restricted but effective detail, deceptively simple compression of complex situations, metaphorical meanings, and rhythmic patterns. The best writers and artists create children's books with these qualities. Their work has the strength to sustain in-depth criticism. Yet there is a lack of consistent scholarship in children's literature that leads to less than consistent standards for publication of both new works and new editions of traditional works. Much current juvenile publishing consists of illustrated adaptations of folk and fairy tales, but there is not enough careful comparison of text and art among the editions. Moreover, many new works have folklore motifs and mythological dimensions of which reviewers, who are the chief critics in the field of children's literature, are unaware or without time to examine. When *Where the Wild Things Are* was published in 1963, it generated much controversial discussion but little comment as the traditional hero's perilous journey.[2]

Sometimes writers themselves are not aware of the stories they are recreating. Zibby Oneal has a telling comment in her acceptance speech for the 1986 Boston Globe-Horn Book Award. After describing a setting that inspired her as fantastical she says:

> How natural, then, that *In Summer Light,* born as it was of this magical landscape, should have turned out to be a fairy tale. How curious that I, having spent many months in the writing, should never have noticed. But I didn't notice. It was only later, well after the book was published, that I saw how much *In Summer Light* shared with these tales.
>
> One day a friend and I were talking about the way that themes from certain tales reappear in the present-day children's books in one disguise or another. I remember having a theory I was eager to argue for. While this might be true for some tales, I said, it wouldn't continue to be true for all. Surely certain tales—"Cinderella," for instance, "Snow White," "Rapunzel"— were no longer relevant to the present day. Surely these passive heroines, content to wait for their princes to arrive, had become anachronisms in the wake of the women's movement. How could these tales continue to interest modern girls, intent on careers and achievement? How could the themes found in these stories mean anything to them at all? It was at about this point that I faltered, as suddenly it occurred to me that, in fact, I had just written something suspiciously like "The Sleeping Beauty" myself.
>
> One doubts the relevance of tales at one's peril, as I have discovered.[3]

Oneal goes on to contradict the interpretation of traditional heroines as passive. Story has again proved flexible enough to accomodate a shift in social values, here to become a paradigm for a newly defined ideal of woman fully realizing herself. Certainly writers such as Margaret Mahy, whose novel *The Changeover* draws both image and structure from "Sleeping Beauty," have projected heroines who activate themselves. Although the protagonist has a loving male partner who supports her rite of maturation, it is she who undertakes the hazards and wins the way: "She saw plainly that she was remade, had brought to life some sleeping part of herself, extending the forest in her head. . . . Through the power of charged imagination, her own and other people's, [she] had made herself into a new kind of creature."[4] Far from being sexist, the fairy tale here becomes a paradigm for a woman's inner voyage.[5] Text has adjusted to context in the story's constant dialectic between the elemental and the cultural.

Heroes, too, can change within the fairy tale paradigm, as Leon Garfield's does in *The Wedding Ghost*.[6] Haunting in both art and narrative, this sophisticated modern elaboration on "Sleeping Beauty" speaks to adults as much as it does to preadolescents. It opens with the wedding shower of an ordinary young couple, Jack and Gillian, who will be married the following Sunday. Jack's old nurse is not invited, but an anonymous gift—an old map—arrives addressed to Jack, and he becomes obsessed with following it. Along city streets enshrouded with fog, down a river, through a dense forest full of human bones, Jack makes his way to a castle and kisses the sleeping woman awake; but his marriage to the princess is superimposed on his wedding to Gillian, and he is left married to the homely real as well as the romantic ideal. Keeping's black pen-and-wash drawings are mysterious and sinister, projecting the power of Garfield's densely packed writing with a relentless force of their own (fig. 24). The book is deceptively formatted in the size of a large picture book. Illusions of time, allusions to literature, and some terrifying graphic images make it a supernatural tour de force.

Fantasies that consciously draw on folklore are too numerous to mention—a few examples should make the point: Lloyd Alexander's use of Welsh lore in his Prydain cycle and Susan Cooper's in *The Dark Is Rising* series; Molly Hunter's use of Scottish lore in *The Wicked One, The Kelpie's Pearls*, and *A Stranger Came Ashore*, and Rosemary Harris's in *The Seal-Singing* (aside from several picture book adaptations of the selkie tale by Jane Yolen, Susan Cooper, and Mordicai Gerstein); Alan Garner's use of British lore in *The Weirdstone of Brisingamen* and *The Moon of Gomrath*, and William Mayne's in *Earthfasts*; Laurence Yep's use of Chinese lore in *Dragon of the Lost Sea* and *Dragon Steel*; Patricia Wrightson's use of Aborigine myths in *The Nargun and the Stars* and its successors; Virginia Hamilton's use of African and Afro-American legends in *The Magical Adventures of Pretty Pearl*. This list could fill a book itself and does not even touch on the folklore and legendry directly adapted into illustrated collections and single editions, a trend that has escalated in the 1970s and 1980s into a canon of graphic variants. These include numerous relatives of "Beauty and the Beast"—for example *Sir Gawain and the Loathly Lady* (fig. 25), which is a British monster-bride story akin to Chaucer's Wife of Bath Tale, and *Mufaro's Beautiful Daughters*, an animal groom tale from Africa that, in picture-book format, was a Caldecott Honor Book in 1988 (fig. 26).

Natalie Babbitt talks about following, not always knowingly, paths of mythic heroes in her contemporary fantasy for children.[7] Paula Fox, throughout her realistic novel *The Moonlight Man,* plays with the tricks of looking and the pain of seeing—imagery reminiscent of Cocteau's "burning gaze" in *Beauty and the Beast* (see chapter 6). Alas, though the protagonist's

24. From *The Wedding Ghost*, by Leon Garfield. Published by Oxford
University Press, 1987. © Charles Keeping, 1987.

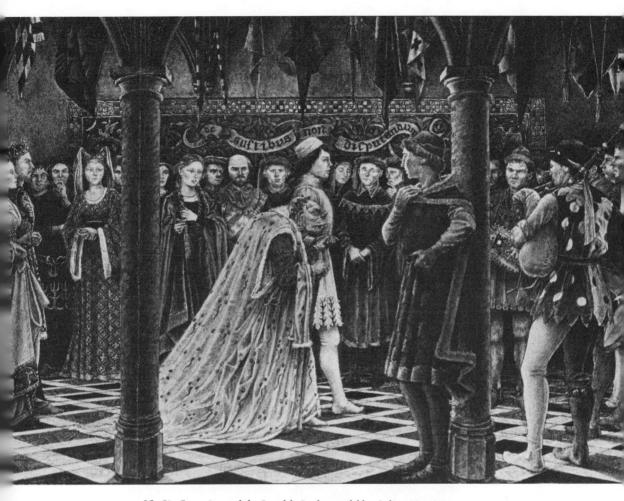

25. *Sir Gawain and the Loathly Lady*, retold by Selina Hastings,
illustrated by Juan Wijngaard, 1985. By permission of Lothrop,
Lee and Shepard Books, a division of William Morrow and Company, Inc.

father acts like a beast, barking on his hands and knees during his drunken bouts, she cannot transform him with her love. "See you," she says at the end of the book as they part in an airport. "Not if I see you first," he whispers.[8] There are strong reverberations of "Beauty and the Beast" in Isabelle Holland's *Man Without a Face*. From redemptive journeys through the underworld, such as *Slake's Limbo* by Felice Holman, to numskull and trickster tales by James Marshall (*The Stupids Step Out, Three Up a Tree, Fox All Week*), old stories survive in new forms through children's books. William Steig's picture books contain many folkloric elements, and his most durable works depend upon them for plot, structure, and characters. An analysis of Steig's work turns up numerous traditional motifs:

Sylvester and the Magic Pebble (1969): magic wishing stone (D1470.1.1); transformation by means of magic stone (D572.5); transformation of man to stone (D231); disenchantment by use of magic object (D771); disenchantment by faithfulness of others (D750)

Rotten Island (1969): monsters (G301); monsters kill each other off at end of world (A1087); world calamities and renewals (A1090)

Amos and Boris (1971): helpful whale (B472); whale-boat (man carried across water on back of whale) (R245); animal grateful for rescue from drowning (B362); reward for rescue (Q53); friendship between the animals (A2493)

26. *Mufaro's Beautiful Daughters: An African Tale*, by John Steptoe, 1987. By permission of Lothrop, Lee and Shepard Books, a division of William Morrow and Company, Inc.

The Amazing Bone (1976): magic bone (human D1007, animal D1013); magic bone gives advice (D1312.2); magic object saves person from execution (D1391); abduction in forest (K1337); abduction by fox (R13.1.11)

Caleb and Kate (1977): witch transforms person to animal (G263.1); transformation of man to dog (D141); man transformed to animal kept as pet by heroine (T33); disenchantment by wounding (D712.6)

Tiffky Doofky (1978): future spouse foretold (M369.2.1); quest for unknown beloved (H1381.2.1.1); magic arrow shot to determine where to seek bride (D1314.1.3); fairies lead traveler astray (F369.7); witch causes person to fall from height (G269.13); love at first sight (T15)

Gorky Rises (1980): magic object gives power of flying (D1531); magic air journey (D2135); transformation of stone to animal (D442.1)

Doctor De Soto (1982): clever physician (J1115.2); small animals dupe larger into trap (L315.15); captor induced to disarm himself (K631); ingratitude punished (Q281)

Brave Irene (1986): dressmaker (P452); task voluntarily undertaken (H945); test of endurance (H1500); filial duty rewarded (Q65)

The Zabajaba Jungle (1987): quest for adventure (H1221); test of going without fear through a wilderness filled with all manner of beasts (H1408); tabu of touching (plucking) flower (C515); bird helper (adviser) on quest (H1233.6.2); son rescues father (R154.2); son rescues mother (R154.1)[9]

Steig, who cartooned "Beauty and the Beast" in *The New Yorker* (fig. 27), surely did not comb through the *Motif-Index of Folk Literature* to create his picture books. Yet the high incidence of motifs that function either as primary to his stories or as points of departure for his own invention suggests how extensively children's literature serves as heir to folk narrative.[10] The challenge of creating a work of art within the relatively restricted forms of children's literature is as great as that of creating any form of literature. There is no historical or cultural limitation on such creation. Periodic revivals of public interest in fairy tales sometimes inspire a nostalgic adulation of Perrault or the Grimms as a cultural peak. The counterreaction that designates such tales as a destructive force can be equally untempered.

Those who create today build on an aesthetic past as certainly as Beaumont did. A "Beauty and the Beast" is rare in any age, but even in a society that neglects the potential greatness of children's literature, the recurrence of such a story inspires sure successors, stories that combine the old and the new for regenerated impact. Of course, there are differences between the oral and written traditions, but writers and artists craft the printed page for effects just as storytellers use voice and body language. Both are elaborating core elements—this study of "Beauty and the Beast" shows

The Beast proposes to Beauty.

27. "The Beast Proposes to Beauty." Drawing by W. Steig;
© 1982. The New Yorker Magazine, Inc.

how children's literature, among other genres, generates literary and graphic variants from folk literature. The oral and literary traditions interact on a continuum.

As contemporary juvenile fiction and picture books recast old stories and develop new ones, it is important that the critical world acknowledge, respect, and respond to them. It was not until the 1970s that the Modern Language Association recognized children's literature in its conferences and journals. Children's literature receives negligible attention not only from those involved with mainstream literature and folklore, but also, ironically, from those concerned with children and education. In the field of reading, textual analysis is more often applied to curricular materials. Although there is at last a growing awareness of the value of literature and storytelling in the development of language and reading motivation, skill drills still dominate our school systems. Even those sympathetic with the "uses" of literature are sometimes unaware of the high quality of art and narrative in today's juvenile publishing. Bettelheim, for instance, dismisses current children's literature completely (his one and only bad example being *The Little Engine That Could,* a 1938 publication) in comparison to folk and fairy tales.[11]

In 1984, a landmark conference on fairy tales at Princeton included a
phalanx of scholars from folklore, anthropology, psychology, comparative
literature, English, Germanic languages and literatures, the graphic arts, Near
Eastern studies, and even architecture. In the book that emerged, *Fairy Tales
and Society: Illusion, Allusion, and Paradigm*[12]—otherwise a model of holistic treatment—no one represented the literature of today's primary fairy
tale consumer, the child, and no one seemed to notice the missing link. At
a 1986 International Grimm Symposium, only one paper out of twenty-four
focused on fairy tales in contemporary children's literature. There seems to
be a reluctance, almost an embarrassment, in associating fairy tales with
children's literature.[13] If children's books and television are the new matrix
for folk and fairy tales, scholars should assess them with the same creative
energy they have applied to past forms.

Fairy tale scholarship itself is a great tradition, and we can learn from its
patterns of development. The very diversity of folk and fairy tale variations
suggests an eclectic or at least open-minded approach to their study. Too
often in the past, critics have used a single theory to account for the cultural-
historical development, psychological-religious interpretation, and aes-
thetic-critical analysis of fairy tales. At best, the theory may be well informed,
well reasoned, and creatively sensitive—but even at best, it may neglect
important aspects of story. The press reported the Princeton conference as
featuring a hundred scholars disagreeing on the nature of the wolf in "Little
Red Riding Hood," which was "variously interpreted as the id, the pleasure
principle, the predatory male, the phallus, an outlaw, a demon, the animal in
all of us, and the inherent dangerousness of a cruel world." (The professor of
architecture quipped that "the real tale was a design flaw: the weak lock on
the grandmother's door.")[14] That the wolf could be all these things, and, for
various audiences, reducible to any one, is the glory of the image, evoking
William Golding's reflection that myth is "a story about which we can finally
do nothing but wonder."[15] Research sometimes loses story to theory. "A
folktale can be interpreted," says Max Lüthi, "but any single interpretation
will impoverish it and will miss what is essential."[16]

Of course, the concentration required by analysis makes it difficult not to
specialize, to the neglect of contributions from other fields. A look at the
critical literature on fairy tales shows that scholars tend to focus too narrowly
on a circumscribed group of stories or too restrictively through the lens of
one discipline and even one theory. A citation of some well-known examples might begin with Bettelheim's aforementioned *Uses of Enchantment*,
which is frequently insightful but which universalizes from the Grimms'

versions and generalizes about "the child." Both the selection—what is studied—and the viewpoint—how it is studied—can limit or even distort conclusions. An enormous amount of research has relied on Jakob and Wilhelm Grimms' work as representation of an oral tradition faithfully

28. "East of the Sun, West of the Moon: A Norwegian Tale." From *The Maid of the North: Feminist Folk Tales from Around the World,* by Ethel Johnston Phelps, illustrated by Lloyd Bloom. Copyright © 1981 by Ethel Johnston Phelps. Reprinted by permission of Henry Holt and Company, Inc.

recorded. However, since it has been documented that Grimm stories were frequently collected from several literate women of French Huguenot background and were altered increasingly from manuscript form through seven editions,[17] some elaborate theoretical constructs appear to have been based on false assumptions, a situation that could have been avoided with a broader representation, such as the collection of 345 "Cinderella" variants provided by Marian Cox as early as 1893.

Jack Zipes's books show an extraordinary sense of his sources' specific sociopolitical contexts—something Bettelheim neglects entirely. Zipes argues from a Marxist position that fairy tales have been shaped into an oppressive sociopolitical force, a charge leveled by many other feminist critics as well,[18] and he champions more recent and liberating stories. Of course, contemporary British, European, and U.S. fantasists have featured active female characters for decades, in trickster tales such as Astrid Lindgren's *Pippi Longstocking*, animal tales such as *Charlotte's Web*, and magic tales such as Patricia McKillip's *The Forgotten Beasts of Eld*. One of the appeals of the high fantasies by Robin McKinley, whose novelization of "Beauty and the Beast" is analysed here and who won a Newbery Award for *The Hero and the Crown*, is her strong women. Zipes's 1986 book, *Don't Bet on the Prince: Contemporary Feminist Fairy Tales in North America and England* finally pays tribute to the clever or lusty heroines who have survived in traditional stories such as "Molly Whuppie," which have starred in story hour programs (mostly conducted by female librarians) since the late nineteenth and early twentieth centuries and in more recent collections by Rosemary Minard (*Womenfolk and Fairy Tales,* 1975), Ethel J. Phelps (*Tatterhood and Other Tales,* 1978; *The Maid of the North: Feminist Folk Tales from Around the World,* 1981) (fig. 28), Alison Lurie (*Clever Gretchen and Other Forgotten Folktales,* 1980), and James Riordan (*The Woman in the Moon and Other Forgotten Heroines,* 1985). Zipes sometimes shortchanges consideration of the tales' aesthetic effects, however, for emphasis on their propagandistic impact and leaves unattended variants that are at odds with his theory. The interpretation of "Beauty and the Beast" as a vehicle of eighteenth-century French male chauvinist repression, for instance, disregards Beauty's role as savior/hero and does not account for related stories that appear in totally different cultural and temporal contexts, with male and female roles sometimes reversed. (Animal wives are almost as common as animal husbands!)

Cultural historian Robert Darnton, in "Peasants Tell Tales: The Meaning of Mother Goose," argues that French fairy tales are strictly literal, given the threatening context of contemporaneous life, and certainly more cautionary than symbolic. Starvation and violence were everpresent, childhood was difficult to survive, and the best way to avoid being tricked was to master deceit. "The human condition has changed so much since then that we can hardly imagine the way it appeared to people whose lives really were nasty, brutish, and short."[19] Darnton's documentation is impressive, but the fact remains that the stories he describes do have relevance at different levels in a radically different period. Whether or not they have been misconstrued by modernists, their elements nevertheless maintain consistent vitality to an average reader in modern times.

J. R. R. Tolkien's classic "Tree and Leaf" is a brilliant essay that has served, with justification, as an ultimate definition of fairy tales and fantasy in literature. His impeccable literary judgement seems to lead, nevertheless, to some rigid opinions about adaptation and illustration based on a Platonic ideal. Sample opinions on adaptation: "The old stories are mollified or bowdlerized, instead of being reserved; the imitations are often merely silly, Pigwiggenry without even the intrigue; or patronizing; or (deadliest of all) covertly sniggering, with an eye on the other grown-ups present."[20] On drama: "I once saw a so-called 'children's pantomime,' the straight story of *Puss-in-Boots*, with even the metamorphosis of the ogre into a mouse. Had this been mechanically successful it would either have terrified the specta-tors or else have been just a turn of high-class conjuring. As it was, though done with some ingenuity of lighting, disbelief had not so much to be suspended as hanged, drawn, and quartered" (p.71). On art: "However good in themselves, illustrations do little good to fairy stories" (p. 95). His insis-tence on purity and protest against bowdlerizing are especially ironic in light of the nonelite progenitors of the fairy tale genre. Tolkien does not have much use for folklorists in general ("They are inclined to say that any two stories that are built round the same folk-lore motive [sic], or are made up of a generally similar combination of such motives, are the 'same stories'"; p. 45).

From the folklore department, Max Lüthi says flat out that "The true guardians of the folktale are neither literary scholars nor psychologists, but folklorists,"[21] a sentiment reflected by Alan Dundes in his essay, "Fairy Tales from a Folkloristic Perspective."[22] Each of these commentators has much of value to contribute to this study of "Beauty and the Beast," to the study of fairy tales in general, and to children's literature of the future. Yet there does seem to be a need for greater flexibility and even humor—both fairy tale staples—in the critical literature. Even if the scope is limited (as this study is to French, British, and U.S. versions of one story, and to text rather than context) the point of view need not be. Story is multidimensional. One of the reasons for the power of Northrop Frye's ideas on archetypal criticism is their broad range (at the risk of being vague: "All art is equally conventional"[23]). Dundes, in *Cinderella: A Folklore Casebook*, incorporates as much diversity into his commentary as marks the story itself. He shows how much can be synthesized from a cross section of scholarship including structural analysis, psychoanalysis, literary criticism, anthropology, and historical schools of folklore—all brought to bear on versions of a story broadly varied across time and place.

The problem of rigidity is not only a current one, as Stith Thompson points out in a summary complaint.

> Each generation of scholars has had its favorite theory. A century ago these scholars were talking with the utmost certainty and dogmatism of these supernatural spouses, telling us that they represented now this, now that phenomenon of sky or cloud or seasonal change. A generation later these creatures were dogmatically described as always essentially animals and as related to primitive totemistic ideas. Still later, the ritualistic school had its inning and all these stories became embodiments of ancient rites. And even today there remain some scholars who assert that they have the key that unlocks this mystery. This key they find in the interpretation of dreams.[24]

Claude Lévi-Strauss delivers a funny example, in his own serious manner, of the same problem.

> If a given mythology confers prominence to a certain character, let us say an evil grandmother, it will be claimed that in such a society grandmothers are actually evil and that mythology reflects the social structure and the social relations; but should the actual data be conflicting, it would be readily claimed that the purpose of mythology is to provide an outlet for repressed feelings. Whatever the situation may be, a clever dialectic will always find a way to pretend that a meaning has been unravelled.[25]

After warning readers that "multi-dimensional frames of reference cannot be ignored, or naively replaced by two- or three-dimensional ones,"[26] he goes on to construct his own inviolable method of analysis.

The compartmentalization of fairy tale scholarship has implications for children's literature. A survey of research in children's literature in the United States and Canada shows a lack of communication between scholars, who tend to concentrate by discipline: librarians and educators on practical and

sociological aspects, English and comparative literature scholars on historical and aesthetic aspects, psychologists on therapeutic aspects.[27] The study
of children's literature needs the cross-ventilation of all these disciplines for a
holistic consideration of art, text, context, and connection with readers or
listeners.

Children's books challenge us to apply new vision to a new literature for
the newly born. To meet that challenge, critics must examine old patterns
open-mindedly, recognizing the dynamic of continuity and fluctuation
exercised by each storyteller and listener. The tale in focus here, "Beauty and
the Beast," has been told many times, with many intentions. It represents
aspects of the worst and best in society, story, and self. It is shaped for
survival.

APPENDIX ONE

Literary Beauties and Folk Beasts
Folktale Issues in *Beauty and the Beast*

Larry DeVries

The Beauty and the Beast: Thinking about Tales

"I now enter from untruth into truth." So begins one of the commonest rituals in early India. Saying this, one "passes from man to the gods."[1] More recently, the Romanian folklorist Mihai Pop has shown that the opening formulas of folktales symbolically express a transition from the true to the untrue.[2] With such a formula the folktale narrator leads the audience from man to fairies, dragons, and wise and helpful animals. This striking contrast is introduced here not to adduce a difference in the working of ritual and folktale, but to underscore a fundamental similarity. In fact, the difference may be only apparent, a difference of words, not meaning. The formulas express transition, and one might ask, with the fairytale poet Joan Swift, "Is it into, or out of, illusion?"[3]

Although apparently opposite in content, these formulas are the same in form. Structure is an issue for both the ritualist and the raconteur—Mircea Eliade has commented on the initiatory structure of the fairy tale[4]—for the sphere of operation is strictly defined and is set off from the ordinary one. One effect of this separation is that it makes the fairy tale easy to define. It is everything that happens between the opening and closing formulas inclusively. This is an overly facile definition, but it has implications for the study of the tale. One may study the beginnings and endings as Pop has done, or the story in the middle, or any one of a number of contexts in which the tale occurs.

A comparative study such as the present one is necessarily limited in its attention to context in direct proportion to the number of versions considered. This is a classic approach, employed by both scholars of the historic-geographic school interested in reconstruction and diffusion and those

155

attempting to discover stylistic and structural features of the tale itself. This approach neglects features of context that deserve the minute scrutiny brought to bear upon them by other methods. But Anna Tavis, in discussing ways in which stories have meaning, has claimed that folktales today are disengaged from their context, and, because of this, open to more interpretations.[5] Symbols are subject to revaluation. Fairy tales have been and are being introduced into new contexts at a rapid rate in such phenomena as cartoons, fairy tale poetry, novels, children's literature, and, one must not forget, essays such as this one.

The survival, indeed the flourishing, of fairy tales in new contexts may be a result of what can be thought of as an iconic character, or the ability to evoke a whole picture with one or more key parts. For example, the scene of a girl with seven small men cannot fail, in a certain cultural context, to bring a specific pattern to mind. This pattern, then, in the *langue* of tales is revivified in the *parole* of the actual telling of the story. The patterns have been reorganized by folklorists and catalogued as motifs and tale types, or described on the basis of forms such as fairy tale or ballad. "Beauty and the Beast," for example, is known scholastically as subtype C of type 425, known in its turn "iconically" as "Cupid and Psyche." Although their results are different, the aims of the scholar and the raconteur are akin to the extent that the work of each results in a retelling of the story. In each case a form is used, the analytical essay, the catalogue, or the fairy tale itself to re-present underlying ideas in the tale.

In the re-presentation of the tale, one may suppose that it undergoes a reinterpretation. The variation of elements in a given folk tale is striking. The power to vary the story while remaining within the type is the interpretive power of the storyteller. There are many variables in a tale. One sees, for example, in a modern cartoon,[6] a picture of a princess and a frog. But here the princess is homely and she is in pursuit of the fleeing frog. Two variables have been altered in this reinterpretation, the beauty of the princess, and the point of view, or perspective from which the story is told. The audience is invited to sympathize with the frog, a change probably already desired by nonviolent hearers of the original tale. One may speculate that humor may be found in the somewhat overdue nature of the interpretation. In any event, the entire effect depends on the recognition of a variation in an underlying pattern.

The persistence of the tales and their susceptibility to variation raise a number of issues, one of the most important of which is the use of the tales, or why they are told. This is particularly interesting in the present case, for with "Beauty and the Beast" we are left with little doubt at least as to the conscious or stated intent of its most seminal narrator. Beaumont's purpose was didactic. Her motive is not appreciably different from that articulated by traditional folktale raconteurs. The Navaho Yellowman said "If my children hear the stories, they will grow up to be good people."[7] Clearly, the motives of Beaumont and Yellowman in tale choice and interpretation could be subjected to deeper analysis. But one cannot deny a convergence in purpose in, on the one hand, the author of a literary tale, and on the other, a narrator in the oral tradition.

"The spiritual tradition of the folk, particularly oral tradition" is the way folklore was defined by the congress at Arnhem, Holland, in 1955.[8] Folklorists make a fundamental distinction between oral and written forms, referring to the latter as literary, and the relation between the two has been a matter of discussion. *La Belle et la Bête* of Beaumont, the story of her predecessor, Villeneuve, in fact all of the versions discussed in the foregoing study are literary versions. The hypothesis of Swahn, that tale type 425 "subtype C is entirely dependent upon literary influence,"[9] exemplifies the distinction. Swahn believes that the folk borrowed the written story to retell as a folktale. That the range of distribution of 425C coincides fairly well with the incidence of translations of Beaumont is what Swahn terms "an essential condition for the reasoning."[10] It is not, of course, a sufficient condition. Literary versions are often removed from consideration by folklorists on the ground that they provide but a single variant. Meanwhile, the text scholar struggles to deal with the multiplicity of variants in this single version. One has the feeling it would be a good idea for these scholars to meet each other.

Actually, oral literature, the Rigveda for example, may vary less than written literature, over a much longer time. If variation is a poor test of orality, and one might note other nondifferentiating features such as length, distribution, and directionality of influence, similar difficulties are presented by style, which may vary dramatically from teller to teller even in a limited tradition area.[11] Certainly one can and should define styles in oral or written literature. But, these may also blend, such as in the case of Wilhelm Grimm's attempt to create a pure folk style. Indeed, one may wonder to what extent the well-known features of orality are inherent in oral literature itself, rather than simply reflexes in discourse of cultural tendencies. An example of this is "the law of three," obeyed by scholars no less than folk narrators, indeed by an entire society.[12] Phenomena such as publishing culture and mass communication and education make it less desirable to restrict the idea of narrative tradition to the oral mode. A tendency in this direction is expressed in a more recent definition of folklore which states "even written and mass media forms are folklore to the extent that variations occur."[13] Interestingly, in reviewing definitions of folklore Lauri Honko has emphasized folklore as a process, recapitulating the move from taxonomy to formalism in the field.[14]

Before proceeding to the formal analysis of "Beauty and the Beast," which is the subject of the first part of this essay, let us view the tale in terms developed by the first generations of folklore scholars in the nineteenth and early twentieth centuries. Aside from consideration of mode and motive, an aspect of all tellings of tales is the conveyance of ideas through an artistic medium. One approach to the analysis of this medium is the notion of motif, "the smallest element in a tale having the power to persist in tradition."[15] Catalogues of such motifs are available for both oral and written tradition. In the case of "Beauty and the Beast," the central motif is T118 Girl (man) married to (enamoured of) a monster. But this does not entirely capture the situation in the general type, which also includes A188 ff. God(dess) in love with mortal. The two values of the latter bridge the gap between two tale types, 400 The man on a quest for his lost wife (the Swan Maiden, for example) and 425 The search for the lost husband (the so-called animal bridegroom). Intuition protests the relatedness of the two types, as do shared motifs such as the gossip taboo[16] and the formula of the "old key."[17] It is a matter of regret, though understandable, that Swahn did not treat tale type 400, which he intended to deal with separately,[18] at the same time as 425.

But the two motifs, T118 and A188, which seem to apply to the present case, do not exhaust the topic in the Motif Index. One finds similarities in a number of other categories such as F300 ff. Liaison with a fairy, K1301 Mortal woman seduced by a god, B600 ff. Marriage of person to animal, T93.5 Tragic love between pari (fairy) and mortal man, G264 La Belle dame sans merci, E474 Cohabition of human and ghost, and the somewhat paradoxical K1325.0.1 Hero, feigning death, copulates with divine maiden. At first glance, the basic notion seems to be that of affective relationship between a human and a nonhuman. But this is not strictly true, for it fails to describe stories like the Kusa Jātaka, with two human principles, or an American "Cupid and Psyche," for example, in which the male is a prize fighter.[19] The principle, then, seems to subsist in the relationship between the humanity of one actor and a nonhuman dimension in the other, that may appear as sub- or superhuman.

A simple step in generalization may be taken, such that this relationship is comprehended by T91 Unequals in love. How are we to understand this asymmetry? The above examples deal with, or at least may be provisionally regarded as dealing with ontological categories—animal, god or goddess, ghost, human. The claim has been made by Meletinsky that these phenomena in the tales represent "reconstituted . . . marriage and wedding customs."[20] In the inequality of the amorous pair we are to see marriage selectional rules, exogamy and endogamy. What we are confronted with in this case is a specific instance of the attempt to explain the origin of the tale, here on the basis of ritual. Both the story of "Cupid and Psyche" and Apuleius' frame story, *Metamorphoses*, have been interpreted as based on initiation rituals.[21] This is an approach which may be neither affirmed, nor flatly denied here. After all, in Megas' reconstruction of the original (Greek) "Cupid and Psyche," the man's mother, a dragon herself, does wish that her son would marry a dragon.[22] Another etiology is offered by Tegethoff in the dream of the incubus (and presumably the succubus when sex is inverted), citing the intensity of the experience to explain the lover's nonhuman, specifically, animal form. Here again, with the theory of dream origin (a nightmärchen?) a general explanation with wider implications is approached. Even if one finds it difficult to accept such phenomena as custom or dream as the cause of folktales, it seems less unreasonable to admit their potential influence in maintaining the tale. Interest in telling and hearing folktales might be less keen without such experiental cognates. Such an artless art form as the folktale is bound to be in constant interplay with life.

The conception of the unequal lovers in terms of social, psychological, or ontological categories, however, seems insufficient to describe the tales under consideration because of certain characteristics of the narrative medium itself. One of these characteristics is that of character development, a central feature of the fairy tale. If, for example, as is often supposed, such tales deal with the process of maturation, then there must be more than one state of a character in the tale, as well as the change from one to the other. Hence, the tale deals with ontogeny as well as ontology. In addition, ideas in the tale are represented by realia such as objects and locations, and especially by the reaction of the characters to these and each other. To take an example of the latter, one sees in the Kusa Jātaka, an early Indic cognate of "Beauty and the Beast," that it is Pabhāvatī who expresses literally Kusa's demonic nature: "A goblin is catching hold of me." Hence, the tale deals with perception as well as the categories already mentioned.

To illustrate some of the complexity inherent in the tale, let us briefly examine one motif found in "Beauty and the Beast", that of the wish for a rose. Beauty wishes for a beautiful flower. She herself has "blossomed," as the Greek translation of La Belle as *Oraia*,[23] literally '*ripe*,' makes clear.

Further, in a French oral version the flower bleeds when it is plucked, suggesting the notion of deflowering. But the scene is played between the father and the Beast. When the flower is cut, it evokes the Beast. It is his garden, his rose, and therefore, his blood and his injury. With no one present to experience the Beast's threat but the father, one might regard the Beast as a hypostatization of the father's fear. One might even wish to see the rose as a metasymbol, suggesting in itself symbolic complexity.

At the early stage of the encounter, the view of the Beast is polarized into that of the father, who fears him, and that of Beauty, who is not afraid. The threat of the Beast is quite clear; it is that of death. While it has this general form in Beaumont, in the folk version mentioned the Beast is specifically an anthropophage. It is interesting that children's drawings of another animal bridegroom, the Frog Prince, reflect this specific quality with open-mouthed and crocodilian frogs.[24]

A polarization of perception between Beauty and her father is also found in the wish for a rose. Apropos of this motif, Swahn has stated that it "is quite unknown in the genuine folk tradition which the other subtypes represent."[25] Such a statement depends on the scope of one's evidence, and when this is widened to include 425R (AT 432), it fails. In Afanas'ev 234, "The Feather of Finist, the Bright Falcon," precisely this motif occurs. A father about to leave for town solicits requests from his daughters. The youngest, who is exceptionally beautiful, asks for a "red flower." The father deplores this wish, calling her "little dunce." The humble wish for a rose is, in a way, no different from the wish for a marvelous object, or an ambigious one ("I know not what"—Afanas'ev 212). The point is the contrast between the ordinary and the extraordinary. The mechanism by which the tale expresses this is to contrast the point of view of the father (and the older sisters, one might add) with the point of view of the heroine.

It is possible to see, in the wish for a rose, a symptom of the heroine's humility, a theme that has attracted the attention of modern commentators, particularly those inclined toward social exegesis. To ascertain the nature of this aspect of Beauty it is helpful to compare other central figures in the animal spouse type. In a number of these one may see, at a certain stage in the development of the story, what may be described as an abasement of one or both of the central characters. Thus, in the Kusa Jātaka the king serves at menial tasks. This is also true of the princess in "King Thrushbeard" (tale type 900). The difference lies in the fact that King Kusa's abasement is voluntary, but the princess has it forced upon her.[26] In contrast to the latter, Beauty willingly accepts her lowly position at home and a dangerous one in the

Beast's castle. Humility in one case corresponds to humiliation in the other. What is internal or inherent in one case is external or causative in the other.

This brief consideration of the motif of the wish for a rose illustrates some of the variation in the narrative interpretation of a specific motif. Other kinds of variation occur, such as change in the wished-for object or the appearance of the motif in a different tale. Variation and the ability to vary seem crucial factors in the life of the tale. Not only are the individual features of the tale variable, but so is the overall view of the story. In the animal husband tale we find, in fact, antithetical morals, points drawn from essentially the same story. The narrator in Apuleius begins: "But I will tell thee a pleasant old wives' tale to put away all sorrow and to revive thy spirits."[27] But the narrator in the Jātaka has a quite different point to make. "Verily, through passion for woman the sages of old, mighty though they were, became weak and fell into distress and destruction."[28] A study of variation in the folktale or the literary tale depends first on the identification of the variables. Two are selected for this study—the events of the story, and the actors.

"Beauty and the Beast": An Analysis of Form

One of the most productive methods of analysis employed by folklorists in the latter half of the present century is that of examining the events of the tale and their sequence. This method was invented by Vladimir Propp, who termed these events "functions." One may imagine asking questions such as "Who is involved?" "Where did the story take place?" or "What happened?" The functions answer the last question. One of the criticisms of this approach has been that one simply cannot speak of pure events without some reference to the performers.[29] In fact, Propp never achieved the level of abstraction his idea seemed to promise, for many functions name specific categories of actor such as member of the family, hero, victim, false hero, donor, and others, each of which seems to contain strong cues for the action of the story. To summarize this approach, Propp claimed to have exhaustively catalogued the functions, which he found to number thirty-one. He further claimed that the order in which they occurred was invariant, though all need not occur in a given tale. The invariant order hypothesis is one that he hedged in his notion of "assimilation,"[30] and, in fact, he did not follow it rigorously in his own analysis.[31]

Nevertheless, what emerges under this approach is a skeletally clear view of the tale, an understanding of how the bones of the narrative are joined one to the other, and a demonstration of the articulation of the joints, defining the possible and impossible, and, hence, the movement characteristic of the whole organism.

At the end of his study, Propp assures us that "new material adds nothing"[32] to the scheme as given. Since he did not analyse the tales in the Afanas'ev collection of the "Cupid and Psyche" type it is doubly interesting to cast a tale of the type 425C "Beauty and the Beast" in functional terms. The source version used here is Beaumont's 1756 edition. Implied functions are bracketed.

a	Initial Situation	Father - 3 sons - 3 daughters.
[g]	Interdiction	[Do not wish for rose.]
d	Violation	Wish for rose.
b	Family Member Absent	Father leaves home.
[g]	Interdiction	[Do not pick rose.]
d	Violation	Father picks rose.
	Consequence	Beast threatens.
		Father promises daughter.
[A]	Lack	[Beauty lacks husband.]
C	Hero leaves	Beauty leaves home.
K	Lack Liquidated	Beast sues for marriage.

This sequence of events in the tale comprises a "move" in that the action reaches a certain level of completion, in this case a proposed marriage, corresponding to the actual marriage of Cupid and Psyche in that story.

The analysis as given is not strictly Proppian in that the functional sequence Interdiction – Violation – Consequence is repeated. The sequence of events is analyzed in this way on the basis of two considerations. The first is that a function may be implicit.[33] Second, the form of an implicit function, or any function, always depends on the point of view of one or another of the dramatis personae. The latter consideration results in an analysis entailing a doubling of the functional sequence Interdiction – Violation – Consequence such that the Consequence of the first sequence is the Interdiction – Violation of the second. Beauty's Violation results in her father's Violation. For the initial implicit Interdiction, one may compare Afanas'ev 235 "Feather of Finist, the Bright Falcon" in which the father overtly deplores his daughter's wish for a red flower.[34]

The first move of "Beauty and the Beast" closes with the meeting of the two principal characters in the Beast's castle. In the action of the tale this functions as the liquidation of Beauty's Lack of a husband. This is particularly cogent, I think, if one views the action with respect to the goal of the tale, namely the final uniting or reunion of Beauty and Beast. It is interesting to note that Beauty's implicit Lack of a husband may be viewed as her father's implicit surfeit of daughters.

In addition, there appears to be a morphological similarity between the overt Violation and the implicit Lack. Beauty's expressed wish for a rose corresponds to an implicit wish for a husband. Dundes points out a case of assimilation of Violation with Lack in his analysis of the American Indian "Star Husband" tale. Here the violation of an implicit interdiction against the wish for a star husband is assimilated to the heroine's lack of such a spouse.[35] If Lack is implicit, it is very hard to see it at a specific and invariant point in the sequence of functions. Its effect is precisely that mentioned by Propp in his discussion of Interdiction as "spectre of misfortune" that "hovers invisibly"[36] over the scene of the story, inevitably impelling the action to its destination.

If one may speak of Beauty's Lack as her father's surfeit, it seems even more reasonable to countenance Lack vis-à-vis the Beast, namely his lack of a (disenchanting) wife. "Nous refusons d'eliminer de la structure du récit la référence aux personages [We refuse to remove reference to characters from the structure of the tale]," said Claude Bremond in criticism of Propp's principle.[37] Actually, the present application of Lack to the Beast certainly oversteps the notion of Lack entertained in *Morphology of the Folktale*. But one may consider a notion of the function which includes the element of point of view, and allows the adduction of morphologically similar material that might not otherwise be associated with the present tale.

Let us consider certain features of the first move of the Russian tale "The Enchanted Princess" (Afanas'ev 272). In this story, a discharged soldier in need of a livelihood encounters a remote castle where food and drink are magically provided. In the castle is a bear, the enchanted princess, who proposes a test of endurance to the soldier. He is successful, disenchantment ensues, and they are married.

In this tale it is relatively easy for one to think in terms of the beast's Lack. The reason for this seems to be that here, as often with female figures, we are made aware of her true nature early in the story. A functional analogy between this story and "Beauty and the Beast" is as follows:

	Beauty and Beast	Enchanted Princess
Lack (beast)	(disenchanting) wife	(disenchanting) husband

The question naturally arises of the soldier's Lack in "The Enchanted Princess." Initially, it seems the soldier is seeking a livelihood. However, the outcome of the move, and indeed the whole tale, is a marriage. Working backwards, it is apparent that the implicit lack with respect to the hero is his lack of a wife. Indeed, Propp's final function, Marriage, often is accompanied or even replaced by the acquisition of wealth and power.[38] This leads to the following comparison.

	Beauty and Beast	Enchanted Princess
Lack (hero figure)	husband	wife

It is easy to see that the roles of the bear and the beast in the two tales are functionally equivalent. What is striking is that the hero figure in "The Enchanted Princess" is equivalent to the beast in "Beauty and the Beast." From this comparison there emerges an ambivalence in both the hero and the beast figures. The two figures meet in an enchanted castle. In "Cupid and Psyche," Cupid is sent by his mother, Psyche by her father, a feature to be analyzed in greater detail in a discussion of characterization below. The value that each of the principal actors will assume in the encounter, whether enchanted beast or disenchanting hero figure, depends strictly on the point of view of the tale. The ambivalence is highlighted in "The Enchanted Princess" in which the first move outlined above is followed first by a quest of the princess for the hero, and then a quest by the hero for the princess.

The second move in Beauty and the Beast also opens with the function Interdiction, and may be outlined as follows.

g	Interdiction	Not to wish to go home.
d	Violation	Wish to go home.
g	Interdiction	Not to overstay.
d	Violation	Overstaying.
A	Lack	Violation caused by sisters leads to lack of husband.
K	Lack Liquidated	Return to Husband.
M	Task	Revive beast.
N	Task Accomplished	Beast revived.
T	Transformation	Beast transformed.
W	Marriage	Marriage.

Again there is a morphological assimilation of Violation, this time with the stronger form of Lack, namely that caused by a villain.[39]

The most general way to see this, without regard to point of view, is simply as a separation of the two main characters. Another way in which separation may occur is found in the second move of Afanas'ev 159, "Maria Morevna."

b	Family Member Absent	Maria leaves.
g	Interdiction	Not to look in room.
d	Violation	Ivan looks in room.
[g]	Interdiction	[Not to give water to Ogre.]
d	Violation	Ivan gives water to Ogre.
A	Lack	Ogre abducts Maria Morevna.
C	Hero Leaves	Ivan looks for his lost wife.
K	Lack Liquidated	Ivan finds Maria Morevna.

One may observe the causal connection between Violation and Lack, where the villain is essentially *ex machina*, even more split off than in "Beauty and the Beast." This is not the case in "The Enchanted Princess." In that tale, the second move draws to a close with the reunion of the princess and the hero. But, she is unable to awaken him from his magical sleep. Frustrated, she brings about his transportation through ill-considered words (cf. tale type 813 "Careless word summons the devil") to "a point between two seas . . . on the very narrowest little wedge."[40] The functional ambivalence of the princess here is obvious.

In "Maria Morevna," separation results from abduction, whereas in "The Enchanted Princess" and "Beauty and the Beast" the hero figure first leaves and then is detained through sleep, or the allied notion of forgetting. These mechanisms of separation also occur from such taboo violations as the hero's kissing his mother in tale type 313, or eating food proffered by a rival wife in tale type 400 (III g). In fact, Swahn suggests that the Interdiction against overstaying in "Beauty and the Beast" is a borrowing from tale type 400, "The Man on a Quest for his Lost Wife."[41] However, one is equally well reminded of Cupid's return to his mother, and his ensuing torpor.

Given what has been said about the role of point of view in determining the functional role of an actor in the tale, it may be unattractive to speak of motif borrowing in this case. A simpler description would result from seeing tale types 400, 425, and related types as one type characterized as tales of the form Union – Separation – Reunion. The exact form the story takes would then depend upon the point of view of the hero figure, who is human, the enchanted spouse being less than human, that is, animal, or more than human, divine. Certainly the identification of type cannot depend on the sex of the hero figure, this being notoriously variable, as in the case of male

Psyches, Swahn's 425N,[42] male Cinderellas, Rooth's type C,[43] and men who wish for star wives.[44]

The Beast and the Beauty: Point of View in the Tale

To understand the role that the perspective of the main character plays in the tale, let us consider the story from the Beast's point of view. This requires no imaginative effort at all, for the story was current in early India, and survives in a number of recensions in early Buddhist texts. The version given here is the Pāli Kusa Jātaka.[45] The "tradition bearers" in this case are Buddhist monks, and this may play a certain role in the choice of point of view at the narrative level. The main characters are a king and princess. Yet their supernatural character is hinted at by a description of the princess as beautiful as a *devacchara*, divine nymph, and her own view of the king as *yakkha*, roughly equivalent to 'spook' or 'ogre'. The story opens with the familiar situation of the childless couple.

At a certain time a king Okkāka ruled with his chief queen Sīlavatī and a harem of 16,000. The king ruled well but had no heir. In a desperate effort to obtain a son, the king opened the doors of his harem to all his subjects. A disgusting beggar, Indra in disguise, chose Sīlavatī. She was transported to heaven and obtained a boon from the god. Her wish for a son was answered by a grant of two sons, one wise but ugly, the other handsome but foolish. When the former, Kusa by name, was sixteen years old, his mother approached him with the suggestion that he marry. After considerable reluctance he fashioned a golden image of a "daughter of the gods," and sent this forth in the world as a bride test. When the image arrived in the Madda kingdom, it was there mistaken for the princess Pabhāvatī. With this testimony to the bride's beauty, the marriage was arranged. A condition was imposed by Kusa's mother, that the princess meet Kusa only in a darkened room until a son is born. At this point, Kusa is anointed king in his own right, his father retiring from both his kingdom and the story. The marriage ensues, and all goes well for a time until Kusa enlists his mother's help in clandestinely viewing his bride. On the first two occasions, Kusa pelts Pabhāvatī with elephant and horse dung. Finally, the king sequesters himself among the lotuses in a pond where his wife is to bathe. She duly arrives and, while in the water, reaches out to pick a lotus. Kusa rises up from behind the flower, announcing himself as her husband. Pabhāvatī is horrified and returns to her father's kingdom. Kusa follows, now, against his mother's advice, making the journey of nearly one thousand miles in a day. He enters the service of Pabhāvatī's father, where he is finally recognized and reviled by Pabhāvatī. Indra intervenes to the effect that seven kings arrive as suitors to Pabhāvatī with their armies. Pabhāvatī's father suggests cutting her up and dividing her among them. Pabhāvatī relents to Kusa, who "roars" so loudly that the kings submit. Indra bestows a transforming jewel as an additional prize. The kings marry Pabhāvatī's younger sisters, and Kusa and Pabhāvatī return to his kingdom.

The relationship of the Kusa Jātaka with "Beauty and the Beast" was remarked by its translator[46] who was aware of Ralston's translation into English of Schniefner's German translation of the Tibetan version.[47] Ralston's discussion, however, totally ignores the crucial difference in point of view in the two tales.

A complete analysis of the sequence of functions in the Kusa tale is unnecessary. Two points, however, seem to call for discussion. The first is a similarity in the two moves of all tales of the type Union – Separation – Reunion. In both moves the Lack is either implicitly or explicitly that of a spouse, with Lack Liquidated being the attainment of a spouse. In the first move of the tales, Lack – Lack Liquidated may be brought about, as we have seen, by Violation. But, in these tales the function is assimilated to the final function, Marriage. In this case, we may expect this to be preceded by the functional pair Task – Task Accomplished (M-N), as in the second move of the Kusa Jātaka and "Cupid and Psyche." This is also familiar from the first move of such tales, for example, Welsh stories of the Lady of the Lake won by the test of recognition and later lost. (See tale type 400 II, c-e.) Thus, we see the pair Interdiction – Violation playing the same role in the logic of the narrative as Task – Task Accomplished—they both lead to Lack Liquidated. This is all the more striking since Violation in the second move of the same tales produces the separation (Lack).

A possible solution to the dilemma is to see the tale as a set of associated functions with the potential for the addition of other associated functions. Thus, taking Lack – Lack Liquidated, Interdiction – Violation, Task – Task Accomplished, and others as AB, A_1B_1, etc., the tale could be represented as : $((AB) + (A_1B_1) \ldots)$, where pairs may be nested in a main pair such that $(A(A_1B_1)B)$.[48] The main pair would obviously be determined by the outcome of the tale. Such a description defines the minimal tale, namely, one unit of associated functions AB,[49] and allows for addition, deletion, and permutation in a way that escapes some of the shortcomings of the invariant order hypothesis. To see the tale as a composite of embedded tales is to see it as the result of a process familiar from longer forms such as epic, with its structure of frame story and ancillary episodes.

But such a description may be too general, in predicting tales that do not exist. More specifically, while positing tales of the type (AB) and (A(A₁B₁)B), we do not know the relationship between them, how one is derived from the other. We have already encountered the phenomenon of assimilation, such that a function becomes collapsed with another function, defined in terms of its consequent. An inverse process, *dissimilation*, would provide the mechanism for the addition and ordering of functions in the tale. Consider the basic set L–LL in the first move of the "Star Husband" tale and "Beauty and the Beast." In the former, Violation is assimilated to Lack. The wish for a star husband results in abduction by a star husband. This is the simplest form, and hence may be considered basic. The functional system of "Beauty and the Beast" may be derived from this by the process of dissimilation. Here the heroine does not wish for a husband, but for a rose, so that Violation does not express the lack of a husband, but the lack of precisely that which leads to obtaining a husband. The functions Interdiction and Lack are in both cases implied by Violation and Lack Liquidated, and may be ignored at a certain point in the description, as indeed they sometimes are in the actual narrative. The process of dissimilation provides a method for deriving one form from another in this case. Its general application cannot be considered in full here. One may see the operation of this principle in such fairy tales as "Maria Morevna," where obtaining a magic bird and horse are inserted before obtaining the princess. Likewise dissimilation accounts for the successive embeddings found in cumulative tales such as that of the woman with the pig that will not jump over the stile (tale type 2030).

The other notable feature of the functional description of what one may think of as a Beauty and Beast/Kusa Jātaka tale is that of transformation. Propp defines this function (his number 29) as "the hero is given a new appearance."[50] The orthodox form of the function transformation is found in the Kusa Jātaka. The hero receives a magic jewel with the power to make him handsome. But in "Beauty and Beast," it is the Beast who is transformed. It follows from the definition of Transformation as a change in the hero, that the Beast is the hero of "Beauty and Beast." This potential interpretation had already been suggested in the previous section. But the beast as hero does not exhaust the beast's functionality. He also corresponds, in a way, to villains such as the Ogre in the second move of "Maria Morevna" or the witch in "Rapunzel" in causing a Lack in the original family situation. In addition if one sees the first move of "Beauty and Beast" from the father's perspective, the Beast has qualities corresponding to a Donor, inasmuch as in their encounter the father acquires the use of a magical agent,[51] the rose, that resolves his problem of a surfeit of daughters. It is not unreasonable to take this position, since whole tale types, such as 331 "The Spirit in the Bottle," are based simply on the associated functions D – E – F, Test by potential Donor – Reaction – Reward.

What seems to result from the discussion of the Beast as hero, villain, and donor is an apparent ambiguity in the character. But this is not really the case, since the various aspects of an actor are strictly the result of a point of view represented by another actor in the tale. Point of view is a factor in the whole tale, in one of its moves, or even within a single function, such as a challenge by a villain and response by the hero. A striking example of the latter is found in a feature that the Kusa Jātaka shares with another early Indic tale, the story of Purūravas and Urvaśī, and a common feature of many ballads, of a verbal duel between the main characters. Functionally this resembles the form of the Task as a riddle contest. Here competing points of view are juxtaposed:

Pabhāvatī: She will be cut into seven pieces before she weds Kusa.
Kusa: She will marry Kusa or no one else.

Such shifting of the point of view is a dramatic feature of the tale, and the perspective expressed at this level may be referred to as the *dramatic* point of view. In general, each character introduced into the tale represents a potentially distinct *dramatic* point of view.

In a specific tale, or a single move, the narrator chooses a character whose action is followed most closely. This is the main character, or the actor Propp has designated as the hero. Since this choice influences the entire characterization of the tale, its broader scope may be accounted for by designating it as the *narrative* point of view. These two levels of perspective, the dramatic and the narrative, may compete, resulting in a kind of tension on which the tale thrives. This may account for such familiar phenomena as the success of the unlikely son, the unlikeliness being only an expression of the point of view of the father, at the dramatic level. The analysis of the well-known concern of the fairy tale for expressing the contrast of appearance with reality,[52] as in such figures as the "wise fool," is easily reducible to one of point of view.

The narrative point of view in the Kusa Jātaka is that of a hero figure, a man whose appearance really is as frightful as Psyche's sisters' deceitful claim. In "Beauty and the Beast" and related types, the tale is told from the perspective of the one who marries the animal bridegroom. Each point of view is essentially latent in the tales in which it is not the narrative point of view. The potential to develop the point of view of a character is shown by tales which include subtales, such as one telling the story of the animal bridegroom's enchantment, found both in folk forms[53] and in Villenueve. In short, variations in point of view are a kind of narrative relativity present both within a tale and between types of tales, and accounts for an enormous variety of meaning and effect possible in the fairy tale.

Beauties and Beasts: The Tale Roles

An interesting aspect of the tale is the apparent ability of a given tale to survive with a varied cast of actors. In the present case it does not seem likely that the story would be told with less than two characters. Thus it may not be unreasonable to see Olrik's principle of "two to a scene"[54] as expressing a maximum, but also a minimum in some cases and, perhaps, a minimal tendency in general. The mere situation of the despair of a lone character, for example, is usually sufficient to evoke a helper. Incidentally, it would probably be a mistake to see a logically simple form as historically original, since both simplification and complication seem to be at work in the evolution of the tale. Before inquiring into the mechanism of addition and deletion of characters in the tale, it is worthwhile observing some alternations that exist with respect to this variable, along with the effect variation has on the tale.

In tale type 930[55] there are present two basic forms which differ strikingly in the number of principal characters required in the narrative. In the first form, a king attempts to avert a prophesied marriage of his daughter and a poor boy by attempting to kill him. In the second (930A), a prince tries similarly to avoid marrying a peasant girl. Ignoring the differences in sex, it can be said that in the latter tale the prince himself accomplishes the deeds, attempted murder and marriage, which require two actors in the former tale. This may be expressed in the following way:

$$\text{actor}_1 - \text{action}_1 + \text{actor}_2 - \text{action}_2 : \text{actor} - \text{action}_1 + \text{action}_2$$

It is clear that there is an assimilation of character roles, like the assimilation of functions discussed in the above analysis of "Beauty and the Beast."

An examination of the second move of "Beauty and the Beast" has shown that two factors contribute to the Lack of a husband. The first is Beauty's Violation of an implicit Interdiction not to leave the Beast. The villainous sisters then cause overstaying. In some variants, for example tale type 432, classified by Megas as 425R,[56] the sisters of the heroine intervene directly to bring about the husband's injury and flight. One of the commonest motifs in tales of the animal spouse type is that of burning the hide that conceals the human. Swahn gives this as IV,3 "Prohibition against destroying her husband's animal skin. The heroine burns it."[57] While there are numerous cases in which Violation takes precisely this form, in "The Three Daughters of King O'Hara" it is the girl's mother who burns the animal skin.[58] In the case considered general by Swahn, there is a substitution of the heroine herself for the villain of the move. The husband may also simply leave, as in Sgiathán Dearg. The possibilities that result in Lack are here somewhat more complex:

$$\text{actor}_1 \ (+ \ \text{actor}_2) \ (+ \ \text{actor}_3) - \text{action}$$

This formula may be expanded in four ways: the husband leaves, the heroine or the villain cause him to leave, or the villain causes the heroine to cause him to leave. A fifth form is possible, in which the husband is absent because he has not yet appeared, but this is limited to the initial situation.

The effect of expansion or contraction of the number of characters in these two instances is easy to see. The fewer the number of characters, the greater the number of possible expansions. In such a compression the characters do not seem to gain complexity, but rather, potential energy. In the reduced situation the characters bear within themselves the potential to act in more character roles.

Propp identified the function Lack as arising in two bases, one (his function 8) requiring a villainous agent, and the other (his function 8a) being simple absence of a needed or desired object. Since the two forms function identically in the sequence of action in the tale, substitution of one for the other is possible. One may say that the causative form (8) is latent or potential in the simple form (8a). But it would be wrong to say that where the heroine alone causes Lack, as in the above example, she has become a villain. Rather, the latter is simply absent and, hence, because of the characteristic structure of the genre, potential. Thus, it would seem correct to say that the heroine in this situation contains a villainous potential or the ability to split into parts, causally connected, according to the strategy of the raconteur.[59]

Not just villainy but other roles may be taken over by an actor if the actor associated with a particular action (function) is absent. Swahn lists a Breton form of 425B[60] in which the vanishing husband provides the valuable objects, normally obtained from helpers of the heroine. The purpose of these objects is to obtain the lost husband. But the objects themselves are not necessary, since the heroine may bring about release of her husband on her own with, for example, tears, kissing, etc., as in "Beauty and the Beast." Thus, the actions of the Donor in the former case appear in the husband role, while in the latter case, they do not appear at the surface of the story, but seem potential in the role of the heroine. Heda Jason notes a similar shift in a Yemenite Jewish tale, "When the dragon gives Hero the sword, the dragon momentarily switches the tale role he plays from Villain to Donor."[61] These phenomena may be connected with what Max Lüthi refers to as the "isolation and universal interconnection"[62] of folktale actors. The lack of contextual detail of a spatial, temporal, or emotional nature in the folktale tends to isolate the personae. But this isolation in itself results in a potential for reconnection that gives the impression of great spontaneity, of being possible at all times, and hence, universal. One may test this in the role of the Beast in "Beauty and the Beast." In providing the father with a chest of gold, an economic "magic object," he acts as a Donor. He is a Villain in his part in removing Beauty from her home, but a Hero in rescuing her from an untenable family situation, a kind of "enchantment." Finally, he plays a role analogous to the Princess who is ultimately rescued by the Hero-figure, Beauty.

Perhaps the clearest case of variation in the number of dramatis personae is that of the multiplication of a single character. A simple form is that of multiplication by three. The Donor, for example, may be a single figure, as in "The Spirit in the Bottle" (tale type 331), or three animals.[63] Here the familiar "law of three" is an optional change, applied such that the functional role of the complex form is the same as that of the simple.[64] The result is quite different when one of a group of three receives special attention in the tale. In this case, a contrast is established between one character and the other two, such that the latter appear as a duality in characterization, but function indifferently. The two sisters of the heroine in the "Cupid and Psyche" type play the same role in the tale, but a similar contrast with the main character is accomplished with a single sister in other tales, such as Frau Holle (tale type 480).

When two characters appear in the same role they may be reduced to what Olrik called the "law of the twins."[65] This appears as a duplication of a single character. In the story of Kusa, the hero has a brother in whom Kusa's qualities of wisdom and ugliness are inverted. Although in this case, the duplicate, really a complement, plays only an attenuated role, in other tales, the two characters function in an identical way. In a certain tale of the animal husband type, "The Two Girls, the Bear, and the Dwarf" (tale type 426), and in a number of versions of the "Star Husband" tale,[66] there are two complementary heroines in a part played, in other versions, by a single actor. Aspects which are combined or latent in one form are differentiated in another.

A stronger form of differentiation is rivalry. In the quest for the lost husband, one possible resolution is that the heroine simply finds him and they are reunited.[67] Another possibility, common to both lost husband and lost bride tales, is that the seeker encounters a rival at the conclusion of the search. The formula of the "old key," sometimes presented as a riddle to the rival, is found in both types (400 and 425).[68] There are further similarities, such as nocturnal visits by the spouse in animal form (tale types 425E and 403, part V), associated with the presence of a child of the couple. One possible resolution of the duplication, the one suggested by designating the relationship as rivalry, is reduction to a single character. The rival is simply eliminated, blown away, as in "Soria Moria Castle." In "The Crow Bride," a Bengali version of the lost wife tale, the role ends so that "the king's son and his two wives began to live happily ever after."[69] Since the rival can only be viewed as such in his or her redundancy in a role often either played by a single character, reduced to one in the end, or resolved by a simple maintenance of both, it seems likely that the doubled form expresses aspects combined or latent in the simple form. The relationships between characters in the tale, in fact, form a spectrum of differentiation: similarity, complementarity, contrast, rivalry, opposition. The phenomenon of multiplication of characters seems to result from two factors, spontaneous reduplication and subsequent differentiation.

To illustrate what has been said concerning the dramatis personae, the minimal form of the present story, that of a single male and a single female character may be represented:

$$m - w.$$

This simple situation is potentially expandable in three possible ways:

$$
\begin{array}{ll}
& m_1, m_2 - w \\
m - w: & m_1, m_2 - w_1, w_2 \\
& m - w_1, w_2.
\end{array}
$$

The duplicated characters may be complementary or contrasting, according to the degree of differentiation, and each is susceptible, in its turn, to a repetition of the pattern.

With this pattern established, an observation may be made concerning the relationship between the reduplicated characters. In the more differentiated form, they are commonly realized as parents, or parent figures. Given the domesticity of the fairy tale, this is scarcely surprising. Taking the main characters, not the initial situation, from Rapunzel, for example, the redundant female actor is the witch, who states, in fact, her motherly intention toward Rapunzel. Representing this figure as wM for woman's mother, the expansion of the basic form is

$$m - w : m - w_1, w_2 = m - w_1, wM.$$

In tale type 426 "The Two Girls, the Bear and the Dwarf," since one may regard the sisters as a complementary unit ("twins"), equivalent to a single actor, the relationship of the characters may first be represented as

$$m, mF - w, wM,$$

where mF is the man's father. This is essentially correct, for the dwarf has usurped the place of the father of the hero. The role of the heroine is then subdivided into "twins":

$$m, mF - w_1, w_2, wM.$$

An expansion of the minimal form which seems to characterize a large part of the animal spouse tales is that in which the parental relationship to the main actor is that of the opposite sex, what may be thought of as a kind of oedipal relationship. The sense in which this term seems appropriate is that of the narrative relationship in which there is a tendency to reduce or eliminate the role of the parent of the same sex, and a corresponding expansion of the role of the opposite-sex parent. Hence, this situation may be termed the *narrative oedipal* relationship. The possibilities inherent in this configuration may be represented as

$$m_1, w_2 - w_1, m_2.$$

Here w$_2$ is the man's mother (mM) and m$_2$ is the woman's father (wF). In the second move of "Maria Morevna," the hero discovers a male figure in Maria's castle. This figure is introduced without apparent motivation, and is functionally the Villain, being the agent in Lack and Pursuit. But economy of description is achieved by regarding this figure as inherent in the simple form, in the following way:

$$m - w : m_1, m_2 - w : m_1 - w, m_2 = m - w, wF.$$

Other indications may be found in the narrative to support this description. It seems to be contradicted by constellations of dramatis personae where the king, for example, is present and the princess has been abducted by a dragon. In this situation, however, the abductor has effectively usurped the king's position, and the king, in his inability to act, is absent from the fundamental situation of the story. One may see how extremely common this is in the animal spouse tales, by observing that the complication of the second move of these tales, featuring Separation – Reunion, often opens with the mere desire of one of the central pair of actors to return home. Thus, in "Beauty and the Beast" and "Soria Moria Castle" the hero-figures return to their original homes. Beauty returns because of her father. The hero of the other story is cautioned to obey his father's advice and not his mother's. The inevitable violation presents the mother as the effective actor in this part of the tale.

Having established the importance of the narrative oedipal relationship in the animal spouse tales, the discussion may conclude with some observations of the influence of this relationship in selected tales of this type, and a brief suggestion as to its origin. In the Bengali story of the Crow Bride mentioned above, the tale ends with the simple juxtaposition of the two women. Yet, although they are "both his wives at par," the narrator has made it unmistakably clear that the first wife is to be differentiated in a maternal role. The first wife takes on a nurturing role, feeding her husband before he sets out to search for the lost Crow Bride. The tale of Kusa takes little account of his father; in all versions he is essentially or really absent. His mother, by contrast, is the motive factor in both his acquisition and his loss of a bride. On the other hand, while Pabhāvatī's mother is present, it is her father's threat to chop her into seven pieces that largely motivates the ultimate reunion. These two tales mirror society each in its own way, in that marriage in North India is, from the man's perspective, *āvaha*, the term used in the Kusa Jātaka, that is, bringing the bride into the household of the man's mother, a form somewhat deceptively termed "patrilocal."

Turning to Western forms of the animal bridegroom story, the role of the man's mother is notoriously prominent in such tales as "Cupid and Psyche," with Aphrodite sending Cupid on her mission by kissing her son long and fervently with parted lips. In Basile's tale II, 9 "The Padlock," the animal bridegroom's mother appears only at the end, but at the most critical moment, where "as soon as he was in his mother's arms, the charm broke."[70] In another tale of this type in the same collection, "The Serpent" (II, 5), the influence of the woman's father over her is clear in her acquiesence, "Do as it shall please you, my Lord and Father. I will not gainsay you in anything."[71] In "Beauty and the Beast," the father and daughter relationship is clearly of the same nature, and needs no more comment than it has already received.[72] The man's father, in addition, suits the pattern, for in the Villeneuve version he has died, as in his early removal in the Kusa Jātaka.[73] One may note Beauty's similar deprivation of her mother, the Fairy Queen, in Villeneuve.

Perhaps the most interesting aspect of the Villeneuve version is the multiplication of female actors in the tale, and this provides an interesting test of the narrative oedipal system of the dramatis personae. The situation of the female actors associated with the main male actor is clear. The Bad Fairy as protectress of the prince represents a splitting of the role of wM. This maternal figure attempts to seduce the prince, and thus acts essentially as the rival of the heroine, a role played also by the queen mother of the prince, in opposing the final marriage. The treatment of female characters associated with the main female actor is more complex, and seems to violate the oedipal typification. As in the case of the man's father, Beauty's mother (stepmother) is removed from the narrative cast, as required by the oedipal paradigm. However, this loss is compensated by such an elaboration of female personae associated with Beauty, that one must conclude that unlike the man's father role (mF), the role of woman's mother (wM) held great interest for the teller of this tale, giving the effect of indelibility to this feature of the narrative. This is perhaps due to a tendency of the story toward elaboration of the feminine. The character role of woman's mother is distributed over three areas, namely, the villainous sisters (attenuated in Villeneuve), the Fairy Queen, who emerges as the "real" mother, and the Dream Fairy, nominally the sister of the latter, but considerably differentiated in her role. The Dream Fairy's activity is to a large extent similar to that of a hero figure in the animal spouse type in her killing of the representatives (emissaries) of the rival Bad Fairy, and especially in her bear guise. The presence of an animal heroine seems to be striking confirmation of the essential unity of the animal or nonhuman husband and wife types and the latency of one in the other.

Finally, the fact that a parental figure here acts as helper in animal form shows the absorption of features of the Donor into this role and may help to explain its persistence. This figure may be thought of as a donative parent. In "Maria Morevna" one sees the absence of mF compensated by the acquisition of older brothers-in-law, who are themselves animal bridegrooms of the hero's sisters. In subsequent moves these became the helpers of the hero. A number of other tales feature a strong donative parent, such as one who has died but lives on in a magically providing form, and this may have influenced the present tales.

It remains only to suggest why the animal spouse story tends toward the narrative oedipal paradigm. For this, let us return to the basic representation of these tales as

$$m - w.$$

From this form, it has been suggested, the following may be derived

$$m_1 \, m_2 - w_1 \, w_2.$$

This becomes

$$m_1 \, w_2 - w_1 \, m_2,$$

where the duplicating figures may be parental. But each set in this group is merely a replication of the original pair, suggesting the conclusion that it is inherent in the basic forms which, as easily as husband and wife, may represent child and parent of opposite sexes. If this is true, one may expect to see not only, for example, uxorial tendencies in the man's mother, but also maternal elements in the wife. This is certainly the case in tales such as the Bengali "Crow Bride." But there is some indication that it may also hold for such tales as "Beauty and the Beast." Here the wife becomes a symbolic mother in restoring the Beast to life. The same view may be taken of disenchantments of other actors by hero figures of either sex.

Beauty and Bestiality: Motifs and Ideas in the Tales

In the preceding sections I have been concerned with the analysis of actors and actions, that is, tale roles and tale functions. One of the points I made in the introduction to the study, however, is the convergence of literature and folktale in artistic and imaginative expression. I have discussed how this expression occurs and in whose words and deeds it is articulated. What remains is the question of what is expressed in this way. Accordingly, I now turn from the idea of the tale to the ideas in the tale.

The discussion of the principles of variation in the number of characters in the tale has already been applied to some aspects of the Villeneuve version of "Beauty and the Beast." The variety in expression of the feminine was found to be a notable feature of this telling. Here we find a hostile queen and a benevolent, loving fairy queen, an ostensible protectress who becomes a seductive temptress of youth, an innocent beauty victimized by harsh powers and a weak father, a mother who turns out not to be a real mother, spiteful step-sisters, and a kind and powerful dream fairy who can also turn into a bear. One of the characteristics held in common by these characters seems to be change and manifestation of latent potential, precisely the principle which brought about the proliferation in the first place. In more contracted forms, the potential for elaboration may be felt more keenly. An excellent example of a contracted form is the lyric poem of Heath-Stubbs in which the dramatis personae are reduced to the two principals, the minimal form given in the analysis of the actors. The poetic medium allows for elaboration of the individual characters in a way impossible in the folktale. In spite of this, one of the appealing aspects of the poem is a kind of similarity to the folktale in its clarity and suggestiveness.

A version of the story with these same features is the film version by Cocteau,[74] and this may serve as an example of the contribution of folklore analysis to the appreciation of art forms other than the folktale. In the first place, we find a number of motifs in Cocteau's version not in the text available to him, but familiar enough from the range of folktale variation. This is an interesting kind of confirmation of the notion that versions of the story may somehow be potential or inherent in one another. Cocteau's approach seems particularly to emphasize the intuitive, and this may account for some of the apparently independent inventions of motifs, or what is known to folklorists as polygenesis. Cocteau entered the task of telling the story at a deep level of personal involvement, keeping a diary of the filming, finding his "personal mythology" and his "childhood memories" in the story, dreaming during the telling of a story of a dream, even referring to the story as "sleep."[75] His emphasis on clarity and cutting of clutter is reminiscent of the process of self-correction in folklore proposed by Walter Anderson.[76] Cocteau refers to himself as an "archaeologist," and the sense in which this seems appropriate is as an archaeologist of ideas. The notion of evoking a forgotten childhood is interesting as a sort of reversal of the process of maturation embodied in the fairy tale. Unless Cocteau is a unique teller of tales in this respect, the recapitulation that such a regression permits may account for some of the appeal of the telling and hearing, and in this case, seeing of fairy tales.

Some of the motifs of note in Cocteau's film version of "Beauty and the Beast" are that of the house which may only be entered through the roof, that of the key, and that of the terrifying castle. The Beast's castle in the film is not simply magically providing as in many other versions, but also eerie and terrifying, as in tales such as tale type 326 "The Youth Who Set Out to Learn What Fear Is," or a number of versions of tale type 400, such as "Soria Moria Castle," in which a masculine hero must overcome frightful denizens of the castle. Cocteau's key substitutes for Beaumont's ring as a magically transporting object. It is the key to the Beast's treasure and is, in fact, one of the sources of his power. It is through possession of the key by Beauty's real-life lover, Avenant, that the incident leading to final transformation occurs. (In fairy tales, the ring is also a token given by the lover before parting which ultimately brings about recognition and subsequent reunion.) A house without windows or doors is found in a Romanian version of the animal spouse tale. The house is the dwelling of the lost husband, and entrance is only possible through the roof, something that is apparently no barrier to the supernatural husband, but is the culmination of an arduous sacrifice on the part of the wife. Cocteau's use of the motif also occurs immediately before the final reunion. Here it is not the woman, but the lover Avenant, who must enter through the roof, leading to the treasure of the Beast. So entering, he dies and is transformed along with the Beast with whom he is apparently identified. The elaboration of the masculine here, rather uncharacteristic of other versions of the story, may be due to Cocteau's personal identification with the story. By splitting the main masculine character into the Beast and the human lover, he approximates the situation of tales in which the bride is abducted by a nonhuman actor.

The role of point of view receives perhaps its most interesting treatment in the film. As a story of an ugly animal married to a beautiful woman, the tale takes the feminine point of view. The problem for the heroine in these tales is the animal in someone else. Cocteau, however, takes a step, for which the twentieth century was no doubt prepared, in requiring his Beauty to confront the "animal" in herself when she says "I am the monster, my Beast." One might say that with this statement she beautifies the Beast. This essentially states the relationship found in the animal wife tales, such as "The Frog Princess" (tale type 402). A complementary point of view is introduced which alternates, like an optical illusion, with the first. The resolution is probably to be found in the greater awareness of self and the other that develops in both characters. In a curious restatement of the issues of intellect and beauty in the Kusa Jātaka, Cocteau's Beast says, "Aside from being ugly, I have no wit," a point also made by Beaumont's Beast. But, to say "I have no wit" is evidence of the contrary, as noted in Plato's Apology, the Kena Upaniṣad, the Dhammapada, and the Book of Proverbs. Here, it is Beauty who points this out. Presumably the insight of both characters is deepened.

Cocteau's treatment of the theme of seeing is emblematic of the folktale. One way in which this is introduced into traditional tales is through the "look taboo." There are a number of variations on this, such as those suggesting concentration by forbidding looking from side to side or backwards, but the one occurring in the animal spouse tales takes the form of an interdiction against seeing the mate in his or her true form. Inevitably, seeing does occur and this leads to complication before final reunion. As Betsy Hearne suggests, the complication of "Beauty and the Beast" is, itself, the task of seeing, which, when it occurs, leads to transformation and reunion. In Cocteau, as in earlier versions, there is a mirror, an instrument of perception, especially self-perception. Like the picture of Dorian Gray, or any good magic mirror, the mirror tells the truth. It shows the sisters, for example, as ugly and beastly. The significance of the image of the mirror may even be inherent in Cocteau's characterization of his creative process in making the film as polishing old silver.[77] It is when Beauty approaches the mirror that its profoundest reflection occurs. It says to her "Reflect for me." If Beauty reflects the mirror as truly as it reflects, the image is that of a mirror reflecting its own image. One is reminded of the Sāṃkhya notion of the *puruṣa* "man, spirit" as pure witness, or the mystic poet Rumi's invitation to "become wholly clear of heart, like the face of mirror without image and picture." In the image of the self-reflecting mirror may lie the clearest image of the power of the tale to reflect the "spiritual tradition of the folk" or the human spirit, for in the self-reflecting state it is contracted to pure potential or nothingness, while if an image is introduced it is repeated infinitely.

The theme of seeing in these stories is intimately connected to the theme of loving. One might make a case for love being the central theme, with all others subordinate to it. While some tales of this kind may not mention love directly, it may be inferred from the efforts of the actors. One wonders what might keep the narrator from being explicit in such cases. Be that as it may, love is mentioned often enough in the story, not only from the developed literary levels, but also in the earliest example of the type, which opens "Urvaśī loved Purūravas," as well as tribal examples, such as the tales of the bonga, or supernatural lover, collected by William George Archer from the Santals of East Central India.[78] One may draw material on love even from such an unemotional source as the Motif Index which characterizes these tales as stories about "unequals in love" (T 91).

An interesting relation between the themes of love and seeing may be found in comparing the roles that these play in "Cupid and Psyche," and in "Beauty and the Beast." To discover this we must look only at the facts of the story as given by the narrator and avoid interpretation, for the time being. Apuleius has Psyche address Cupid early in the marriage, "whoever you are, I love you and adore you passionately." Upon seeing him, likewise, "she cast herself upon him in an ecstasy of love." The change that occurs in this tale is one of seeing, namely from Psyche's not seeing Cupid to her seeing him. In "Beauty and the Beast," on the other hand, the heroine is never deprived of literally seeing the Beast. In fact, here it is his appearance that is the problem for her, not his disappearance, as in the case of Psyche. Beauty is able to overcome her fear, but not her repugnance, until the final transformation in which she expresses her love for the Beast. In "Cupid and Psyche" there is a development of seeing in the context of love, while in "Beauty and the Beast" love develops in the context of seeing.

The act of seeing, as it occurs at crucial points in the narrative with such powerful consequences, seems to imply much more than bare perception. Seeing creates an alliance in other tales, such as "The Speckled Bull." Here, a king's daughter is fated to marry the first man she lays eyes on. An extraordinary bull appears in the land, and the king, taking care that no man is present, leads her outside to view it. Upon removing her blindfold, the king bids her look at the remarkable creature. "That's not a bull," she replies, for she sees that it is really a prince, and, indeed, her future husband. In stories of the Swan Maiden type, the hero views the heavenly damsel at her bath. He sees her in her real form and is able to marry her by concealing her avian garment, thus forcing her to remain in human form. In each case, the human actor sees what others do not, that is, he has gained knowledge that is in some sense secret and, hence, powerful and ambivalent. The power of this knowledge is clear from the influence of its possessor and the fact that it is often interdicted. Ambivalence lies in the fact that the result of knowing is far from certain. A scenario similar to the opening of the Swan Maiden tale is found in the encounter of Actaeon and Artemis. Here, however, the human is punished for taboo viewing by being transformed into a stag, in effect, into subhuman form. This shows, incidentally, the connection, at least at the conceptual level, between the animal husband and heavenly bride tales. In "Pururavas and Urvaśi" and "Cupid and Psyche," the taboo viewing likewise results in separation.

If, in the so-called look taboo, the underlying issue is seen as knowledge, a relationship may be found with another form of interdiction common in the tales under consideration, namely the "gossip taboo." In this case, the principal actor, hero or heroine, is warned not to discuss the spouse with his or her family. The knowledge of the nonhuman or otherworldly spouse is secret. The look taboo effectively says the spouse may not be known in full; the gossip taboo says the knowledge may not be shared with others.

The taboo in such tales, then, is a taboo against knowing. The hero must be kept or must keep himself in the dark, often quite literally. The object of the forbidden knowledge is not one's self, it would seem, but the other, the creator of the blissful ignorance. In this dreamlike darkness, all is according to Beauty's or Psyche's wish, to take an example. The effect of this is to reduce the other to an aspect of the main character, yet with a certain independence. Without the reality testing which is essentially at play in the taboo violation, the other remains little more than a dream, a wish, a figment of the imagination. As such, this character is portrayed with great ambivalence, a terrible beast, or an ambrosial deity. In "Cupid and Psyche," it is particularly apparent that this is a reflection of Psyche's own ambivalence as lover, on the one hand, and murderer, on the other.

The origin of ambivalence in these tales is a matter for study in its own right and will be discussed below. For the moment, one may note simply that the ambivalence is always resolved. In the early part of the tale, the happiness of the initial union is compromised by the sense of threat implied in the interdiction. This is, no doubt, an expression of underlying ambivalence. Resolution occurs when the implied danger becomes real, and separation occurs. That this is a kind of resolution is shown by the fact that many tales of unequals in love end here. La Belle Dame Sans Merci disappears, the woman flees from the star husband, the neglected animal husband dies from grief—

the unhappy ending. Or, the lover toils and is transformed. Both Pururavas and Psyche become immortal, as do, by the way, fairy tale heros in our own culture, who do not die, but live happily ever after.

Ambivalence, or two-valuedness, is generally expressed on the surface of the story in action or states of being. The Donor figure provides a good example of ambivalence in action. Approached in one way, the Donor provides assistance, while another approach provokes his hinderance. The change of state characteristic of the tale hero may also be seen as ambivalence. Kusa, for example, is ugly but becomes beautiful. In this case, one sees the frequent phemonenon of splitting of the character, as in the tale of "The Two Brothers" (tale type 303), or "The Black Bride and the White Bride" (tale type 403), discussed above in the analysis of tale actors. Kusa, as a character, is really two-fold, ugly and beautiful, wise and foolish, the complement being expressed in his brother, whose role in the tale seems to be little more than to express this complementarity. Kusa becomes the complementary character when he impersonates his brother. Ambivalence runs so strongly through the Kusa story that even the final transformation is reversible. He may alternately be handsome or repulsive, depending on the context. Two-valuedness in the tale, or what seems to be an analytic tendency inherent in the tale, incidentally, makes the tale particularly susceptible to interpretations stressing bivalence.

Even ambivalence in perception is expressed as an action. The taboo is not to look, or not to speak, and it requires an act of interpretation to understand this as a prohibition against knowing. One is encouraged to probe deeper, and to inquire whether the origin of the tales' surface ambivalence may not lie in ambivalence of feeling. After all, many narrators are quite frank about the existence of feeling in the stories, although it is rarely described for its own sake as it might be in other genres. Indeed, the very notion of the happy ending gives some indication of a perhaps unexpressed, but nevertheless, pervasive motive and goal of feeling. The reluctance of some raconteurs to mention feelings directly shows that not only is there ambivalence of feeling in the tales, but there is also ambivalence about feeling in the tellers.

The affective dimension of narrative is often the topic of interpretations of tales along psychological lines with the inherent inclination of that discipline to look behind the scenes. While such exercises often seem prejudiced (they already know what the tale is about) and ignorant (they ignore most of the folkloristic data on the tale), they are perhaps most engagingly seen as retellings of the stories, as narratives in their own right, with the right of the narrator to vary the tale according to his or her own inclinations and those of the audience. These variations may be subtle, such as highlighting an incidental feature for the sake of its polemical value; less subtle, as in the case of the Jungian process known as "amplification," in which the contextual disposition of the narrator is bypassed in favor of the free association of the hearer; or quite blatant, such as Neumann's reading of the incident of the lamp in "Cupid and Psyche." Since Neumann wishes to see this as a story of consciousness raising, he is irresistibly drawn to the flame of symbolism in the lamp. Psyche sees Cupid and falls into a presumably enlightened form of love, freed from the matriarchal inclination to see this as rape. She then, more or less as an afterthought, pricks herself on Cupid's arrow. The luster of the thought appears to have blinded Neumann to the fact the Psyche had actually expressed her love for Cupid long before this. There is a development in Psyche's love in the episode of the lamp, but a careful reading of the story, and one which gives credence to the ancient mode of understanding, reveals that the development is not the result of perception or awareness, but magical compulsion. Psyche does not prick her finger because she is in love; rather, she falls irreversibly in love, as Apuleius' audience knew, because of the prick. A Freudian would have understood this immediately.

Although psychological exegesis of the tales often turns on the concept of love, there is a reluctance to explore the topic for its own sake, with its rich and vast literature, before analysing love in the tale. For example, one might think of Irving Singer's categories of *eros, philia, nomos* and *agape* in *The Nature of Love,*[79] of June Singer's contrast between being in love and loving in *Energies of Love,*[80] or of Paul Helwig's elegant distinction in *Liebe und Feindschaft* between love and hate as oriented toward the other, and fear as oriented away.[81] One may cite Kenneth Pope's definition of love in *On Love and Loving* :

> A preoccupation with another person. A deeply felt desire to be with the loved one. A feeling of incompleteness without him or her. Thinking of the loved one often, whether together or apart. Separation frequently provokes feelings of genuine despair or else tantalizing anticipation of reuniting. Reunion is seen as bringing feelings of euphoric ecstasy or peace and fulfillment.[82]

There seem, in any case, to be implicit views on love in the psychological analyses which might be brought out. It is certainly simplistic, but affords a beginning to say that the Freudians are interested in sexuality, and the Jungians in consciousness. One of the dangers of this simplicity lies in a peculiar kind of overlap in the two approaches. Bettelheim wishes to explain "Cupid and Psyche" in such a way that "naive sexual enjoyment is very different from mature love based on knowledge, experience and even suffering."[83] In a way, this is similar to Claude Rambaux' attempt in *Trois analyses de l'amour* to explain the tale on the basis of "personal maturation" leading to "adult love."[84] He alludes to Psyche's "capacity to learn from her experiences,"[85] an ability based on her possessing the cardinal virtues, namely, lucidity, generosity, and courage, as well as beauty. What a contrast, by the way, with Zipe's view of the heroine as a toadying nonentity who aspires only to obey. For Rambaux, it is the troubles (tasks) of Psyche that bring out her personal qualities. But, in fact, the difficulties of the hero(ine) in fairy tales elicit, not personal qualities (at least not at the literal level), but magical helpers. And Psyche, far from learning from experience, violates the look taboo at least twice, simply playing the part of a typical fairy tale hero.

Bettelheim perhaps goes even farther than Rambaux, into seemingly very un-Freudian territory, when he suggests the reading that "the highest psychic qualities (Psyche) are to be wedded to sexuality (Eros) . . . spiritual man must be reborn to become ready for the marriage of sexuality with wisdom."[86] In fact, Psyche is ingenuous and under the influence of magic, a victim of bad advice who succeeds in spite of herself. One should perhaps not underestimate the attractiveness to the psychoanalyst of the allegorical element introduced by Apuleius into the tale with the figure of Psyche. Bettelheim speculates in *Freud and Man's Soul* [87] that Freud himself was influenced by the story.

For Marie-Louise von Franz, also, the story of "Cupid and Psyche" turns on the point of the imputed illumination of Psyche. "Light, in mythological contexts, symbolizes consciousness," she says,[88] raising Psyche out of the ignorance or unconsciousness symbolized by the liaison in darkness. Having begun with a defiant, individuating act of knowing, Psyche then strives with various aspects of unconsciousness to win her ultimate reward of divinization. However, since von Franz considers Olympus to be a representation of the collective unconscious,[89] it is difficult to follow her interpretation of the story as Psyche's "process of becoming conscious."[90] Turning to the theme of love, one feels a similar uncertainty in von Franz's exegesis. On the one hand, she seems to say that knowing depends on loving. "At the moment she [Psyche] begins genuinely to love, she is no longer lost in . . . unconsciousness."[91] On the other hand, von Franz defines love as "the reverential awe which a human being can give to some thing greater than himself."[92] One feels here that the understanding of a tale of ambivalence is thwarted by an ambivalence in the understanding. Psyche strives in a seemingly enlightened condition and ultimately "falls into complete unconsciousness, into the state of the Gods."[93] Thus, von Franz sees in "Cupid and Psyche" a "solution," but not a resolution.[94]

Despite these obscurities in von Franz's analysis, she has captured something of the dilemma characteristic of tales of unequals in love in what she says of the love relationship in general as "a moving, unique mystery, and at the same time just an ordinary human event."[95] This amounts to seeing the relationship from two different points of view, which correspond, but for a single omission, to the nature of the two "unequal" protagonists, one human, the other divine. What is missing is the animal spouse. The tale is, inevitably, told from the human perspective, narrators being human, so that the point of view presented is that of one looking either up to or down on another. The human hero(ine) loves one who is either sub- or super-human. The oracle in "Cupid and Psyche" warns, "Do not look for a son-in-law sprung from mortal root."[96] Apuleius has often been connected with Platonism, and the Platonic view of love is strikingly similar:

> Socrates: What then, I asked, can Love be? A mortal?
> Diotima: That least of all.[97]

Now, in the fairy tale one is not simply left with a conundrum. Rather, contradictions are frequently resolved in a happy ending. To take one view of this, we might consider Melanie Klein's view of the happy marriage as that in which "the unconscious minds of the love partners correspond,"[98] a solution that would probably have been agreeable to von Franz. But, this is not quite sufficient to explain the tale. It leaves open the possibility that the correspondence may develop at an unacceptable level. The tale never resolves downward; the princess does not become a frog. The transformation function of the tale changes unequals in love to equals only in the upward direction. Purūravas and Psyche become divine; the husband of the fairy becomes superhumanly lucky; the Beast becomes a beauty.

The notion of point of view is reminiscent of Melanie Klein's "positions," stages of psychological ontogeny, which may be recapitulated throughout life. The two orientations are the schizoid position, which, as its name suggests, is analytical and differentiating, and the depressive position, in which fragmentation is transcended in favor of an awareness of the whole. It is in this synthesizing and integrating activity of the depressive position that Klein believes love develops. Prior to this, in the schizoid phase, relationship to the other is characterized by splitting and projection of the self. The other is experienced as entirely good or entirely bad parts. Like the fairy tale figure who suffers the interdiction against knowing, one cannot get the whole picture, and hence, greatly undervalues or equally greatly overvalues the other. In the depressive orientation, the schism is overcome, but with less of the control than the reductionistic tendencies of the earlier view afforded. With the wholeness of the other, the independence of the other is also encountered. Indeed, the single most vivid experience of the depressive phase is the one found in all tales of unequals in love, the loss of the other. This loss calls forth the work of mourning, a very active process in Kleinian thought, which is expressed in the external terms of the tale as striving for reunion with the other, and in inner psychological terms as restoration of the good internal object.

It is clear that the work of restoring the good internal object consists of seeing the other as a whole and internalizing this whole. One sees the value of and feels the need for the other, or one may feel the need for, and thus, see the value of the other. A fine example of internalizing the other is found in the final resolution in Tagore's *King of the Dark Chamber*, a play based on the Kusa Jātaka:[99]

> Sudarshana: That fever of longing has left my eyes for ever. You are not beauti
>   ful, my lord —you stand beyond all comparisons!
> King: That which can be comparable with me lies within yourself.
> Sudarshana: Your love lives in me — you are mirrored in that love, and you see
>   your face reflected in me.

The origin of love in overcoming the contradictions in the other and in the internalization of the other may occur on a variety of levels, depending on the relationship of self to other. Some psychologists, emphasizing early development, tend to concentrate on the parent-child relationship. Klein found this largely in the mother. She is quite clear about the ambivalence in this relationship. For her, those who have "turned away from their mother, in dislike or hate" still retain "a beautiful picture of the mother" within them-selves.[100] Von Franz created a larger picture of the other, but also found the origin of the inner presence of the other to begin with the parent. For the male, the inner other in Jungian thought is the anima, "a derivative of the mother figure," von Franz says, and, at the same time, "his disposition for reaction toward women."[101] Another level on which relationship may occur is that of human with the divine. One may encounter the divine in the father-teacher role, for example, as Moses and Yahweh, or Naciketas and Yama in the Kaṭha Upaniṣad, but the divine in tales of unequals in love appears as a lover or spouse.

In the development of love in these stories, Verena Kast in *Mann und Frau im Märchen* has emphasized the element of communion in the work of restoring the lost other.[102] She points out that in the story of "The Singing, Springing Lark" (Grimms no. 88) the animal husband leaves a trail by shedding, at intervals in his flight, a white feather and a drop of blood. Kusa in his search for Pabhāvatī plays music to make her aware that he is at hand. One is reminded of Rapunzel's singing in the desert which leads her lover to her, and also of Purūravas, whose name probably means "loudly raving," or of Lancelot's "grizzly groan" at the moment of his flight from the false Guinevere. These expressions of despair and loss in love appear to assist restoration of the other through a bond of awareness and knowing. It is clear that the tale of the search for the lost husband contains in nascent form the tale of the search for the lost wife, and vice versa. Hence, the awareness and restoration always has the dimension of mutuality. The hero and heroine restore each other.

The iconicity of tales allows interpretation, a kind of retelling, at a fascinating variety of levels. The relationship in the tale may represent parent and child, human and divine, male and female, or any of these in combination. One might even wish to interpret the relationship as that of a person to him- or herself, a relation which the seemingly isolated yogi expresses in similar terms. I have by no means exhausted the exegetical possibilities of this group of tales. I have bypassed entire types of explana-tions, such as interpretation in naturalistic terms. A recent example of the latter is found in A. T. Hatto's study of the swan maiden story (MT 400). Hatto attempts to trace the tale to a time of the domestication of migratory fowl,[103] deriving the animal wife story from a story of animal husbandry. What a wealth of variety this tale supports—bonga lovers, King Kong, futuristic stories of gorgeous androids. The tale of the lover of the other that is not what it seems might be the tale of the love of tales themselves.

APPENDIX TWO

Beaumont's Eighteenth-Century Version
in Facsimile

The following facsimile includes selections from a 1783 English edition of Madame Le Prince de Beaumont's work, *The Young Misses Magazine*, which was translated from her original 1756 French edition, *Le magasin des enfans*. Represented here are the title page, first page, and pages forty-four through sixty-seven containing Dialogue 5, in which appears the tale "Beauty and the Beast."

Appendix 2. Facsimile of Madame Le Prince de Beaumont's tale "Beauty and the Beast," from *The Young Misses Magazine*, 1783 (reprinted from her English translation of the 1756 French edition). By permission of the E. W. and Faith Collection of Juvenile Literature, Miami University Libraries, Oxford, Ohio.

THE

YOUNG MISSES

MAGAZINE,

CONTAINING

DIALOGUES.

BETWEEN

A GOVERNESS and several Young
LADIES of QUALITY her Scholars:

IN WHICH

Each Lady is made to speak according to her particular
Genius, Temper and Inclination;

Their several Faults are pointed out, and the easy Way to mend
them, as well as to think, and speak, and act properly; no less
Care being taken to form their Hearts to Goodness, than to
enlighten their Understandings with useful Knowledge.

A short and clear Abridgment is also given of Sacred and Profane
History, and some Lessons in Geography.

The Useful is blended throughout with the Agreeable, the Whole
being interspersed with proper Reflections and Moral Tales.

By Madam LE PRINCE DE BEAUMONT.

THE FOURTH EDITION.

VOL. I.

LONDON:
Printed for C. NOURSE, opposite Catherine-
Street, in the Strand.

M.DCC.LXXXIII.

DIALOGUES

BETWEEN

Young Ladies of Quality

AND THEIR

GOVERNESS.

DIALOGUE I.

Lady TRIFLE, *coming to visit Lady* SENSIBLE.

MY dear Lady Sensible, how do you do? you cannot think how delighted I am to spend the afternoon with you. They tell me you have got from Paris the prettiest doll that ever was seen. Oh! how merry we shall be.

Lady Sensible. With all my heart, my dear; I am glad I have any thing to entertain you. But somebody knocks.——'Tis Lady Witty; she sent me word she would come and drink tea.

Lady Witty. Your servant, ladies:——But, bless me! did not I see Lady Sensible playing with

VOL. I. B

have become of you, if you had died before you had asked God Almighty pardon? he is very good to give you time to repent and amend; pray thank him this very night for so great a mercy, and tell him you will love him with all your heart for the future. Good night, my dear children, I am very well pleased with your attention; and next time, to make you amends, you shall have some fine stories, and a pretty tale.

DIALOGUE V.

The Third Day.

Mrs. Affable.

YOU are come very soon to-day, ladies: we have but just this moment got up from table.

Lady Witty. Mrs. Affable, I dined with these ladies, and we were so impatient to see you, that we were not above ten minutes at dinner.

Mrs. Affable. Then I must chide you, dear children, nothing is worse for your health than to eat too quick. To punish you, there shall be stories before tea, but we will go and walk in the garden.

Lady

Lady Mary. I like walking in the garden very well, but I like stories still better; pray, Mrs. Affable, forgive us this time; upon my conscience, I did not know it was a fault to eat so quick.

Mrs. Affable. And it is another fault to swear upon your conscience, you must not say so again. I will not let you repeat your lessons now, ladies, left it should hurt you to think of your lessons so soon after dinner.

Lady Charlotte. Well, Mrs. Affable, we will say nothing, but you will tell us something; you promised us a pretty tale, will it hurt us to hear it?

Mrs. Affable. I see I must do as you would have me: when you are good children, I have not the heart to deny you any thing: come, we will go and sit in the garden, and I will tell you the tale I promised you last time.

BEAUTY and the BEAST; a Tale.

There was once a very rich merchant, who had six children, three sons, and three daughters; being a man of sense, he spared no cost for their education, but gave them all kinds of masters. His daughters were extremely handsome, especially the youngest; when she was little

little every body admired her, and called her
'*The little Beauty*;' fo that, as fhe grew up,
fhe ftill went by the name of *Beauty*, which
made her fifters very jealous. The youngeft, as
fhe was handfomer, was alfo better than her fifters. The two eldeft had a great deal of pride,
becaufe they were rich. They gave themfelves ridiculous airs, and would not vifit other merchants
daughters, nor keep company with any but per-
fons of quality. They went out every day upon
parties of pleafure, balls, plays, concerts, &c.
and laughed at their youngeft fifter, becaufe fhe
fpent the greateft part of her time in reading good
books. As it was known that they were great
fortunes, feveral eminent merchants made their
addreffes to them; but the two eldeft faid, they
would never marry, unlefs they could meet with
a duke, or an earl at leaft. Beauty very civilly
thanked them that courted her, and told them
fhe was too young yet to marry, but chofe to
ftay with her father a few years longer.

All at once the merchant loft his whole fortune,
excepting a fmall country houfe at a great diftance
from town, and told his children with tears in his
eyes, they muft go there and work for their living.
The two eldeft anfwered, that they would not
leave the town, for they had feveral lovers, who
they were fure would be glad to have them, tho'
they

they had no fortune; but the good ladies were
miftaken, for their lovers flighted and forfook
them in their poverty. As they were not beloved
on account of their pride, every body faid, they
do not deferve to be pitied, we are very glad to
fee their pride humbled, let them go and give
themfelves quality airs in milking the cows and
minding their dairy. But, added they, we are
extremely concerned for Beauty, fhe was fuch a
charming, fweet-tempered creature, fpoke fo
kindly to poor people, and was of fuch an affable,
obliging behaviour. Nay, feveral gentlemen
would have married her, tho' they knew fhe had
not a penny; but fhe told them fhe could not
think of leaving her poor father in his misfortunes, but was determined to go along with him
into the country to comfort and attend him.
Poor Beauty at firft was fadly grieved at the lofs
of her fortune; but, faid fhe to herfelf, were I to
cry ever fo much, that would not make things
better, I muft try to make myfelf happy without
a fortune. When they came to their country-
houfe, the merchant and his three fons applied
themfelves to hufbandry and tillage; and Beauty
rofe at four in the morning, and made hafte to
have the houfe clean, and dinner ready for the family. In the beginning fhe found it very difficult,
for fhe had not been ufed to work as a fervant,
but

but in lefs than two months fhe grew ftronger and healthier than ever. After fhe had done her work, fhe read, played on the harpfichord, or elfe fung whilft fhe fpun. On the contrary, her two fifters did not know how to fpend their time; they got up at ten, and did nothing but faunter about the whole day, lamenting the lofs of their fine cloaths and acquaintance. Do but fee our youngeft fifter, faid they, one to the other, what a poor, ftupid, mean-fpirited creature fhe is, to be contented with fuch an unhappy difmal fituation. The good merchant was of a quite different opinion; he knew very well that Beauty outfhone her fifters, in her perfon as well as her mind, and admired her humility and induftry, but above all her humility and patience; for her fifters not only left her all the work of the houfe to do, but infulted her every moment.

The family had lived about a year in this retirement, when the merchant received a letter with an account that a veffel, on board of which he had effects, was fafely arrived. This news had like to have turned the heads of the two eldeft daughters, who immediately flattered themfelves with the hopes of returning to town, for they were quite weary of a country life; and when they faw their father ready to fet out, they begged of him to buy them new gowns, head-dreffes,

dreffes, ribbands, and all manner of trifles; but Beauty afked for nothing, for fhe thought to herfelf, that all the money her father was going to receive, would fcarce be fufficient to purchafe every thing her fifters wanted. What will you have, Beauty? faid her father. Since you have the goodnefs to think of me, anfwered fhe, be fo kind to bring me a rofe, for as none grows hereabouts, they are a kind of rarity. Not that Beauty cared for a rofe, but fhe afked for fomething, left fhe fhould feem by her example to condemn her fifters conduct, who would have faid fhe did it only to look particular. The good man went on his journey, but when he came there, they went to law with him about the merchandize, and after a great deal of trouble and pains to no purpofe, he came back as poor as before.

He was within thirty miles of his own houfe, thinking on the pleafure he fhould have in feeing his children again, when going through a large foreft he loft himfelf. It rained and fnowed terribly; befides, the wind was fo high, that it threw him twice off his horfe, and night coming on, he began to apprehend being either ftarved to death with cold and hunger, or elfe devoured by the wolves, whom he heard howling all round him, when, on a fudden, looking through a long walk of trees, he faw a light at fome diftance, and

going

going on a little farther perceived it came from a palace illuminated from top to bottom. The merchant returned God thanks for this happy discovery, and hasted to the place, but was greatly surprized at not meeting with any one in the outcourts. His horse followed him, and seeing a large stable open, went in, and finding both hay and oats, the poor beast, who was almost famished, fell to eating very heartily; the merchant tied him up to the manger, and walking towards the house, where he saw no one, but entering into a large hall, he found a good fire, and a table plentifully set out with but one cover laid. As he was wet quite through with the rain and snow, he drew near the fire to dry himself. I hope, said he, the master of the house, or his servants, will excuse the liberty I take; I suppose it will not be long before some of them appear.

He waited a considerable time, till it struck eleven, and still nobody came: at last he was so hungry that he could stay no longer, but took a chicken and eat it in two mouthfuls, trembling all the while. After this he drank a few glasses of wine, and growing more courageous he went out of the hall, and crossed through several grand apartments with magnificent furniture, till he came into a chamber, which had an exceeding good bed in it, and as he was very much fatigued, and

and it was past midnight, he concluded it was best to shut the door, and go to bed.

It was ten the next morning before the merchant waked, and as he was going to rise he was astonished to see a good suit of clothes in the room of his own, which were quite spoiled; certainly, said he, this palace belongs to some kind fairy, who has seen and pitied my distress. He looked through a window, but instead of snow saw the most delightful arbours, interwoven with the beautifullest flowers that ever were beheld. He then returned to the great hall, where he had supped the night before, and found some chocolate ready made on a little table. Thank you, good Madam Fairy, said he aloud, for being so careful as to provide me a breakfast; I am extremely obliged to you for all your favours.

The good man drank his chocolate, and then went to look for his horse, but passing thro' an arbour of roses, he remembered Beauty's request to him, and gathered a branch on which were several; immediately he heard a great noise, and saw such a frightful beast coming towards him, that he was ready to faint away. You are very ungrateful, said the Beast to him, in a terrible voice; I have saved your life by receiving you into my castle, and, in return, you steal my roses, which I value beyond any thing in the universe; but

but you shall die for it; I give you but a quarter of an hour to prepare yourself, and say your prayers. The merchant fell-on his knees, and lifted up both his hands: My lord, said he, I beseech you to forgive me, indeed I had no intention to offend in gathering a rose for one of my daughters, who desired me to bring her one. My name is not, My Lord, replied the monster, but Beast; I don't love compliments, not I; I like people should speak as they think; and so do not imagine, I am to be moved by any of your flattering speeches: but you say you have got daughters; I will forgive you, on condition that one of them come willingly, and suffer for you. Let me have no words, but go about your business, and swear that if your daughter refuse to die in your stead, you will return within three months. The merchant had no mind to sacrifice his daughters to the ugly monster, but he thought, in obtaining this respite, he should have the satisfaction of seeing them once more; so he promised, upon oath, he would return, and the Beast told him he might set out when he pleased; but, added he, you shall not depart empty handed; go back to the room where you lay, and you will see a great empty chest; fill it with whatever you like best, and I will send it to you home, and at the same time Beast withdrew. Well, said the good man

to

to himself, if I must die, I shall have the comfort, at least, of leaving something to my poor children.

He returned to the bed-chamber, and finding a great quantity of broad pieces of gold, he filled the great chest the Beast had mentioned, locked it, and afterwards took his horse out of the stable, leaving the palace with as much grief as he had entered it with joy. The horse, of his own accord, took one of the roads of the forest, and in a few hours the good man was at home. His children came round him, but instead of receiving their embraces with pleasure, he looked on them, and holding up the branch he had in his hands, he burst into tears. Here, Beauty, said he, take these roses; but little do you think how dear they are like to cost your unhappy father, and then related his fatal adventure: immediately the two eldest set up lamentable outcries, and said all manner of ill-natured things to Beauty, who did not cry at all. Do but see the pride of that little wretch, said they; she would not ask for fine clothes, as we did; but no truly, Miss wanted to distinguish herself, so now she will be the death of our poor father, and yet she does not so much as shed a tear. Why should I, answered Beauty, it would be very needless, for my father shall not suffer upon my account, since the

monster

monster will accept of one of his daughters, I will deliver myself up to all his fury, and I am very happy in thinking that my death will save my father's life, and be a proof of my tender love for him. No sister, said her three brothers, that shall not be, we will go find the monster, and either kill him, or perish in the attempt. Do not imagine any such thing, my sons, said the merchant, Beast's power is so great, that I have no hopes of your overcoming him: I am charmed with Beauty's kind and generous offer, but I cannot yield to it; I am old, and have not long to live, so can only lose a few years, which I regret for your sakes alone, my dear children. Indeed father, said Beauty, you shall not go to the palace without me, you cannot hinder me from following you. It was to no purpose all they could say, Beauty still insisted on setting out for the fine palace, and her sisters were delighted at it, for her virtue and amiable qualities made them envious and jealous.

The merchant was so afflicted at the thoughts of losing his daughter, that he had quite forgot the chest full of gold; but at night when he retired to rest, no sooner had he shut his chamberdoor, than, to his great astonishment, he found it by his bed-side; he was determined, however, not to tell his children, that he was grown rich, because

because they would have wanted to return to town, and he was resolved not to leave the country; but he trusted Beauty with the secret, who informed him, that two gentlemen came in his absence, and courted her sisters; she begged her father to consent to their marriage, and give them fortunes, for she was so good, that she loved them, and forgave heartily all their ill usage. These wicked creatures rubbed their eyes with an onion to force some tears when they parted with their sister, but her brothers were really concerned. Beauty was the only one who did not shed tears at parting, because she would not increase their uneasiness.

The horse took the direct road to the palace, and towards evening they perceived it illuminated as at first: the horse went of himself into the stable, and the good man and his daughter came into the great hall, where they found a table splendidly served up, and two covers. The merchant had no heart to eat, but Beauty, endeavouring to appear chearful, sat down to table, and helped him. Afterwards, thought she to herself, Beast surely has a mind to fatten me before he eats me, since he provides such a plentiful entertainment. When they had supped they heard a great noise, and the merchant, all in tears,

bid

bid his poor child, farewel, for he thought Beaſt was coming. Beauty was ſadly terrified at his horrid form, but ſhe took courage as well as ſhe could, and the monſter having aſked her if ſhe came willingly; y—e—es, ſaid ſhe, trembling: you are very good, and I am greatly obliged to you; honeſt man, go your ways to-morrow morning, but never think of coming here again. Farewel Beauty, farewel Beaſt, anſwered ſhe, and immediately the monſter withdrew. Oh, daughter, ſaid the merchant, embracing Beauty, I am almoſt frightened to death; believe me, you had better go back, and let me ſtay here; no, father, ſaid Beauty, in a reſolute tone, you ſhall ſet out to-morrow morning, and leave me to the care and protection of providence. They went to-bed, and thought they ſhould not cloſe their eyes all night; but ſcarce were they laid down, than they fell faſt aſleep, and Beauty dreamed, a fine lady came, and ſaid to her, I am content, Beauty, with your good will; this good action of yours in giving up your own life to ſave your father's ſhall not go unrewarded. Beauty waked, and told her father her dream, and though it helped to comfort him a little, yet he could not help crying bitterly, when he took leave of his dear child.

As ſoon as he was gone, Beauty ſat down in the great hall, and fell a crying likewiſe; but as ſhe

ſhe was miſtreſs of a great deal of reſolution, ſhe recommended herſelf to God, and reſolved not to be uneaſy the little time ſhe had to live; for ſhe firmly believed Beaſt would eat her up that night.

However, ſhe thought ſhe might as well walk about till then, and view this fine caſtle, which ſhe could not help admiring; it was a delightful pleaſant place, and ſhe was extremely ſurpriſed at ſeeing a door, over which was wrote, " BEAUTY's APARTMENT." She opened it haſtily, and was quite dazzled with the magnificence that reigned throughout; but what chiefly took up her attention, was a large library, a harpſichord, and ſeveral muſic books. Well, ſaid ſhe to herſelf, I ſee they will not let my time hang heavy upon my hands for want of amuſement. Then ſhe reflected, " Were I but to ſtay here a day, " there would not have been all theſe prepara- " tions." This conſideration inſpired her with freſh courage; and opening the library ſhe took a book, and read theſe words in letters of gold:

" Welcome Beauty, baniſh fear,
" You are queen and miſtreſs here:
" Speak your wiſhes, ſpeak your will,
" Swift obedience meets them ſtill."

Alas,

Alas! faid fhe, with a figh, there is nothing I defire fo much as to fee my poor father, and know what he is doing; fhe had no fooner faid this, when cafting her eyes on a great looking-glafs, to her great amazement fhe faw her own home, where her father arrived with a very dejected countenance; her fifters went to meet him, and notwithftanding their endeavours to appear forrowful, their joy, felt for having got rid of their fifter, was vifible in every feature: a moment after, every thing difappeared, and Beauty's apprehenfions at this proof of Beaft's complaifance.

At noon fhe found dinner ready, and while at table, was entertained with an excellent concert of mufic, though without feeing any body: but at night, as fhe was going to fit down to fupper, fhe heard the noife Beaft made, and could not help being fadly terrified. Beauty, faid the monfter, will you give me leave to fee you fup? That is as you pleafe, anfwered Beauty trembling. No, replied the Beaft, you alone are miftrefs here; you need only bid me be gone, if my prefence is troublefome, and I will immediately withdraw: but, tell me, do not you think me very ugly? That is true, faid Beauty, for I cannot tell a lie, but I believe you are very good-natured. So I am, faid the mon-ſter,

ster, but then, befides my uglinefs, I have no fenfe; I know very well that I am a poor, filly, ftupid creature. 'Tis no fign of folly to think fo, replied Beauty, for never did fool know this, or had fo humble a conceit of his own underftanding. Eat then, Beauty, faid the monfter, and endeavour to amufe yourfelf in your palace, for every thing here is yours, and I fhould be very uneafy, if you were not happy. You are very obliging, anfwered Beauty; I own I am pleafed with your kindnefs, and when I confider that, your deformity fcarce appears. Yes, faid the Beaft, my heart is good, but ftill I am a monfter. Among mankind, fays Beauty, there are many that deferve that name more than you, and I prefer you, juft as you are, to thofe, who, under a human form, hide a treacherous, corrupt, and ungrateful heart. If I had fenfe enough, replied the Beaft, I would make a fine compliment to thank you, but I am fo dull, that I can only fay, I am greatly obliged to you. Beauty eat a hearty fupper, and had almoft conquered her dread of the monfter; but fhe had like to have fainted away, when he faid to her, Beauty, will you be my wife? She was fome time before fhe durft anfwer, for fhe was afraid of making him angry, if fhe refufed. At laft, however, fhe faid, trembling, No, Beaft. Imme-diately

diately the poor monster went to figh, and hiffed fo frightfully, that the whole palace echoed. But Beauty foon recovered her fright, for Beaft having faid, in a mournful voice, " then farewel, Beauty," left the room; and only turned back, now and then, to look at her as he went out.

When Beauty was alone, fhe felt a great deal of compaffion for poor Beaft. Alas, faid fhe, 'tis a thoufand pities, any thing fo good-natured fhould be fo ugly.

Beauty fpent three months very contentedly in the palace: every evening Beaft paid her a vifit, and talked to her during fupper, very rationally, with plain good common fenfe, but never with what the world calls wit; and Beauty daily difcovered fome valuable qualifications in the monfter, and feeing him often had fo accuftomed her to his deformity, that, far from dreading the time of his vifit, fhe would often look on her watch to fee when it would be nine, for the Beaft never miffed coming at that hour. There was but one thing that gave Beauty any concern, which was, that every night, before fhe went to bed, the monfter always afked her, if fhe would be his wife. One day fhe faid to him, Beaft, you make me very uneafy, I wifh I could confent to marry you, but I am too fincere to make you believe that will ever happen: I fhall

I fhall always efteem you as a friend, endeavour to be fatisfied with this. I muft, faid the Beaft, for, alas! I know too well my own misfortune, but then I love you with the tendereft affection: however, I ought to think myfelf happy, that you will ftay here; promife me never to leave me. Beauty blufhed at thefe words; fhe had feen in her glafs, that her father had pined himfelf fick for the lofs of her, and fhe longed to fee him again. I could, anfwered fhe, indeed promife never to leave you intirely, but I have fo great a defire to fee my father, that I fhall fret to death, if you refufe me that fatisfaction. I had rather die myfelf, faid the monfter, than give you the leaft uneafinefs: I will fend you to your father, you fhall remain with him, and poor Beaft will die with grief. No, faid Beauty, weeping, I love you too well to be the caufe of your death: I give you my promife to return in a week: you have fhewn me, that my fifters are married, and my brothers gone to the army; only let me ftay a week with my father, as he is alone. You fhall be there to-morrow morning, faid the Beaft, but remember your promife: you need only lay your ring on a table before you go to bed, when you have a mind to come back: farewel, Beauty. Beaft fighed as ufual, bidding her good night, and Beauty went to bed very fad at feeing him fo afflicted.

afflicted. When she waked the next morning, she found herself at her father's, and having rang a little bell, that was by her bedside, she saw the maid come, who, the moment she saw her, gave a loud shriek, at which the good man ran up stairs, and thought he should have died with joy to see his dear daughter again. He held her fast locked in his arms above a quarter of an hour. As soon as the first transports were over, Beauty began to think of rising, and was afraid she had no clothes to put on; but the maid told her, that she had just found, in the next room, a large trunk full of gowns, covered with gold and diamonds. Beauty thanked good Beast for his kind care, and taking one of the plainest of them, she intended to make a present of the others to her sisters. She scarce had said so, when the trunk disappeared. Her father told her, that Beast insisted on her keeping them herself, and immediately both gowns and trunk came back again.

Beauty dressed herself, and in the mean time they sent to her sisters, who hasted thither with their husbands. They were both of them very unhappy. The eldest had married a gentleman, extremely handsome indeed, but so fond of his own person, that he was full of nothing but his own dear self, and neglected his wife. The second

cond had married a man of wit, but he only made use of it to plague and torment every body, and his wife most of all. Beauty's sisters sickened with envy, when they saw her dressed like a princess, and more beautiful than ever, nor could all her obliging affectionate behaviour stifle their jealousy, which was ready to burst when she told them how happy she was. They went down into the garden to vent it in tears; and said one to the other, in what is this little creature better than us, that she should be so much happier? Sister, said the eldest, a thought just strikes my mind; let us endeavour to detain her above a week, and perhaps the silly monster will be so enraged at her for breaking her word, that he will devour her. Right, sister, answered the other, therefore we must shew her as much kindness as possible. After they had taken this resolution, they went up, and behaved so affectionately to their sister, that poor Beauty wept for joy. When the week was expired, they cried and tore their hair, and seemed so sorry to part with her, that she promised to stay a week longer.

In the mean time, Beauty could not help reflecting on herself for the uneasiness she was likely to cause poor Beast, whom she sincerely loved, and really longed to see again. The tenth

tenth night she spent at her father's, she dreamed she was in the palace garden, and that she saw Beast extended on the grass plat, who seemed just expiring; and, in a dying voice, reproached her with her ingratitude. Beauty started out of her sleep, and bursting into tears, am not I very wicked, said she, to act so unkindly to Beast, that has studied so much to please me in every thing? Is it his fault that he is so ugly, and has so little sense? He is kind and good, and that is sufficient. Why did I refuse to marry him? I should be happier with the monster than my sisters are with their husbands; it is neither wit, nor a fine person, in a husband, that makes a woman happy, but virtue, sweetness of temper, and complaisance, and Beast has all these valuable qualifications. It is true, I do not feel the tenderness of affection for him, but I find I have the highest gratitude, esteem and friendship; and I will not make him miserable; were I to be so ungrateful I should never forgive myself. Beauty having said this, rose, put her ring on the table, and then laid down again; scarce was she in bed before she fell asleep, and when she waked the next morning, she was overjoyed to find herself in the Beast's palace. She put on one of her richest suits to please him, and waited for evening with the utmost impatience,

tience, at last the wished for hour came, the clock struck nine, yet no Beast appeared. Beauty then feared she had been the cause of his death; she ran crying and wringing her hands all about the palace, like one in despair: after having sought for him every where, she recollected her dream, and flew to the canal in the garden, where she dreamed she saw him. There she found poor Beast stretched out, quite senseless, and, as she imagined, dead. She threw herself upon him without any dread, and finding his heart beat still, she fetched some water from the canal, and poured it on his head. Beast opened his eyes, and said to Beauty, you forgot your promise, and I was so afflicted for having lost you, that I resolved to starve myself, but since I have the happiness of seeing you once more, I die satisfied. No, dear Beast, said Beauty, you must not die; live to be my husband; from this moment I give you my hand, and swear to be none but yours. Alas! I thought I had only a friendship for you, but the grief I now feel convinces me, that I cannot live without you. Beauty scarce had pronounced these words, when she saw the palace sparkle with light; and fireworks, instruments of music, every thing seemed to give notice of some great event: but nothing could fix her attention; she turned to her dear Beast,

Beast, for whom she trembled with fear; but how great was her surprise! Beast was disappeared, and she saw, at her feet, one of the loveliest princes that eye ever beheld; who returned her thanks for having put an end to the charm, under which he had so long resembled a Beast. Though this prince was worthy of all her attention, she could not forbear asking where Beast was. You see him at your feet, said the prince: a wicked fairy had condemned me to remain under that shape till a beautiful virgin should consent to marry me: the fairy likewise enjoined me to conceal my understanding; there was only you in the world generous enough to be won by the goodness of my temper, and in offering you my crown I can't discharge the obligations I have to you. Beauty, agreeably surprised, gave the charming prince her hand to rise; they went together into the castle, and Beauty was overjoyed to find, in the great hall, her father and his whole family, whom the beautiful lady, that appeared to her in her dream, had conveyed thither.

Beauty, said this lady, come and receive the reward of your judicious choice; you have preferred virtue before either wit or beauty, and deserve to find a person in whom all these qualifications are united: you are going to be a great queen,

queen, I hope the throne will not lessen your virtue, or make you forget yourself. As to you, ladies, said the fairy to Beauty's two sisters, I know your hearts, and all the malice they contain: become two statues, but, under this transformation, still retain your reason. You shall stand before your sister's palace gate, and be it your punishment to behold her happiness; and it will not be in your power to return to your former state, till you own your faults, but I am very much afraid that you will always remain statues. Pride, anger, gluttony, and idleness are sometimes conquered, but the conversion of a malicious and envious mind is a kind of miracle. Immediately the fairy gave a stroke with her wand, and in a moment all that were in the hall were transported into the prince's dominions: his subjects received him with joy; he married Beauty, and lived with her many years, and their happiness, as it was founded on virtue, was compleat.

Lady Charlotte.   And were her two sisters always statues?

Mrs. Affable.   Yes, my dear, because their hearts were never changed.

Lady Witty.   I could hear you a whole week together without being tired; I love this Beauty prodigiously, yet, methinks, if I had been in her place,

APPENDIX THREE

A Twentieth-Century Oral Version

La Belle et La Bête

Il était une fois un marchand d'habits qui avait trois filles. Un jour, il s'en va à la ville pour acheter des affaires. Alors, il dit à une de ses filles, à l'aînée . . .

– Qu'est-ce qu'il faudra que je t'apporte?

– Oh, elle lui dit, mon père, j'aimerais bien une belle robe.

– Bien, je t'apporterai ta robe.

A la deuxième il dit:

– Et toi, qu'est-ce que tu voudras que je t'apporte?

– Oh, elle dit, mon père, moi, je voudrais un joli corsage.

Alors il lui dit:

– Bien, je t'apporterai ton corsage.

A la troisième il dit:

– Qu'est-ce qu'il faudra que je t'apporte?

– Oh, elle dit, mon père, comme on n'est pas bien riche, tu m'apporteras seulement une rose.

– Oh, il lui dit, je t'apporterai une rose, mais ce n'est pas grand'chose!

Alors, voilà le marchand parti en ville: il achète sa robe, il achète son corsage, mais il n'avait pas trouvé de rose. En revenant, qu'est-ce qu'il voit? Un joli château avec plein de roses dans le jardin. Il se dit:

– Ma foi, tant pis! Je vais demander si on veut me donner une rose.

Paul Delarue and Marie-Louise Tenèze, *Le conte populaire française: Catalogue raisonné des versions de France et des pays de langue française d'outre-mer; Canada, Louisiane, Ilots française des Etats-Unis, Antilles française, Haïti, Ile Maurice, La Réunion*, vol. 2 (Paris: Editions G.-P. Maisonneuve et Larose, 1964) forme C.

Il rentre, il approche: il ne voit personne.

– Eh bien, il diet, tant pis! Je coupe la rose!

Il coupe une rose. Mais, en coupant la rose, il est sorti du sang. Alors, une grosse bête apparaît qui lui dit:

– Tu as coupé une rose sans me le demander.

Le marchand lui répond:

– Eh bien, c'est pour ma fille qui m'en avait demandé une. Ma foi! n'en trouvant nulle part, j'en ai pris une ici.

Alors la Bête lui dit:

– Puisque tu as une fille, tu reviendras avec elle pour que je la mange, ou toi-même! Si dans deux jours tu n'es pas là, il t'arrivera un grand malheur.

Violà le marchand parti, bien ennuyé En arrivant chez lui, il donne la robe à sa première fille; ensuite il donne le corsage à la deuxième; alors il dit à la troisième:

– Voici ta rose, mais, tu sais, elle m'a causé de graves ennuis. Il faudra que toi ou moi nous revenions où je l'ai prise, car il y a une grosse bête qui veut nous manger toi ou moi parce que j'ai coupé la rose.

Les deux soeurs de la jeune fille là l'ont disputée:

– Tu vois, avec tes manières de ne pas être comme tout le monde! Si notre père est mangé, qu'est-ce qu'on fera, nous seules?

– Ce n'est pas mon père qui sera mangé, ce sera moi!

Violà le père et la fille partis. En arrivant à la porte du château, la jeune fille, elle rentre; puis le père s'en va. La jeune fille regarde partout, ne trouve personne. Partout où elle regarde, c'était marqué:

Tout est à toi. Mais surtout, ne t'en va pas, car il arriverait un grand malheur à ton père.

Arrive le soir. La jeune fille, ne voyant rien, se couche dans un beau lit. Et, dans la nuit, violà qu'apparaît la Bête. La Bête lui dit:

– Si tu veux te marier avec moi, tu seras très heureuse.

Alors, la jeune fille dit:

– Avant, je veux réfléchir.

Elle ne pouvait pas dire non!

Les jours passèrent. La jeune fille ne se décidait pas. Alors, elle dit à la Bête:

– Si tu étais bien gentille, tu me laisserais aller voir mes parents.

La Bête lui dit:

– Vas-y, mais, sois rentrée à neuf heures!

Voilà la jeune fille partie et qui revient juste à neuf heures.

Une autre fois, la jeune fille lui dit:

– Je voudrais bien encore une fois aller voir mes parents!

La Bête lui dit:

– Vas-y, mais, comme tu as été raisonnable, tu rentreras à dix heures.

Et la jeune fille, le soir, revient à dix heures.

Une autre fois, elle dit:

– Je voudrais bien encore une fois aller voir mes parents.

Alors la Bête lui dit:

– Vas-y, mais tu seras là à onze heures.

Mais les soeurs lui disent au moment de partir:

– Tu nous embêtes avec ta Bête! Tu as bien le temps de rentrer!

La jeune fille se laisse faire et ne rentre que le lendemain.

Le lendemain, en arrivant, ne trouve plus sa Bête . . . mais, tout à coup, qu'est-ce qu'elle entend? La Bête qui était dans la rivière et qui pleurait! Elle voulait se noyer parce qu'elle croyait que la jeune fille ne rentrerait pas. Alors la jeune fille lui dit:

– Reviens, ma Bête, je me marierai avec toi!

Et la Bête se transforme en un prince charmant. (C'était un prince que les sorcières avaient changé en Bête, comme autrefois.)

Alors la Belle et la Bête se sont mariés. Il y a eu un grand mariage. Puis, la jeune fille a pris son père avec elle. Elle a dit à ses soeurs:

– Vous n'avez pas été très bonnes pour moi mais je veux l'oublier. Je vous donnerai un appartement dans mon palais et vous n'aurez plus besoin de travailler. Et nous serons tous très heureux!

Et c'est fini!

[Collected by Mlle A. de Félice in 1944 from Jeanne Meiraud, 41 years old, a native of Fromental (Creuse). This story had first been recorded in dialect; then the storyteller herself translated it into French.—MS A. de Félice, Bas-Poitou, MS ATP 59.2, 85–87.]

APPENDIX FOUR

A Sampling of Nineteenth-Century Editions

1804   *Beauty and the Beast; or, The Magic Rose,* with elegant coloured engravings. A new edition revised, and adapted for juvenile readers, By a Lady. London, Dean and Munday. 36 pp.

Strictly adapted Beaumont version, but with the sisters restored after several years of good conduct. A note at the end tells of the Eastern origin of good and bad genii, who, for each person, prompt the "proper course of life" or "evil actions"; one's future destiny depends on obeying the good or yielding to the evil. Beauty's filial devotion counteracts an evil genii's plot, revealing Prince Azin to be the real prince. Colored engravings, two to a page, tiny with clear blue, red, and yellow hues, illustrate the text in a well-balanced design. The monster has scaled legs and paws, with clawed hands and arms, its face a combination of human and beast. Men are in French costumes, with feathered hats, tights, puffy sleeves, and belted tunics; women are in Greek costume, all with serious countenances.

1804   *Tabart's Improved Edition of Beauty and the Beast: A Tale for the Nursery* with coloured plates. A New Edition. London, Tabart & Co. 37 pages, suede binding. Three copperplates, 6 pp., Beaumont text.

Middle Eastern costume; Greek Revival backgrounds. Beast has gorilla-wolf head with hairy human figure. Pink, green, brown, red, yellow, blue, with earth-tones predominant, make a surprisingly colorful early edition.

1811   *Beauty and the Beast: or A Rough Outside with Gentle Heart, A Poetical Version of an Ancient Tale.* Illustrated with a Series of

Elegant Engravings and Beauty's Song at Her Spinning Wheel, Set to Music by Mr. Whitaker. London: Printed for M. J. Goodwin, at the Juvenile Library, 41, Skinner Street, United Kingdom. 5s. 6d. coloured, or 3s. 6d. plain.

Discussed in the text.

1815 *Beauty and the Beast: A Tale Ornamented with Cuts.* Bristol: Philip Rose. 39 pp., 6p.

Beaumont text. Full-page woodcuts are oval framed and stilted. Empire costumes; Greek backgrounds with Italianate touches. Beast looks like a mastodon cow.

1816 *Beauty and the Beast: A Tale.* London: Printed for the Booksellers. New Juvenile Library. A New and Correct Edition. Four copperplates by Lizars. 34 pp., 6p.

The text is smooth, a formal Beaumont translation with occasional dialogue and comfortable style. Black-and-white, fine-lined illustrations are textured with crosshatch. Restrained composition. Greek Revival/Empire styles. Beast appears as a dragon-like reptile with horns. The father looks to be of the same age as the prince, with the same figure and costume.

1818 *Popular Fairy Tales; or, a Lilliputian Library Containing Twenty-six Choice Pieces , by Those Renowned Personages King Oberon, Queen Mab, Mother Goose, Mother Bunch, Master Puck, and Other Distinguished Personages at the Court of the Fairies.* Now first collected and revised by Benjamin Tabart. With twenty-six coloured engravings. London: Sir Richard Phillips, ca.1818.

A 16-page story, Beaumont's version, in a collection. The beast appears to be a cross between wolf and bear, the humans sport "Moorish" costumes.

1824 *Beauty and the Beast; or, The Magic Rose.* Emb. with Coloured Engravings. London: Dean & Munday. 34 pp., 6p. [This may be a new edition of the 1804 version.]

Beaumont text. Three-panel, fold-out illustrations. French Empire costume; elaborate palace room settings; bear-like Beast. The fairy is grouped with the court ladies. The father is similar to the prince. Plum-pink, yellow, blue, and flesh tones predominate.

1836 *The Child's Own Book.* Illustrated with 300 engravings. 5th ed. London: Thomas Tegg and Son. Pp. 33–50.

Beaumont text. Persian costume and hints of Greek Revival

in architecture. Beast is part dog, part lion. Editor's note on the author: "It is to be trusted . . . that . . . she has delighted the imagination without corrupting the heart" (p. viii).

1840   *The Interesting Story of Beauty and the Beast with a Coloured Engraving.* Derby: Thomas Richardson. 12 pp. 2*p.*

Beaumont text. Empire clothes. Furry Beast with human hands, feet, and face.

1841   *Beauty and the Beast: A Grand, Comic, Romantic, Operatic, Melodramatic, Fairy Extravaganza, in Two Acts,* by J. R. Planché as Performed at the Theatre Royal, Covent Garden, on Easter-Monday, April 12, 1841. London: G. Berger, Holywell St., Strand; And All Book sellers. Price one shilling.

Discussed in the text.

1842   *Beauty and the Beast.* A Manuscript by Richard Doyle. Translated by Adelaide Doyle. Printed by the Pierpont Morgan Library, New York, 1973.

Beaumont's text. Black-and-white pen sketches, fine line and crosshatch. Serio-comic cartoon style, miniature figures, fanciful borders, initials, tail-pieces. Bear Beast. Handwritten.

1843   *Beauty and the Beast: An entirely new Edition* with new pictures by an Eminent Artist. Edited by Felix Summerly. The Home Treasury. London: Joseph Cundall. 35pp.

Eastern setting and costume. Beast is a furry, upright, bearded dog. Long notes on other folk/fairy tale versions and editor's adaptation. Modernized text: ports and commerce of merchant's ships are named. Beauty's cottage garden is elaborated; roses' magic is added. Verses are scattered throughout. The merchant bathes in rose-water. Beauty's room is richly imagined. The Beast is witty, asks for marriage only once. Affection developed carefully. The magic rose is a vehicle of travel and a binding symbol. Beauty respects the week's limitation, but her sisters take the rose. The prince is shown kneeling, and the side-view of his face is the same shade as the Beast's. It avoids anti-climax since no features are visible.

Undated   (This edition, in the Victoria and Albert Museum Library, appears to be pre-1850.)

Beauty and the Beast, To Which is Added the Punishment of Ingratitude. A New Edition. With Elegant Engraving. London:

Printed for S. Maunder. Engraving by W. Layton, Published by Hodgson. 36pp.

Beaumont text. Attached separate "Greek" story of a physician and a tyrant, a somewhat gruesome tale irrelevant except by contrast to "Beauty and the Beast's" reward-for-gratitude theme.

1850   *The History of Beauty and the Beast.* Glasgow: Francis Orr and Sons.

No illustrations. Similar edition to Richardson Chapbook Series.

1853   *Beauty and the Beast.* With illustrations by Alfred Crowquill. New York: Leavitt and Allen.

Satirical drawings cartoon the characters in a graphic foil of a traditional text.

1854   *Beauty and the Beast: An Entertainment for Young People, the First of the Series of Little Plays for Little People.* By Miss Julia Corner and Alfred Crowquill. London: Dean & Son. 46pp. 1*s.* boxed.

The characters named: Beast = Azor (Bear); Merchant = Zimri; Daughters = Anna, Lolo, Beauty; Fairy = Silverstar. Rhyming couplets in iambic pentameter. This is a didactic lessonbook series. Fairy has large role, and is assisted by four fairy attendants. Stiff pen drawings look "child conscious" with doll-like figures that are foreshortened. Elaborate costume, turbans, tunics, etc. Instructions and stage directions. All dialogue. Victorian version of Persian costumes. For amusement and moral instruction of children 8 to 12 years old.

1856   *Beauty and the Beast.* Aunt Mary's Series. McLoughlin Bros. & Co., New York. 14pp.

Beaumont's text with a cleaned-up ending—the sisters are restored after repenting of their folly. Beast is a bear. Colonial backgrounds. Eight full-page pen-and-ink pictures with red, yellow, and blue (hand-colored?), and an illustrated cover.

[1867]   *Beauty and the Beast.* Aunt Mavor's Toy Books. London, George Routledge & Sons. 8pp. 6*p.*

The Beaumont version in a shortened, simple, bold, absorbing style, with elements of the Beauty/Beast relationship presented strongly and immediately. Art is simply composed, large, dramatic, and effective, with brilliantly clear colors in gold, red, green, and blue. Pictures are advertised to sell separately, "strongly mounted on cloth," for 1 shilling each. Large print and pictures. Eastern turban and robes. Beast is reflected in a bearlike prince with full beard and hair (vaguely reminiscent of Prince Albert). Many lines made with color draw in the eye with an absorbing effect. Direct, powerful, kept to the simplest elements and language. (The text omits the merchant's misfortunes, compressing his losses, journey, and retrieval of the rose into the first few sentences.)

Undated *Beauty and the Beast.* Second Series of Aunt Mavor's Picture Books for Little Readers. London, George Routledge. 6*p*.

Inferior pictures compared to the first edition. The colors are dull, the words are divided by hyphens into syllables for educational purposes. The story is fuller though still pared down (the merchant's misfortunes are described but abbreviated). The art shows miniaturized adults in Victorian dress with turbans. The Beast is a bear and the prince is French.

1867 *Beauty and the Beast.* (Loring's Tales of the Day). By Miss Thackeray, Author of "The Village on the Cliff." From "The Cornhill." Boston: Loring, 1867. 22 pp. 15 cents.

More fiction than fairy tale, this unillustrated, seven-part love story presages, in many ways, Angela Carter's twentieth-century version about Mr. Lyon.

1875 *Beauty and the Beast.* Walter Crane's Toy Books. Shilling Series. London & New York: George Routledge & Sons.

Discussed in the text.

1886 *Gordon Browne's Series of Old Fairy Tales no. 2: Beauty and the Beast.* Drawings by Gordon Browne. Story retold by Laura E. Richards. London: Black & Son. 32pp., 1*s*.

Black-and-white line drawings are full-page and scattered throughout. Victorian dress. Beast is a wolf with mule and griffin characteristics. The story is set within a story: in the absence of the fairy, a tree tells children the tale. Cute, condescending text. Sisters named Gracilia, Superba, Beauty. Children interrupt story with questions as in Uncle Remus stories. The merchant is successful on his trip; there are many explanations, e.g., for why he could not get a rose (the king's daughter's wedding took all the flowers). Conflict between the sick father and the dying beast is emphasized: crossed loyalties. The prince was changed by a malicious witch because he refused to marry an ugly daughter (one-eyed, hump-backed). The children are dismissed by the tree.

1889   "Beauty and the Beast" in *The Blue Fairy Book,* edited by Andrew Lang. London: Longmans, Green Co. 21pp.

     Discussed in the text.

1891   La Belle et la Bête in *Contes de fées,* edited by Edward S. Joynes. Boston: D. C. Heath.

     An educational collection adapted to help young readers practise their French.

1892   "Beauty and the Beast" in *Favorite Fairy Tales.* With new pictures by Maud Humphrey. Frederick A. Stokes Company. 2 pp.

     One of the briefest versions for children, this tells the story in two pages with large print and a picture of Beauty confronting a creature cloaked, fanged, and considering her with wolfish intentions.

1894   *Jack the Giant Killer and Beauty and the Beast.* The Banbury Cross Series prepared for children by Grace Rhys. Vol. 11. London: J. M. Dent.

     Warmly personalized characters appear in small but dramatic black and white drawings scattered throughout the text.

Notes

Chapter 1

1. "I love innocent games with those who are not," a quote from an unidentified lady of the court in Andrew Lang, *Blue Fairy Book,* rev. ed. (Middlesex: Kestrel, 1975), 354.

2. I examined them in 1980.

3. Roger Sale, *Fairy Tales and After: From Snow White to E. B. White* (Cambridge: Harvard University Press, 1978), 45.

4. Jane Yolen, "America's Cinderella," in *Cinderella: A Folklore Casebook*, ed. Alan Dundes (New York: Garland Publishing, 1982), 303.

5. The International Youth Library in Munich has the following editions: one picturebook each in English (1983), French (1986), and Spanish (1982), with two in German (1969, 1986). One fairy tale collection in German (1946) contains "Beauty and the Beast"; nine collections in French include it with fairy tales by Perrault and d'Aulnoy (1910, 1930, 1950, 1951, 1962, 1976, 1978, 1979, 1980). The library also has three editions of *Le magasin des enfans* (1779, 1802, 1846) and a copy of *Le vrai magasin des enfans* (1960), illustrated by Paul Gavarni, Jean Guerin, and Adolphe Mouilleron (Lausanne: Guildes des jeunes, 1960).

Chapter 2

1. Summarized from "The Small Tooth Dog" in Katharine M. Briggs and Ruth L. Tongue, *Folktales of England* (Chicago and London: University of Chicago Press, 1965), 3–5.

2. Summarized from "The Enchanted Tsarévitch" in Aleksandr Nikolaevich Afans'ev, *Russian Folktales* (republished in Detroit: Gale Research Company, 1974), 283–286.

3. Jan-Öjvind Swahn, *The Tale of Cupid and Psyche* (Lund: Gleerup, 1955), 311.

4. Literary motifs that disappear are those without an epic function: the three brothers, the merchant's second bankruptcy, the Beast's gift to the merchant, and the pretended sorrow of the sisters. Those motifs that live on are the theft of the flower, the forced marriage to the animal, the taboo, and the breaking of it, plus the detail of the horse and the devices in the magic palace (Swahn, *The Tale of Cupid and Psyche*, 309).

5. Ibid., 297–298.

6. "Beauty and the Beast" has been compared to "Riquet à la Houppe" from a psychoanalytic perspective by Jacques Barchilon in his article "Beauty and the Beast," *Psychoanalysis and the Psychoanalytic Review* 46, no. 4, (Winter 1959): 19–29 and from a socio-political viewpoint by Jack Zipes in *Fairy Tales and the Art of Subversion: The Classical Genre for Children and the Process of Civilization* (New York: Wildman Press, 1983), 31–41 and "The Dark Side of Beauty and the Beast: The Origins of the Literary Fairy Tale for Children," *Proceedings of the Eighth Annual Conference of the Children's Literature Association,* ed. Priscilla P. Ord, University of Minnesota, March 1981 (Boston: Children's Literature Association, 1982), 119–125

7. Although the primary focus of this study is literary, the essay by Larry Devries in appendix 1 further explores the folkloristic aspects of this tale, including a Proppian analysis of "Beauty and the Beast."

8. Stith Thompson, *Motif-Index of Folk-Literature: A Classification of Narrative Elements in Folktales, Ballads, Myths, Fables, Mediaeval Romances, Exempla, Fabliaux, Jest-books, and Local Legends,* 6 vols. (Bloomington: Indiana University Press, 1956), 2:85.

9. Antti Aarne, *The Types of the Folktale: A Classification and Bibliography*, trans. and rev. by Stith Thompson, Folklore Fellows Communications no. 184 (Helsinki: Academia Scientiarum Fennica, 1961), 143.

10. Ibid.

11. Ibid.

12. Paul Delarue and Marie-Louise Tenèze, *Le conte populaire français: Catalogue raisonné des versions de France et des pays de langue française d'outre-mer: Canada, Louisiane, Ilots française des Etats-Unis, Antilles françaises, Haïti, Ile Maurice, La Réunio,* vol. 2 (Paris: Editions G.-P. Maisonneuve et Larose, 1964), 86, 92–107.

13. Katharine M. Briggs, *A Dictionary of British Folktales in the English Language,* 2 vols. (Bloomington: Indiana University Press, 1970), 1:41.

14. These are listed in *The Types of the Irish Folktale* by Sean O'Suilleabhain and Reidar Th. Christiansen (Helsinki: Suomalainen Tiedeakatemia, 1967) and are accessible through an updated listing at the Folklore Commission Archives, University College, Dublin. The first is unpublished, a story handwritten from a telling by John Power in Ballymahon in 1932. The latter two appear, respectively, in Jeremiah Curtin, *Irish Folk-Tales*, ed. Séamus O'Duilearga (Dublin: Folklore of Ireland Society,

1943), 95–102; and in Curtin's *Myths and Folk-Lore of Ireland* (Boston: Little, Brown & Co., 1906), 50–63.

15. Francis James Child, ed., *The English and Scottish Popular Ballads*, vol.1 (1882, reprint New York: Dover Publications, 1965), 306–313.

16. The Opies cite two early Italian versions of "Beauty and the Beast," one about a Pig Prince in Straparola's *Piacevoli notti* (night 2, story 1) in 1550; the other, "The Serpent," in Basile's *Pentamerone* (day 2, tale 5) in 1634. Iona and Peter Opie, *The Classic Fairy Tales* (London: Oxford University Press, 1974), 137.

17. Sources for these stories are listed in the Bibliography. One of the most systematic listings of folktales as they appear in modern printed sources is D. L. Ashliman's invaluable book, *A Guide to Folktales in the English Language: Based on the Aarne-Thompson Classification System* (Westport, Conn.: Greenwood Press, 1987). 425A and 425C appear on pages 87–89.

18. Strictly speaking, "Cupid and Psyche" is not a myth, which is defined folkloristically as "a narrative explaining how the world and humans came to be in their present form" (quoted from Alan Dundes, in unpublished correspondence, 1987). However, the word myth has now acquired a broader literary and popular meaning as cultural metaphor. The point here is the strength of story underlying arbitrarily defined categories of folktale, fairy tale, myth, etc.

19. R. D. Jameson, "Cinderella in China," in *Cinderella: A Folklore Casebook*, ed. Alan Dundes (New York: Garland Publishing, Inc., 1982), 93.

20. Claude Lévi-Strauss, "The Structural Study of Myth," in *The Structuralists from Marx to Lévi-Strauss*, ed. Richard and Fernande De George (New York: Doubleday/ Anchor Books, 1972), 174.

21. W. R. S. Ralston, "Beauty and the Beast," *The Nineteenth Century* (December 1878): 1010.

22. Stith Thompson, *The Folktale* (Berkeley: University of California Press, 1977), 100.

23. The serpent is an obvious symbol of sexuality and one that appears in many animal groom stories, including "Monoyohe" (Botswana, Lesotho, and Swaziland), "The Serpent of Kamushalanga" (Tanzania), "The Serpent and the Grape-Grower's Daughter" (France), and "The Enchanted Tsarévitch" (Russian, summarized earlier).

24. Apulée *Les métamorphoses ou l'asne d'or de L.* (Apulée Philosophe Platonicien. Paris, 1648). This is listed in Mary Elizabeth Storer, "Les sources des contes de fées," in *Un épisode littéraire de la fin du XVII siècle: La mode des contes de fées (1685–1700)* (Paris: Librairie Ancienne Honore Champion, 1928), 281. Storer has an extensive discussion of the popular and literary sources of seventeenth-century French fairy tales, including Madame d'Aulnoy's and Perrault's.

25. Erich Neumann, *Amor and Psyche: The Psychic Development of the Feminine, A Commentary on the Tale of Apuleius*, trans. Ralph Manheim (New York: Pantheon, 1956), 7. Preceding Neumann's discourse is an excellent translation of the tale, which was used for this analysis.

26. Ibid., 22.

27. Georgios A. Megas, *Das Märchen von Amor und Psyche in der griechischen Überlieferung (Aarne-Thompson 425, 428, and 432)* (Athēnai: Grapheion Dēmosiegmatōn tes Akademias Athēnōn, 1971). Debate over the origins of "Cupid and Psyche" has a history among folklorists. In his introduction to Adlington's 1887 translation of "Cupid and Psyche," Andrew Lang has a long discussion of the origins of the myth, including a repudiation of Cosquin's belief that India was the "birthplace" of the primitive form of "Cupid and Psyche." Lang believed that the essential ideas and incidents of the tale were to be found "universally."

28. Jane Tucker Mitchell, *A Thematic Analysis of Madame d'Aulnoy's Contes de Fées.* Romance Monographs, no. 30 (Oxford, Miss.: University of Mississippi, 1978), 67.

29. Madame Le Prince de Beaumont, *The Young Ladies Magazine, or Dialogues between a Discreet Governess and Several Young Ladies of the First Rank under Her Education,* 4 vols. in 2 (London: J. Nourse, 1760), 1: xxi–xxii.

30. "He spared nothing for the education of his children and gave them all sorts of teachers," translated from Madame Le Prince de Beaumont's *Magasin des enfans* (London: J. Haberkorn, 1756), 71.

31. An issue discussed in the last chapter of this book.

32. Quoted from Mitchell, *A Thematic Analysis,* 28.

33. Madame Le Prince de Beaumont, "Beauty and the Beast," in *The Classic Fairy Tales,* eds. Iona and Peter Opie, 145.

34. For extensive—and sometimes conflicting—psychological interpretations of "Cupid and Psyche," see Marie-Louise von Franz, *A Psychological Interpretation of The Golden Ass of Apuleius* (Irving, Tex.: Spring Publications, Inc., University of Dallas, 1980), 61–109; Erich Neumann, *Amor and Psyche,* cited earlier; and Phyllis B. Katz, "The Myth of Psyche: A Definition of the Nature of the Feminine?" *Arethusa* 9, no.1 (Spring 1976): 11–118.

35. Northrop Frye, *Anatomy of Criticism* (Princeton: Princeton University Press, 1957), 344.

36. Ralston, "Beauty and the Beast," *The Nineteenth Century,* 991.

37. Ernest Dowson, *The Story of Beauty and the Beast: The Complete Fairy Story,* translated from the French by Ernest Dowson with four plates in colour by Charles Condor (London: John Lane, The Bodley Head, 1908), 68. A limited edition of 300 copies, this translation is available at both the British Library and the Newberry Library and is the source for all of the quotations in the following discussion of Villeneuve's story.

38. Folk versions generally classify the Beast as a particular animal.

39. Vladimir Propp, "Morphology of the Folktale," *International Journal of American Linguistics* 24, no.4 (October 1958 [part 3]) (Bloomington: Indiana University Research Center in Anthropology, Folklore, and Linguistics, no. 10), 29 (p. 30 in

the more readily available revised edition published by University of Texas Press, 1968).

40. Roger Sale, *Fairy Tales and After,* 59.

41. C. S. Lewis, *Of Other Worlds: Essays and Stories,* ed. Walter Hooper (New York: Harcourt Brace Jovanovich, 1966), 17.

42. J. R. R. Tolkien, "Tree and Leaf," in *The Tolkien Reader* (New York: Ballantine, 1966), 87.

43. Ibid., 56, 95.

44. Ibid., 78.

45. Madame Le Prince de Beaumont, "Beauty and the Beast," in Iona and Peter Opie, *The Classic Fairy Tales,* 143. Page numbers of the quotations in the following discussion refer to the translation appearing in the Opies' book.

46. Stephanie Comtesse de Genlis, *The Beauty and the Monster: A Comedy from the French of the Countesse de Genlis Extracted from the Theatre of Education* (Worcester, Mass.: Isaiah Thomas, 1785), 4. Page numbers after the quotations in the following discussion refer to this source.

Chapter 3

1. The examples listed in appendix 4 show the range of versions available in the course of the nineteenth century.

2. Felix Summerly, *Beauty and the Beast* (London: Joseph Cundall, 1843), iii–iv.

3. *Beauty and the Beast: or a Rough Outside with a Gentle Heart, A Poetical Version of an Ancient Tale* (London: M. J. Godwin, 1811), 29. Page numbers after quotations in the following discussion refer to this source.

4. J. R. Planché, *Beauty and the Beast: A Grand, Comic, Romantic, Operatic, Melodramatic, Fairy Extravaganza in Two Acts* (London: G. Berger, 1841), 6. Page numbers after quotations in the following discussion refer to this source.

5. Walter Crane, *Beauty and the Beast and Other Tales* (London: Thames and Hudson, 1982), unpaged introduction by Anthony Crane. Quotations in the following pages are all drawn from Crane's unpaged version of "Beauty and the Beast."

6. Eleanor Vere Boyle, *Beauty and the Beast: An Old Tale New-Told* (London: Sampson Low, Marston, Low, and Serle, 1875), 2. Page numbers after quotations in the following discussion refer to this edition. (Barron's 1988 publication of this book has a truncated adaptation and poorly reproduced art.)

7. Andrew Lang, "Introduction to the Large Paper Edition of the *Blue Fairy Book* (1889)," in Brian Alderson's edition, 354.

8. Ibid., 360.

9. Mrs. E. M. Field, *The Child and His Book* (1892), quoted by Brian Alderson, "Postscript to the 1975 edition," in the *Blue Fairy Book* by Andrew Lang, 359.

10. Ibid.

11. Tolkien, "Tree and Leaf," 65.

12. Brian Alderson excepts Jacobs and Hartland from the many imitators of Lang, claiming that the former's *English Fairy Tales* and the latter's *English Fairy and Other Folk Tales*, both published in 1890, were vigorously supported by the Folk-Lore Society. See "Appendix II," in the *Blue Fairy Book* by Andrew Lang, 359.

13. Andrew Lang, "Beauty and the Beast," in the *Blue Fairy Book*, 111. Page numbers after quotations in the following discussion refer to the 1975 Alderson edition of Lang's 1889 book.

14. Elizabeth K. Helsinger, *Ruskin and the Art of the Beholder* (Cambridge: Harvard University Press, 1982), 53.

Chapter 4

1. Henry and Lila Luce, "Divorce Deco," *Esquire*, November 1983, 79.

2. Fernand Nozière, *Three Gallant Plays: A Byzantine Afternoon, Beauty and the Beast, The Slippers of Aphrodite*, trans. Clarence Stratton (New York: William Edwin Rudge, 1929), xxix. Page numbers after the following quotations refer to this source.

3. *Encyclopaedia Britannica*, 1968, s.v. "Quiller-Couch, Sir Arthur Thomas."

4. Sir Arthur Quiller-Couch, "Beauty and the Beast," in *The Sleeping Beauty and Other Fairy Tales from the Old French*, illus. Edmund Dulac (London: Hodder and Stoughton, 1910), 96. Page numbers after quotations in the following discussion refer to Quiller-Couch's version.

5. David Larkin, *Dulac* (New York: Charles Scribner's Sons, 1975), unpaged intro. by Brian Sanders.

6. Anna Alice Chapin, *The Now-A-Days Fairy Book*, with Illustrations in color by Jessie Willcox Smith (New York: Dodd, Mead, 1911), 67.

7. *Beauty and the Beast*, Aunt Mary's Series (New York: McLoughlin Brothers and Co., 1856), unpaged.

8. Laura E. Richards, *Gordon Browne's Series of Old Fairy Tales no. 2: Beauty and the Beast* (London: Black and Son, 1886), unpaged.

9. Capt. Edric Vredenburg, *Old Fairy Tales* (London: Raphael Tuck & Sons, n.d.), 59.

10. E. Nesbit, *The Old Nursery Stories*, illus. W. H. Margetson (London: Henry Frowde and Hodder & Stoughton, 1908), 28.

11. Margaret Tarrant, "Beauty and the Beast," in *Fairy Tales* (New York: Thomas Y. Crowell, 1978 [1920]), 72. Page numbers after the following quotations refer to this source.

12. John Heath-Stubbs, *Beauty and the Beast* (London: Routledge, 1943), 16–18.

13. Jean Decock, "Preface," in *Beauty and the Beast: Scenario and Dialogs* by Jean Cocteau (New York: New York University Press, 1970), x.

14. Jean Cocteau, *Beauty and the Beast: Diary of a Film* (New York: Dover

Publications, 1972), 65. Page numbers after the following quotations refer to this edition of Cocteau's diary during the filming of "Beauty and the Beast."

15. Jean Cocteau, *Beauty and the Beast: Scenario and Dialogs*, 26. Page numbers after the following quotations refer to this source.

Chapter 5

1. Robert A. Simon, *Beauty and the Beast: An Opera in One Act* for the music of Vittorio Giannini (New York: G. Ricordi and Co., 1951), 2.

2. "Notes," Library of Congress catalogue printout under most "Beauty and the Beast" entries.

3. "Beauty and the Beast," Coronet Films, 1979.

4. *Beauty and the Beast* (Mahwah, N.J.: Troll Associates, 1981), 1.

5. I have examined the area of publishing economics and its historical impact on fairy tale dissemination in a paper called "Booking the Brothers Grimm: Art, Adaptations, and Economics," which appeared in *Book Research Quarterly*, (Winter 1986–1987): 18–32, and in *The Brothers Grimm and Folktale*, ed. James M. McGlathery (Urbana, Il.: University of Illinois Press, 1988), 220–233.

6. Philippa Pearce, *Beauty and the Beast*, illus. Alan Barrett (New York: Thomas Y. Crowell, 1972), 23.

7. Marianna Mayer, *Beauty and the Beast*, illus. Mercer Mayer (New York: Four Winds Press, 1978), 2. Page numbers for the quotations in the following discussion refer to this source.

8. Deborah Apy, *Beauty and the Beast,* illus. Michael Hague (New York: Holt, Rinehart and Winston, 1983), 19. Page numbers after quotations in the following discussion refer to this source.

9. These two remarks were among many written in response to several school library sessions in which a librarian read aloud different picturebook versions of "Beauty and the Beast."

10. Robin McKinley, *Beauty: A Retelling of the Story of Beauty and the Beast* (New York: Harper and Row, 1978), 115. Page numbers after the quotations in the following discussion refer to this source.

11. Tolkien, "Tree and Leaf," 74–75.

12. Julie Brookhart, "Beauty, a New Version of an Old Tale," unpublished paper, University of Chicago, 1979, 20.

13. Robin McKinley, interviewed for this study, 1983.

14. Angela Carter, "The Courtship of Mr. Lyon," *Elsewhere: Tales of Fantasy,* vol. 2, ed. Terri Windling and Mark Alan Arnold (New York: Ace Fantasy, 1982), 121. Page numbers after quotations in the following discussion refer to this source.

15. Tanith Lee, "Beauty," *Red As Blood or Tales from the Sisters Grimmer* (New York: Daw Books, 1983), 179. Page numbers after the quotations in the following discussion refer to this source.

16. The tale of "Cupid and Psyche" has also inspired a religiously charged novel by C. S. Lewis, *Till We Have Faces* (San Diego: A Harvest HBJ Book, 1956), with an ending dominated by Christian mysticism.

17. "Is Prime Time Ready for Fable?" by Steven Oney in the *New York Times*, 20 September 1987; "An Urban Fable Goes Beneath the Surface" by John O'Connor in the *New York Times*, 22 November 1987; "Move Over, Ozzie and Harriet" by Alice Hoffman in the *New York Times*, 14 February 1988. Ron Perlman, who acts the part of the Beast (Vincent), claims to receive a great deal of fan mail: "Women say that Vincent is the ultimate fantasy lover, someone who asks nothing in return but gives 110 percent. . . . He evokes deep unconscious feelings of longing for a connection to someone who understands things on a very emotional level." Associated Press, *Chicago Sun-Times*, 5 July, 1988.

Chapter 6

1. A. K. Ramanujan, "Hanchi: A Kannada Cinderella," in *Cinderella: A Folklore Casebook,* ed. Alan Dundes, 260.

2. Lévi-Strauss, "The Structural Study of Myth," in De George, *The Structuralists*, 173.

3. Wilbur Urban, *Language and Reality*, quoted in Cleanth Brooks, *The Well-Wrought Urn: Studies in the Structure of Poetry* (San Diego: A Harvest/HBJ Book, 1975), 261–262.

4. Robin McKinley, interviewed for this study, 1983.

5. Frye, *Anatomy of Criticism,* 341.

6. Thomas Mintz, "The Meaning of the Rose in 'Beauty and the Beast,'" *The Psycholoanalytic Review,* no. 4 (1969–70): 615–620.

7. *Funk and Wagnalls Standard Dictionary of Folklore, Mythology, and Legend* (New York: Funk and Wagnalls Co., 1949), 2:956.

8. Frye, *Anatomy of Criticism,* 204 and ensuing discussion.

9. The symbolic appearance of earth, fire, water, and air in the tale is an old one. Gilbert Durand classifies Psyche's four trials as representing initiation by the four elements ("Psyche's View," *Spring,* 1981, 12).

10. The "chorus" here refers to the fairy godmother/adviser figure discussed earlier.

11. Joseph Campbell, *The Hero with a Thousand Faces* (Princeton: Princeton University Press, 1973), 98.

12. Madame Le Prince de Beaumont, "Beauty and the Beast," in Opie and Opie, *The Classic Fairy Tales,* 148

13. Bruno Bettelheim's Freudian interpretation is a good example of single-minded theory applied to a multidimensional story. His style of analysis is so stilted compared to the grace of the images themselves that the closer he comes to

explaining it, the farther away he moves from the story's impact. His remorseless pursuit of one meaning almost obliterates the tale's imaginative possibilities. Certainly what he says about the story and its effects on children rings true within a context of Freudian assumptions, though there is some articulate disagreement on his making such a rigid case based upon so many assumptions. A number of psychologists have criticized Bettelheim's universalizing a model from very little clinical evidence. In addition, Jack Zipes challenges his imposition of contemporary theories on historical material in "The Use and Abuse of Fairy Tales," in *Breaking the Magic Spell: Radical Theories of Folk and Fairy Tales* (New York: Methuen, 1984), 160–182.

14. Bruno Bettelheim, *The Uses of Enchantment: The Meaning and Importance of Fairy Tales* (New York: Random House/Vintage, 1977), 309. Jacques Barchilon terms it, more gracefully, the reconciliation of the unconscious with the conscious, the fairy tale "thus establishing the artistic arch of alliance between the kingdom of night and the kingdom of day" (a point reminiscent of Cocteau's filmic contrasts). Barchilon also discusses "Beauty and the Beast" as presenting "the humanization of the beast and the 'bestialization' of his female companion," a balance caught by Heath-Stubbs in his poem (see chapter 4). See Jacques Barchilon, "Beauty and the Beast," *Psychoanalysis and the Psychoanalytic Review* 46, no.4 (Winter 1959): 19–29.

15. C. G. Jung, *The Spirit in Man, Art, and Literature*, trans. R. F. C. Hull (Princeton: Princeton University Press, 1972), 91.

16. Ibid., 90.

17. Ibid., 94. In her Jungian analysis of "Cupid and Psyche," von Franz equates Eros with Osiris, who, she says, "taught men and women genuine mutual love" (*A Psychological Interpretation of The Golden Ass of Apuleius*, 109). "If you think of Psyche as the archetype of the anima and of Eros as the archetype of the animus, it is a strange ultimate reversal of the roles" (108).

18. *Beauty and the Beast: or a Rough Outside with a Gentle Heart*, 29.

19. Cocteau, *Beauty and the Beast: Scenario and Dialogs*, 180.

20. Madame Le Prince de Beaumont, in Opie and Opie, *The Classic Fairy Tales*, 147–148.

21. Cocteau, "Beauty and the Beast," *Scenario and Dialogs*, 250–252.

22. Ibid., 244.

23. Jung, *The Spirit in Man, Art, and Literature*, 82, 95.

24. Cocteau, *Scenario and Dialogs*, 180.

25. Ibid., 95–96.

26. Jean Decock, in the preface to Cocteau's filmscript, xi–xii.

27. John Bierhorst, "Afterword," in Charles Perrault, *The Glass Slipper: Charles Perrault's Tales of Times Past,* trans. and ed. by John Bierhorst (New York: Four Winds Press, 1981), 101.

28. Ibid.

Chapter 7

1. There are some 49,813 children's trade books in print in the United States, according to *Children's Books in Print 1987–88* (New York: Bowker, 1987), v. This does not include textbooks or mass market books.

2. The scholarship is beginning to catch up with the literature. A last section of the bibliography gives a dozen sample sources of criticism, other than those mentioned in the course of this study, that have dealt seriously with the relationship of folklore and children's literature.

3. Zibby Oneal, "In Summer Light," *Horn Book* 63 no. 1 (January/February, 1987): 32.

4. Margaret Mahy, *The Changeover* (New York: Atheneum/Margaret K. McElderry, 1984), 152.

5. For a fuller analysis of *The Changeover*, see Hearne, *Booklist* 82, no.5 (1 November 1985): 410–412.

6. Leon Garfield, *The Wedding Ghost*, illus. by Charles Keeping (Oxford: Oxford University Press, 1987).

7. Natalie Babbitt, "The Fantastic Voyage," *The Five Owls* 1, no. 6 (July/August 1987): 77–80.

8. Paula Fox, *The Moonlight Man* (New York: Bradbury Press, 1986), 179.

9. Folk motifs identified by Leone McDermott in an unpublished paper, "Narrative Elements in the Work of William Steig," Graduate Library School, University of Chicago, 1987.

10. Less imaginatively, current teenage romance outlines (called tip sheets), which authors must follow closely to qualify their work for a series, often conform to fairy tale conventions. Popular literature in other cultures may reflect persisting patterns from oral tradition. Wendy Griswold's work with Nigerian romance novels shows them to have the unreliable heroes, helper figures, episodic structure, and unanticipated or ambiguous endings common to the trickster stories that dominate African oral tradition ("Formulaic Fiction: The Author As Agent of Elective Affinity," a paper presented at a Faculty Colloquium on Communicative Phenomena, University of Chicago, 2 December 1987).

11. Bettelheim, *The Uses of Enchantment*, 2.

12. Ruth B. Bottigheimer, *Fairy Tales and Society: Illusion, Allusion, and Paradigm* (Philadelphia: University of Pennsylvania Press, 1986).

13. One cannot help speculating about the fact that traditional folklore scholarship has been dominated by men and most children's literature specialists are women.

14. "Sex, Death, and Red Riding Hood," *Time*, 19 March 1984, 68.

15. Quoted in the *New York Times Book Review*, 19 February 1984, 11.

16. Max Lüthi, *The European Folktale*, trans. John D. Niles (Philadelphia: Institute for the Study of Human Issues, 1981).

17. The Grimms' rewriting is polemically described in John Ellis's *One Fairy Story Too Many* (Chicago and London: University of Chicago Press, 1983), which charges the brothers with substantial changes of basic elements supposed to reflect universal unconscious patterns and with attributing "folk" sources to stories passed on by well-educated informants. Heinz Rölleke has a more tempered approach in his discussion of the Grimms' informants in "The 'Utterly Hessian' Fairy Tales by 'Old Marie': The End of a Myth," in Bottigheimer, *Fairy Tales and Society,* 287–300.

18. The views of Kay Stone, Madonna Kolbenschlag, Andrea Dworkin, Jane Yolen, and others are now widely cited and well known. Elizabeth Segal has a judicious summary of the feminist controversy over fairy tales in children's literature, especially relating to the work of Elizabeth Fisher, Alison Lurie, Alleen Pace Nilsen, Lenore J. Weitzman, and Marcia Leiberman; see Segal's "Picture Books and Princesses: The Feminist Contribution," in *Proceedings of the Eighth Annual Conference of the Children's Literature Association,* ed. Priscilla A. Ord, 77–83.

19. Robert Darnton, *The Great Cat Massacre and Other Episodes in French Cultural History* (New York: Basic Books, 1984), 29.

20. J. R. R. Tolkien, "Tree and Leaf," in *The Tolkien Reader,* 65.

21. Lüthi, *The European Folktale,* 118.

22. Alan Dundes, "Fairy Tales from a Folkloristic Perspective," in Bottigheimer, *Fairy Tales and Society,* 259–269.

23. Frye, *Anatomy of Criticism,* 96.

24. Thompson, *The Folktale,* 97.

25. Lévi-Strauss, "The Structural Study of Myth," in De George, *The Structuralists from Marx to Levi-Strauss,* 171.

26. Ibid., 183.

27. Hearne, "Problems and Possibilities: Research in Children's Literature, the U.S. and Canada," a paper delivered at the International Youth Library Conference, Munich, April 1988, and reprinted in part in *School Library Journal* (August 1988): 27–31.

Literary Beauties and Folk Beasts

1. Śatapathabrāhmaṇa 1.1.1.4. Trans. by Julius Eggling, *The Śatapatha-Brāhmana,* pt. 1 (repr. Motilal Banarsidass: Delhi, 1978), 4.

2. Mihai Pop, "Die Funktion der Anfangs- und Schlussformeln in rumäischen Märchen," in *Volksüberlieferung: Festschrift für Kurt Ranke,* ed. Fritz Harbort, Karel C. Peeters, and Robert Wildhaber (Göttingen: Verlag Otto Schwartz & Co., 1968), 321–326.

3. In *Disenchantments: An Anthology of Modern Fairy Tale Poetry,* ed. Wolfgang Mieder (Hanover, N.H.: University Press of New England, 1985), 133.

4. In *The Fairytale as Art Form and Portrait of Man,* by Max Lüthi, trans. by Jon Erickson (Bloomington: Indiana University Press, 1984), 160.

5. Anna Tavis, "Fairy Tales from a Semiotic Perspective," in *Fairy Tales and Society: Illusion, Allusion and Paradigm,* ed. Ruth Bottigheimer, (Philadelphia: University of Pennsylvania Press, 1986), 200.

6. Lutz Röhrich, "Metamorphosen des Märchens heute," in *Über Märchen für Kinder von heute: Essays zu ihren Wandel und ihrer Funktion,* ed. Klaus Doderer (Weinheim und Basel: Beltz Verlag, 1983), 107.

7. Barre Toelken, "The 'Pretty Languages' of Yellowman: Genre, Mode and Texture in Navaho Coyote Narratives," in *Folklore Genres,* ed. Dan Ben-Amos (Austin: University of Texas Press, 1976), 155.

8. *International Dictionary of Regional European Ethnology and Folklore,* vol.1 (Copenhagen: Rosenkilde and Bagger, 1960), 135.

9. Jan-Öjvind Swahn, *The Tale of Cupid and Psyche* (Lund: Gleerup, 1955), 311. Designation by tale type follows Antti Aarne, *The Types of the Folktale,* trans. and rev. by Stith Thompson (Helsinki: Academia Scientiaram Fennica, 1961). Motif numbers and titles are from Stith Thompson, *Motif Index of Folk-Literature,* 6 vols. (Bloomington, Indiana: Indiana University Press, 1955–1958). Other tale numbers refer to standard collections in which these tales are found.

10. Ibid.

11. Stith Thompson, *The Folktale* (Berkeley: University of California Press, 1977), 451–453.

12. Cf. Alan Dundes, "The Number Three in American Culture," in *Interpreting Folklore,* ed. Alan Dundes (Bloomington: Indiana University Press, 1980), 134–159.

13. Lauri Honko, "Possibilities of International Cooperation and Regulation in the Safeguarding of Folklore," *Nordic Institute of Folklore Newsletter* 15, no. 1 (May 1987), 8.

14. Ibid.

15. Thompson, *The Folktale,* 415.

16. Swahn, *The Tale of Cupid and Psyche,* 306.

17. Lüthi, *The Fairytale,* 70–71.

18. Swahn, op. cit., 18.

19. Leonard W. Roberts, *South from Hell-fer-Sartin* (Berea, Ky.: The Council of Southern Mountains, Inc., 1964), 60–63.

20. Eleazar Meletinsky, "Marriage: Its Function and Position in the Structure of Folktales," in *Soviet Structural Folkloristics,* vol. 1, ed. P. Miranda (The Hague and Paris: Mouton, 1974), 61. Specific to the present tales, see p. 67 for interpretation of "the archaic marriage theme (AT 400, 425) of the miraculous partners." Does a tale like "The Maiden without Hands" (tale type 706) preserve archaic rites?

21. Several works exploring this theme are cited by C. C. Schlam, "The Scholarship on Apulieus since 1938," *Classical World* 64, no. 9 (May 1971), 285–308. Cf. esp. his reference to Scazzoso's view of the Metamorphoses as a "novel of initiation," and Merkelbach's interpretation of "Cupid and Psyche" as reflecting an

Isis cult initiation myth. A number of interpretative essays have been collected in *Amor und Psyche*, ed. Gerhard Binder and Reinhold Merkelbach, Wege der Forschung, bd. 126 (Darmstadt: Wissenschaftliche Buchgesellschaft, 1968). A recent appraisal of Apuleius is *Unity in Diversity: A Study of Apuleius' Metamorphoses*, by Paula James (Hildesheim, Zurich and New York: Olms-Weidman, 1987), Altertumswissenschaftlichen Texte und Studien, bd. 16.

22. Georgios A. Megas, *Das Märchen von Amor und Psyche in der griechischen Überlieferung (Aarne-Thompson 425, 428 and 432)* (Athēnai: Grapheion Dēmosieumatōn tēs Akadēmias Athēnōn, 1971), 201.

23. Ibid., 138.

24. Röhrich, "Metamorphosen des Märchen heute," 107.

25. Swahn, *The Tale of Cupid and Psyche*, 217.

26. This is also the case with Pabhāvatī in the Kusa Jātaka.

27. Sed ego te narrationibus lepidisque fabulis protinus avocabo

28. mātugāme paṭibaddhacittatāya hi tejavanto pi
   porāṇakapaṇḍitā nittejā hutvā anayavyasanaṁ pāpuṇiṁsū

29. Claude Bremond, *Logique du récit* (Paris: Editions du Seuil, 1977), 132–133.

30. Vladimir Propp, *Morphology of the Folkltale*, 2d ed. rev. and ed. with a preface by Louis A. Wagner, new introd. by Alan Dundes (Austin: University of Texas Press, 1968), 66–70.

31. Cf. Juha Pentikäinen, *Oral Repertoire and World View: An Anthropological Study of Marina Takalo's Life History*, Folklore Fellows Communications no. 219, (Helsinki: Suomalainen Tiedeaktenia, 1978), 287–288.

32. Propp, *Morphology*, 144.

33. Ibid., 27. Cf. also Alan Dundes, *The Morphology of North American Indian Folktales*, Folklore Fellows Communications no. 195, (Helsinki: Suomalainen Tiedeakatemia, 1964), 53.

34. A. N. Afanas'ev, *Narodnye russkie skazki*, vol. 2 (Moskva: Xydozestennaja literatura, 1957), 241.

35. Dundes, *Morphology*, 88.

36. Propp, *Morphology*, 27.

37. Bremond, *Logique*, 132.

38. Propp, op. cit., 63–64.

39. Ibid., 30–35.

40. *Myths and Folk-tales of the Russians, Western Slavs, and Magyars*, trans. by Jeremiah Curtin (Boston: Little, Brown & Co., 1890).

41. Swahn, *The Tale of Cupid and Psyche*, 306.

42. Ibid., 343–345.

43. Anna Brigitta Rooth, *The Cinderella Cycle* (Lund: Gleerup, 1951), 20–22.

44. Cf. Dundes' note 10 p. 457 to Stith Thompson, "The Star Husband Tale" in *The Study of Folklore*, ed. Alan Dundes (Englewood Cliffs, N.J.: Prentice-Hall, 1965).

45. Swahn, *The Tale of Cupid and Psyche*, 387–392. For comparison of the chief Indic textual sources of the tale see Tilak Raj Chopra, *The Kuśa-Jātaka: A Critical and Comparative Study,* Alt- und Neu-indische Studien 13 (Hamburg: Cram, DeGruyter & Co., 1966).

46. E. B. Cowell, *The Jātaka, or, Stories of the Buddha's Former Births: Translated from the Pāli by various hands*, vol. 5 (repr. London: Luzac, 1969), 141 n. 1.

47. W.R.S. Ralston, *Tibetan Tales Derived from Indian Sources: Translated from the Tibetan of the Kah-Gyur by F. Anton von Schiefner, done into English from the German* (London, 1893), xxxvii–xxxix and 21–28.

48. See Propp's analysis of Afanas'ev 159 in appendix 3 for nested moves.

49. Propp himself approached this notion in suggesting that "any tale element . . . can evolve into an independent story" (*Morphology*, 78). Dundes (*Morphology*) analyzes a number of stories of one motifeme, and Thompson (*Folktale*, 439) notes that more than half of the Aarne tale types consist of a single motif.

50. Propp, *Morphology*, 62–63.

51. Propp's function 14 (F).

52. Lüthi, *The Fairytale*, 127.

53. E.g., "Sgiathán Dearg and the Daughter of the King of the Western World," in *Irish Folktales collected by Jeremiah Curtin,* ed with introd. and notes by Séamus O'Duilearga (Dublin: Folklore of Ireland Society, 1943), 95–102.

54. Alex Olrik, "Epic Laws of Folk Narrative," in *The Study of Folklore*, ed. Alan Dundes (Englewood Cliff, N.J.: Prentice-Hall, 1965), 134–135.

55. Antti Aarne, *Der reiche Man und sein Schwiegersohn,* Folklore Fellows Communications no. 23 ([Hamina: Suomalaisen Tiedakatemian Kustantana, 1916], 110–115) gives an analysis of this tale. Cf. also Archer Taylor, "The Predestined Wife," *Fabula* 2 (1959): 45–82.

56. Megas, *Das Märchen von Amor und Psyche*, 12–13.

57. Swahn, *The Tale of Cupid and Psyche*, 22.

58. "The Three Daughters of King O'Hara" in *Myths and Folklore of Ireland,* ed. by Jeremiah Curtin, (Boston: Little, Brown and Co., 1906), 52.

59. Here the situation seems to resemble psychological processes such as defense mechanism or self-deception.

60. Namely, CB 12 in Swahn, *The Tale of Cupid and Psyche*, 52–53.

61. Heda Jason and Dimitri Segal, eds., *Patterns in Oral Literature* (The Hague and Paris: Mouton Publishers, 1977), 275.

62. Lüthi, *The Fairytale*, 37–65.

63. Cf. Propp's function D^4 and D^7 in *Morphology,* 40–41.

64. "Repetition, in and of itself, is a nonstructural phenomenon," Dundes, *Morphology*, 86.

65. Olrik in Dundes, *The Study of Folklore,* 136.

66. Thompson, "Star Husband," in Dundes, ibid., 435–436.

67. The reunion may be lacking, resulting in an unhappy ending.

68. See the tale type index under 425A and Johannes Bolte and Georg Polívka, *Anmerkungen zu den Kinder- u. Hausmärchen der Brüder Grimm,* vol. 2 (Leipzig: Dieterich'sche Verlagsbuchhandlung, 1918), 319 to Grimms no. 92.

69. "The Crow Bride," in *Folktales of Bangladesh*, ed. Abdul Hafiz (Dhaka: Bangla Academy, 1985), 25–34.

70. *The Pentamerone of Giambattista Basile, translated from the Italian of Benedetto Croce . . . by N. M. Penzer,* vol. 1 (New York and London: E. P. Dutton, 1932), 200.

71. Ibid., 163.

72. For a summary and addition to views on this, see Jack Zipes, "Klassische Märchen in Zivilisationsprozess: Die Schattenseite von 'La Belle et la Bête,'" 57–77.

73. In the Sanskrit versions of the Kusa Jātaka the father dies early in the story.

74. Jean Cocteau, *Beauty and the Beast*, Film, 1946.

75. Jean Cocteau, *Diary*, 21.

76. Thompson, *The Folktale* (Berkeley: University of California Press, 1977), 437.

77. Cocteau, *Dairy*, 21.

78. William George Archer, *The Hill of Flutes: Life, Love and Poetry of Tribal India: A Portrait of the Santals* (Pittsburgh: University of Pittsburgh Press, 1974), 279–289.

79. Irving Singer, *The Nature of Love*, 2d ed. (Chicago and London: University of Chicago Press, 1984).

80. June Singer, *Energies of Love* (Garden City, New York: Anchor Press/Doubleday, 1983).

81. Paul Hedwig, *Liebe und Feindschaft* (München/Basel: Ernst Reinhardt Verlag, 1964).

82. Kenneth S. Pope et al., *On Love and Loving: Psychological Perspectives on the Nature and Experience of Romantic Love* (San Francisco, Washington and London: Jossey-Bass Publishers, 1980), 327–328.

83. Bruno Bettelheim, *The Uses of Enchantment: The Meaning and Importance of Fairy Tales* (New York: Random House/Vintage, 1977), 293.

84. Claude Rambaux, *Trois analyses de l'amour* (Paris: Societe d'edition "Les belles lettres," 1985), 206.

85. Ibid., 204.

86. Bettelheim, *Uses of Enchantment*, 293.

87. Bruno Bettelheim, *Freud and Man's Soul* (New York: Alfred A. Knopf, 1983), 12–13.

88. Marie-Louise von Franz, *A Psychological Interpretation of the Golden Ass of Apuleius* (Irving, Texas: Spring Publications, University of Dallas, 1980), 85.

89. Ibid., 63.

90. Ibid., 83.

91. Ibid., 86.

92. Ibid., 104.

93. Ibid.

94. Ibid., 106.

95. Ibid., 89.

96. Nec speres generum mortali stirpe creatum (Metamorphoses 4.33).

97. Tí oùn án, éphēn, eíe ho Érōs; thnētós;

Hēkistá ge (Symposium 202 D).

98. Phyllis Gross-Kurth, *Melanie Klein: Her World and Her Work* (New York: Alfred A. Knopf, 1986), 236.

99. Rabindranath Tagore, *The King of the Dark Chamber* (New York: Macmillan, 1916), 192–193.

100. Ibid., 217. When Melanie Klein's mother lay dying, Klein knelt and begged forgiveness, somewhat as, *mutatis mutandi*, Beauty reacted to the dying Beast (Gross-Kurth, 218).

101. Von Franz, *A Psychological Interpretation*, 70.

102. Verena Kast, *Mann und Frau im Märchen* (Olten und Freiberg im Breisgau: Walter Verlag, 1983), 77–99.

103. A. T. Hatto, "The Swan Maiden: A Folk-Tale of North Eurasian Origin?" *Bulletin of the School of Oriental and African Studies, London University* 24 (1961): 326–352.

Bibliography

Many versions of "Beauty and the Beast" were consulted but not included in the body of this study. Except for those listed in appendix 4, only the editions actually discussed in the text are cited. Story sources are arranged according to the main entry that appears on the title page of the book. Thus editions of "Beauty and the Beast" may be listed under title or adapter in the absence of a cited author or under Le Prince de Beaumont, if she is acknowledged.

Story Sources

Afanas'ev, Aleksandr Nikolaevich. *Narodnye russkie skazki,* vol. 2. Moskva: Xydož-
    estennaja literatura, 1957.
———. *Russian Folktales.* Republished in Detroit: Gale Research Company, 1974.
Aksadov, Sergei. *The Scarlet Flower: A Russian Folk Tale.* Translated by Isadora Levin.
    Illustrated by Boris Diodorov. Harcourt Brace Jovanovich, 1989.
Andersen, Hans Christian. *The Complete Fairy Tales and Stories.* Translated by Erik
    Haugaard. New York: Doubleday, 1974.
Apuleius. *The Most Pleasant and Delectable Tale of the Marriage of Cupid and Psyche,
    done into English by William Adlington of University College in Oxford, with a
    discourse on the fable by Andrew Lang, late of Merton College in Oxford.* London:
    David Nutt, 1887.
———. *Cupid and Psyche and Other Tales from The Golden Ass of Aurelius, newly
    edited by W. H. D. Rouse.* London: Chatto and Windus, 1907.
Apy, Deborah. *Beauty and the Beast.* Illustrated by Michael Hague. New York: Holt,
    Rinehart and Winston, 1983.
Arnott, Kathleen. "The Snake Chief" in *African Myths and Legends.* London: Oxford
    University Press, 1962.
Basile, Giambattista. *The Pentamerone of Giambattista Basile, translated from the*

Italian of Benedetto Croce... by N. M. Penzer. Vol. 1. New York and London: E. P. Dutton, 1932.

Bates, Katherine Lee. *Once Upon a Time: A Book of Old-Time Fairy Tales.* Chicago: Rand McNally, 1921.

Beaumont. See Le Prince de Beaumont, Madame.

Beauty and the Beast. Aunt Mary's Series. New York: McLoughlin Brothers and Co., 1856.

Beauty and the Beast. Coronet Films. 1979.

Beauty and the Beast. Illustrated by Hilary Knight. New York: Macmillan, 1963.

Beauty and the Beast. Illustrated by Karen Milone. Mahwah, N.J.: Troll Associates, 1981.

Beauty and the Beast. Produced by Shelly Duvall. A Faerie Tale Theatre Production. 1984.

Beauty and the Beast Ballet. An ABC Films release, 1966. Produced by Gordon Waldear. Featuring the San Francisco Ballet, music by Tchaikovsky, choreography by Lew Christensen, narration by Haley Mills. With Robert Gladstein, Lynda Meyer, David Anderson. Color, 50 minutes.

Beauty and the Beast: or a Rough Outside with a Gentle Heart, a Poetical Version of an Ancient Tale. (Attributed to Charles Lamb.) London: M. J. Godwin, 1811.

Briggs, Katharine M., and Ruth L. Tongue. *Folktales of England.* Chicago and London: University of Chicago Press, 1965.

Boyle, Eleanor Vere. *Beauty and the Beast: An Old Tale New-Told.* London: Sampson Low, Marston, Low, and Searle, 1875.

Calvino, Italo. "Belinda and the Monster" in *Italian Folktales.* Translated by George Martin. New York: Harcourt Brace Jovanovich, 1980.

Campbell, Marie. "A Bunch of Laurel Blooms for a Present" in *Tales from the Cloud Walking Country.* Bloomington: University of Indiana Press, 1958.

Carter, Angela. "The Courtship of Mr. Lyon" in *Elsewhere: Tales of Fantasy.* 2 vols. Edited by Terri Windling and Mark Alan Arnold. New York: Ace Fantasy, 1982.

———, ed. *Sleeping Beauty and Other Favourite Fairy Tales.* Translated by Angela Carter and illustrated by Michael Foreman. North Pomfret, Vt.: Victor Gollancz/David & Charles, 1982.

Carter, Anne. *Beauty and the Beast.* Illustrated by Binette Schroeder. New York: Potter/Crown, 1986.

Chapin, Anna Alice. *The Now-A-Days Fairy Book.* With Illustrations in Color by Jessie Willcox Smith. New York: Dodd, Mead, 1911.

Chase, Richard. "Whitebear Whittington" in *Grandfather Tales.* Cambridge: Houghton Mifflin, 1948.

Child, Francis James, ed. *The English and Scottish Popular Ballads.* Vol. 1. New York: Dover Publications, 1965 (a republication of the 1882 edition).

Chopra, Tilak Raj. *The Kuśa-Jātaka: A Critical and Comparative Study.* Alt- und Neu-indische Studien 13. Hamburg: Cram, DeGruyter & Co., 1966.

Cocteau, Jean. *Beauty and the Beast.* Film, 1946.

———. *Beauty and the Beast: Scenario and Dialogs.* New York: New York University Press, 1970.

———. *Beauty and the Beast: Diary of a Film.* New York: Dover Publications, 1972.

Cohen, Barbara. *Roses.* New York: Lothrop, Lee and Shepard Books, 1984.

Corneille. "Psyché: Tragédie-ballet" in *Oeuvres complètes.* Préface de Raymond Lebègue, presentation et notes de André Stegmann. Paris: Éditions du Seuil, 1963.

Corner, Julia, and Alfred Crowquill. *Beauty and the Beast: An Entertainment for Young People, the First of the Series of Little Plays for Little People.* London: Dean & Son, 1854.

Cowell, E. B. *The Jātaka, or, Stories of the Buddha's Former Births: Translated from the Pali by various hands.* Vol. 5. Reprint. London: Luzac, 1969.

Cox, Marian. *Cinderella.* London: David Nutt, 1893.

Crane, Walter. *Beauty and the Beast.* London: George Routledge and Sons, 1875.

———. *Beauty and the Beast and Other Tales.* London: Thames and Hudson, 1982.

Curtin, Jeremiah, trans. *Myths and Folk-tales of the Russians, Western Slavs, and Magyars.* Boston: Little, Brown & Co., 1890.

———. "The Three Daughters of King O'Hara" in *Myths and Folk-Lore of Ireland.* Boston: Little, Brown & Co., 1906.

———. "Sgiathán Dearg and the Daughter of the King of the Western World" in *Irish Folk-Tales.* Edited with introduction and notes by Séamus O'Duilearga. Dublin: Folklore of Ireland Society, 1943.

Delarue, Paul. "The Serpent and the Grape-grower's Daughter" in *French Fairy Tales.* New York: Knopf, 1968.

Dowson, Ernest. *The Story of Beauty and the Beast: The Complete Fairy Story.* Translated from the French by Ernest Dowson with Four Plates in Colour by Charles Condor. London: John Lane, The Bodley Head, 1908.

Doyle, Richard. *Beauty and the Beast: A Manuscript by Richard Doyle.* New York: Pierpont Morgan Library, 1973.

Fast, Jonathan. *The Beast.* New York: Ballantine Books, 1981.

Fox, Paula. *The Moonlight Man.* New York: Bradbury Press, 1986.

Garfield, Leon. *The Wedding Ghost.* Illustrated by Charles Keeping. Oxford: Oxford University, 1987.

Genlis, Stéphanie Félicité Ducrest de Saint Aubin, Comtesse de. *The Beauty and the Monster: A Comedy from the French of the Countesse de Genlis Extracted from the Theatre of Education.* Printed at Worcester, Mass. by Isaiah Thomas and Sold at his Book-Store. Boston: Isaiah Thomas, 1785.

Goble, Paul. *The Girl Who Loved Wild Horses.* Scarsdale, N. Y.: Bradbury Press, 1978.

———. *Buffalo Woman.* Scarsdale, N. Y.: Bradbury Press, 1984.

Goode, Diane. See Le Prince de Beaumont.

Gray, Nicholas Stuart. *Beauty and the Beast: A Play for Children.* Illustrated by Joan Jefferson Farjeon. London: Oxford University Press, 1951.

Grimm, Jakob Ludwig Karl, and Wilhelm Karl Grimm. "The Lilting, Leaping Lark" in *Grimms' Tales for Young and Old: The Complete Stories.* Translated by Ralph Manheim. New York: Doubleday, 1977.

Hafiz, Abdul, ed. *Folktales of Bangladesh.* Dhaka: Bangla Academy, 1985.

Halfyard, Lynda, and Karen Rose. *Kristin and Boone.* Boston: Houghton Mifflin, 1983.

Harris, Rosemary. *Beauty and the Beast.* Illustrated by Errol LeCain. New York: Doubleday, 1980.

Hastings, Selina, ed. *Sir Gawain and the Loathly Lady.* Illustrated by Juan Wijngaard. New York: Lothrop, 1985.

Haviland, Virginia. *Favorite Fairy Tales Told in France.* Illustrated by Roger Duvoisin. Boston: Little, Brown, 1959.

Heath-Stubbs, John. *Beauty and the Beast.* London: Routledge, 1943.

Holme, Bryan, ed. *Tales from Times Past.* New York: Viking Press (A Studio Book), 1977.

Hutton, Warwick. *Beauty and the Beast.* New York: Atheneum/A Margaret K. McElderry Book, 1985.

Jones, Olive, ed. *Beauty and the Beast.* Little Box of Fairy Tales, illustrated by Francesca Crespi. New York: Dial, 1983.

Klipple, May Augusta. "African Folk Tales with Foreign Analogues." Dissertation, Indiana University, 1938.

Knappert, Jan. "Monyohe" in *Myths and Legends of Botswana, Lesotho and Swaziland.* Leiden: E. J. Brill, 1985.

Lamb, Charles. See *Beauty and the Beast: or a Rough Outside with a Gentle Heart, a Poetical Version of an Ancient Tale.*

Lang, Andrew. *Blue Fairy Book.* Edited by Andrew Lang with numerous illustrations by H. J. Ford and G. P. Jacomb Hood. London: Longmans, Green, and Co., 1889.

———. *Blue Fairy Book.* Revised and edited by Brian Alderson from the 1889 edition. New York: Viking, 1975.

———. *Red Fairy Book.* Revised and edited by Brian Alderson from the 1890 edition. New York: Viking, 1976.

———. *Green Fairy Book.* Revised and edited by Brian Alderson from the 1892 edition. New York: Viking, 1978.

Le Prince de Beaumont, Madame. *Le magasin des enfans, ou dialogues entre une sage gouvernante et plusiers de ses élèves de la première distinction.* Par Mme. Le Prince de Beaumont. Londres: J. Haberkorn, 1756.

———. *The Young Misses Magazine, containing Dialogues between a Governess and Several Young Ladies of Quality her Scholars.* Vol. 1. 4th ed. London: C. Nourse, 1783.

———. *The Young Ladies Magazine, or Dialogues between a Discreet Governess and Several Young Ladies of the First Rank under her Education.* 4 vols. in 2. London: J. Nourse, 1760. (A sequel to the *Young Misses Magazine.*)

————. *Letters from Emerance to Lucy.* 2 vols. London: J. Nourse, 1766.

————. *Beauty and the Beast.* Translated and illustrated by Diane Goode. New York: Bradbury Press, 1978.

Lee, Tanith. "Beauty." In *Red as Blood or Tales from the Sisters Grimmer.* New York: Daw Books, 1983.

Lenkoff, Irene. *Beauty and the Beast: Yes & Know Invisible Ink Fairy Tale Storybook.* Louisville, Ky.: Lee Publications, 1980.

Lewis, C. S. *Till We Have Faces.* San Diego: A Harvest HBJ Book, 1956.

Lurie, Alison, ed. *Clever Gretchen and Other Forgotten Folktales.* Illustrated by Margot Tomes. New York: Crowell, 1980.

MacDonald, George. *The Princess and the Goblin.* Elgin, Ill.: Chariot Books, 1978.

McKinley, Robin. *Beauty: A Retelling of the Story of Beauty and the Beast.* New York: Harper and Row, 1978.

Mahy, Margaret. *The Changeover.* New York: Atheneum/Margaret K. McElderry, 1984.

Mayer, Fanny Hagin. "The Monkey Son-in-law" in *Ancient Tales in Modern Japan: An Anthology of Japanese Folktales.* Bloomington: Indiana University Press, 1985.

Mayer, Marianna. *Beauty and the Beast.* Illustrated by Mercer Mayer. New York: Four Winds Press, 1978.

Minard, Rosemary. *Womenfolk and Fairy Tales..* Boston: Houghton Mifflin, 1975.

Nesbit, E. *The Old Nursery Stories.* Illustrated by W. H. Margetson. London: Henry Frowde and Hodder & Stoughton, 1908.

Nozière, Fernand. *Three Gallant Plays: A Byzantine Afternoon, Beauty and the Beast, The Slippers of Aphrodite.* Translated by Clarence Stratton. New York: William Rudge, 1909.

Opie, Iona, and Peter Opie, eds. *The Classic Fairy Tales.* London: Oxford University Press, 1974.

Osborne, Mary Pope. *Beauty and the Beast.* Illustrated by Winslow Pinney Pels. New York: Scholastic, 1987

Pearce, Philippa. *Beauty and the Beast.* Illustrated by Alan Barrett. New York: Thomas Y. Crowell, 1972.

Perrault, Charles. *Old Time Stories Told by Master Charles Perrault.* Translated from the French by A. E. Johnson, with illustrations by W. Heath Robinson. London: Constable, 1921.

————. *The Glass Slipper: Charles Perrault's Tales of Times Past.* Translated and edited by John Bierhorst. New York: Four Winds Press, 1981.

Phelps, Ethel Johnston. *The Maid of the North: Feminist Folk Tales from Around the World.* Illustrated by Lloyd Bloom. New York: Holt, Rinehart and Winston, 1981.

Planché, J. R. *Beauty and the Beast: A Grand, Comic, Romantic, Operatic, Melo-dramatic, Fairy Extravaganza in Two Acts.* London: G. Berger, 1841.

Ponsot, Marie, trans. *The Fairy Tale Book.* Illustrated by Adrienne Ségur. New York: Golden Press, 1958.

Provensen, Alice, and Martin Provensen. *The Provensen Book of Fairy Tales*. New York: Random House, 1971.

Quiller-Couch, Sir Arthur Thomas. "Beauty and the Beast." *The Sleeping Beauty and Other Tales from the Old French*. Illustrated by Edmund Dulac. London: Hodder and Stoughton, 1910.

Rackham, Arthur. *The Arthur Rackham Fairy Book: A Book of Old Favourites with New Illustrations*. Philadelphia: J. B. Lippincott, 1933.

Ralston, W. R. S. *Tibetan Tales Derived from Indian Sources: Translated from the Tibetan of the Kah-Gyur by F. Anton von Schiefner, done into English from the German*. London, 1893.

Richards, Laura E. *Gordon Browne's Series of Old Fairy Tales no. 2: Beauty and the Beast*. London: Black and Son, 1886.

Riordan, James, comp. *The Woman in the Moon and other Tales of Forgotten Heroines*. Illustrated by Angela Barrett. New York: Dial, 1985

Roberts, Leonard W. "Bully Bornes" and "The Enchanted Cat" in *South from Hell-fer-Sartin*. Berea, Ky.: The Council of Southern Mountains, 1964.

Sietel, Peter. "The Serpent of Kam Ushalanga," as told by Ma Kelezensia Konstantin in *See So That We May See: Performances and Interpretations of Traditional Tales from Tanzania*. From performances tape-recorded by Sheila Dauer and Peter Seitel. Bloomington: Indiana University Press, 1980.

Simon, Robert A. *Beauty and the Beast: An Opera in One Act for the Music of Vittorio Giannini*. New York: G. Ricordi and Co., 1951.

Smith, Albert. *Beauty and the Beast*. With illustrations by Alfred Crowquill. New York: Leavitt and Allen, 1853.

Southgate, Vera. *Beauty and the Beast*. (Well-Loved Tales.) Loughborough, England: Ladybird Books, 1980.

Steptoe, John. *Mufaro's Beautiful Daughters: An African Tale*. New York: Lothrop, 1987.

Summerly, Felix. *Beauty and the Beast*. London: Joseph Cundall, 1843.

Tarrant, Margaret. *Fairy Tales*. New York: Thomas Y. Crowell, 1978 [1920].

The Tenggren Tell-It-Again Book. Illustrated by Gustaf Tenggren with text edited and adapted by Katharine Gibson. Boston: Little, Brown, 1942.

Theal, George McCall. *Kaffir Folk-lore; or, A Selection from the Traditional Tales Current among the People Living on the Eastern Border of the Cape Colony*. With copious explanatory notes. London: W. Swan Sonnenschein, 1882.

Thomas, Rosemary Hyde. "Prince White Hog" in *It's Good To Tell You: French Folktales from Missouri*. Columbia, Mo.: University of Missouri Press, 1981.

Villeneuve, Gabrielle Susanne Barbot de Gallon (Madame) de. "La belle et la bête." *Le cabinet des fées, ou collection des fées, et autres contes merveilleux, ornés de figures*. À Amsterdam, et se trouve à Paris, Rue et Hotel Serpente, 1786. (Villeneuve's version first appeared in 1740 in *La jeune amériquaine, et les contes marins*, which was unavailable for study, but was reprinted in *Le cabinet des fées*.)

————. *Beauty and the Beast*. Illustrated by Etienne Delessert. Mankato, Minn.: Creative Education Inc., 1984.

Vredenberg, Capt. Edric. *Old Fairy Tales*. London: Raphael Tuck, & Sons, n.d.

Walker, Barbara. "The Princess and the Pig," in *A Treasury of Turkish Folktales for Children*. Hamden, Conn.: Linnet Books, 1988.

Williamson, Duncan, ed. "The Hedgehurst" in *Fireside Tales of the Traveler Children: Twelve Scottish Tales*. New York: Harmony Books, 1985.

Critical Sources

Aarne, Antti. *Der reiche Man und sein Schwiegersohn*. Folklore Fellows Communications, no. 23. Hamina: Suomalaisen Tiedakatemian Kustantana, 1916.

————. *The Types of the Folktale: A Classification and Bibliography*. Translated and revised by Stith Thompson. Folklore Fellows Communications, no. 184. Helsinki: Academia Scientiarum Fennica, 1961.

Abel, Elizabeth; Marianne Hirsch; and Elizabeth Langland. *The Voyage In: Fictions of Female Development*. Hanover, N.H.: University Press of New England, 1983.

Archer, William George. *The Hill of Flutes: Life, Love, and Poetry of Tribal India: A Portrait of the Santals*. Pittsburgh: University of Pittsburgh Press, 1974.

Ashliman, D. L. *A Guide to Folktales in the English Language: Based on the Aarne-Thompson Classification System*. Westport, Conn.: Greenwood Press, 1987.

Babbitt, Natalie. "The Fantastic Voyage." *The Five Owls*, 1, no. 6 (July/August 1987): 77–80.

Barchilon, Jacques. "Beauty and the Beast: From Myth To Fairy Tale." *Psychoanalysis and the Psychoanalytic Review* 46: 4 (Winter, 1959): 19–29.

————. "Beauty and the Beast." *Modern Language Review* 56 (1961): 81–82.

Bettelheim, Bruno. *The Uses of Enchantment: The Meaning and Importance of Fairy Tales*. New York: Random House/Vintage, 1977.

————. *Freud and Man's Soul*. New York: Alfred A. Knopf, 1983.

Binder, Gerhard and Reinhold Merkelbach, eds. *Amor und Psyche*. Wege der Forschung, bd. 126. Darmstadt: Wissenschaftliche Buchgesellschaft, 1968.

Bolte, Johannes, and Georg Polívka. *Anmerkungen zu den Kinder- u. Hausmärchen der Brüder Grimm*. vol. 2. Leipzig: Dieterich'sche Verlagsbuchhandlung, 1918.

Bottigheimer, Ruth B., ed. *Fairy Tales and Society: Illusion, Allusion, and Paradigm*. Philadelphia: University of Pennsylvania Press, 1986.

Boulet, Jean. *La Belle et la Bête*. Paris: Le Terrain Vague, n.d.

Bremond, Claude. *Logique du récit*. Paris: Editions du Seuil, 1977.

Brewer, Derek. "The Battleground of Home: Versions of Fairy Tales." *Encounter*, April 1980, 52–61.

Briggs, Katharine M. *A Dictionary of British Folk-Tales in the English Language*. 2 vols. Bloomington: Indiana University Press, 1970.

Brookhart, Julie. "Beauty, A New Version of an Old Tale." Unpublished paper, University of Chicago, 1979.

Brooks, Cleanth. *The Well-Wrought Urn: Studies in the Structure of Poetry.* San Diego: A Harvest/HBJ Book, 1975.

Campbell, Joseph. *The Hero with a Thousand Faces.* Princeton: Princeton University Press, 1973.

————. *The Way of the Animal Powers.* Vol. 1 of *The Historical Atlas of World Mythology.* New York: Harper and Row, 1984.

Canham, Stephen. "What Manner of Beast? Illustrations of 'Beauty and the Beast.'" In *Image & Maker: An Annual Dedicated to the Consideration of Book Illustration,* edited by Harold Darling and Peter Neumeyer. La Jolla: Green Tiger Press, 1984.

Cumberland, George. *Thoughts on Outline, Sculpture, and the System that Guided the Ancient Artists in Composing Their Figures and Groupes.* Accompanied with free remarks on the practice of the moderns, and liberal hints cordially intended for their advantage. To which are annexed twenty-four designs of classical subjects invented on the principles recommended in the essay by George Cumberland. Illustrated by George Cumberland and William Blake. London: W. Wilson, 1796.

Darnton, Robert. *The Great Cat Massacre and Other Episodes in French Cultural History.* New York: Basic Books, 1984.

De George, Richard, and Fernande De George, eds. *The Structuralists from Marx to Lévi-Strauss.* Garden City, N.Y.: Doubleday/Anchor Books, 1972.

Delarue, Paul, and Marie-Louise Tenèze. *Le conte populaire français: Catalogue raisonné des versions de France et des pays de langue française d'outre-mer; Canada, Louisiane, Ilots française des Etats-Unis, Antilles françaises, Haïti, Ile Maurice, La Réunion.* Tome 2. Paris: Éditions G.-P. Maisonneuve et Larose, 1964.

Dixon, Roland B. *The Mythology of All Races, in Thirteen Volumes.* Vol. 9. *Oceanic.* Boston: Marshall Jones, 1916.

Dundes, Alan. *The Morphology of North American Indian Folktales,* Folklore Fellows Communications no. 195. Helsinki: Suomalainen Tiedeakatemia, 1964.

————. "The Number Three in American Culture." In *Interpreting Folklore,* edited by Alan Dundes. Bloomington: Indiana University Press, 1980.

————, ed. *Cinderella: A Folklore Casebook.* New York: Garland Publishing, Inc., 1982.

————, ed. *The Study of Folklore.* Englewood Cliff, N.J.: Prentice-Hall, 1965.

Durand, Gilbert. "Psyche's View," *Spring* (1981): 1-19.

Eastman, Mary. *Index to Fairy Tales, Myths, and Legends.* Boston: F. W. Faxon, 1926, 1937, 1952.

Ellis, John M. *One Fairy Story Too Many.* Chicago and London: University of Chicago Press, 1983.

Engen, Rodney K. *Walter Crane As a Book Illustrator.* New York: St. Martin's Press, 1975.

Favat, André. *Child and Tale: The Origins of Interest*. No. 19 in a series of research reports sponsored by the NCTE Committee on Research. Urbana, Ill.: National Council of Teachers of English, 1977.

Freud, Sigmund. "Fairy Tale Subjects in Dreams." In *Collected Papers*, vol. 4. New York: International Psycho-analytical Press, 1924–1925.

———. *On Creativity and the Unconscious: Papers on the Psychology of Art, Literature, Love, Religion*. Edited by Benjamin Nelson. New York: Harper and Row, 1958.

Fromm, Erich. *The Forgotten Language: An Introduction to the Understanding of Dreams, Fairy Tales, and Myths*. New York: Holt, Rinehart, and Winston, 1951.

Frye, Northrop. *Anatomy of Criticism*. Princeton: Princeton University Press, 1957.

Funk and Wagnalls Standard Dictionary of Folklore, Mythology, and Legend. 2 vols. New York: Funk and Wagnalls Co., 1949.

Gardner, Howard. "Brief on Behalf of Fairy Tales." *Phaedrus: An International Journal of Children's Literature Research,* 5 (1978): 14–23.

Griswold, Wendy. "Formulaic Fiction: The Author As Agent of Elective Affinity." Paper presented at a Faculty Colloquium on Communicative Phenomena, University of Chicago, 2 December, 1987.

Gross-Kurth, Phyllis. *Melanie Klein: Her World and Her Work*. New York: Alfred A. Knopf, 1986.

Hatto, A. T. "The Swan Maiden: A Folk-Tale of North Eurasian Origin?" *Bulletin of the School of Oriental and African Studies, London University* 24 (1961): 326-352.

Hearn, Michael Patrick. *The Art of the Broadway Poster*. New York: Ballantine Books, 1980.

Hearne, Betsy. "The Changeover." In *Booklist* 82, no. 5 (1 November 1985): 410–412.

———. "Booking the Brothers Grimm: Art, Adaptations, and Economics." *Book Research Quarterly* Winter 1986–87: 18–32.

———. "Problems and Possibilities: U.S. Research in Children's Literature." *School Library Journal* (August 1988): 27–31.

Helsinger, Elizabeth K. *Ruskin and the Art of the Beholder*. Cambridge: Harvard University Press, 1982.

Helwig, Paul. *Liebe und Feindschaft*. München/Basel: Ernst Reinhardt Verlag, 1964.

Henderson, Joseph L. "Ancient Myths and Modern Man." *Man and His Symbols*. Edited by Carl G. Jung. Garden City, N.Y.: Doubleday and Co./A Windfall Book, 1964.

———. "Heroes and Hero Makers." *Through Folklore to Literature*. Papers presented at the Australian National Section of the IBBY Conference on Children's Literature, Sidney, Australia, 1978. Edited by Maurice Saxby. Sidney: IBBY Australia Publications, 1979.

Heuscher, Julius. *A Psychiatric Study of Myths and Fairy Tales: Their Origin, Meaning, and Usefulness*. 2d ed. Springfield, Ill.: Thomas, 1974.

Honko, Lauri. "Possibilities of International Cooperation and Regulation in the Safe-guarding of Folklore," *Nordic Institute of Folklore Newsletter* 15, no. 1 (May, 1987): 4-21.

International Dictionary of Regional European Ethnology and Folklore. vol. 1. Copenhagen: Resenkilde and Bagger, 1960.

Ireland, Norma. *Index to Fairy Tales, 1949–1972, including Folklore, Legends, and Myths, in Collections.* Westwood, Mass.: F. W. Faxon, 1973.

James, Paula. *Unity in Diversity: A Study of Apuleius' Metamorphoses.* Altertumwis-senschaftlichen Texte and Studien, bd. 16. Hildesheim, Zurich, and New York: Olms-Weidman, 1987.

Jason, Heda, and Dimitri Segal, eds. *Patterns in Oral Literature.* World Anthropology. The Hague and Paris: Mouton Publishers, 1977.

Jung, C. G. *Man and His Symbols.* New York: Doubleday, 1964.

——— *The Spirit in Man, Art, and Literature.* Translated by R. F. C. Hull. Princeton: Princeton University Press, 1972.

Kast, Verena. *Mann und Frau im Märchen: Eine tiefenpsychologische Deutung.* Olten und Freiburg im Breisgau: Walter-Verlag, 1983.

Katz, Phyllis B. "The Myth of Pyche: Definition of the Nature of the Feminine?" *Arethusa* 9, no. 1 (Spring 1976): 111–118.

Kolbenschlag, Madonna. *Kiss Sleeping Beauty Goodbye.* New York: Doubleday, 1979.

Laiblin, Wilhelm, ed. *Märchenforschung und Tiefenpsychologie.* Wege der Forschung. bd. 102. Darmstadt: Wissenschaftliche Buchgesellschaft, 1975.

Larken, David. *Dulac.* New York: Charles Scribner's Sons, 1975.

Lévi-Strauss, Claude. *Myth and Meaning.* New York: Schocken Books, 1979.

Lewis, C. S. *Of Other Worlds: Essays and Stories.* Edited, with a preface, by Walter Hooper. New York: Harcourt Brace Jovanovich, 1966.

Luce, Henry, and Lila Luce. "Divorce Deco," *Esquire,* November 1983.

Lüthi, Max. *Once Upon a Time: On the Nature of Fairy Tales.* New York: Frederick Unger, 1970.

———. *The European Folktale.* Translated by John D. Niles. Philadelphia: Institute for the Study of Human Issues, 1981.

———. *The Fairytale as Art Form and Portrait of Man.* Translated by Jon Erickson. Bloomington: Indiana University Press, 1984.

McDermott, Leone. "Narrative Elements in the Work of William Steig." Unpublished paper, University of Chicago, 1987.

McGlathery, James M., ed. with Larry W. Danielson, Ruth E. Lorbe, and Selma K. Richardson. *The Brothers Grimm and Folktale.* Urbana, Ill.: University of Illinois Press, 1988.

MacPherson, Jay. "'Beauty and the Beast' and Some Relatives." A lecture given to the Friends of the Osbourne and Lillian H. Smith Collections. Toronto, 1974. Mimeo.

Mallet, Carl-Heinz. *Fairy Tales and Children: The Psychology of Children Revealed*

Through Four of Grimm's Fairy Tales. Translated by Joachim Neugroschel. New York: Schocken Books, 1984.

Megas, Georgios A. *Das Märchen von Amor und Psyche in der griechischen Überlieferung (Aarne-Thompson 425, 428, and 432).* Athēnai: Grapheion Dēmosieumatōn tēs Akadēmias Athēnōn, 1971.

Meletinsky, Eleazar, "Marriage: Its Function and Position in the Structure of Folktales." In *Soviet Structural Folkloristics,* vol. 1, edited by P. Miranda. The Hague and Paris: Mouton, 1974.

Mieder, Wolfgang, ed. *Disenchantments: An Anthology of Modern Fairy Tale Poetry.* Hanover, N.H.: University Press of New England, 1985.

Mintz, Thomas. "The Meaning of the Rose in 'Beauty and the Beast.'" *The Psychoanalytic Review* 56, no. 4 (1969–70): 615–620.

Mitchell, Jane Tucker. *A Thematic Analysis of Madame D'Aulnoy's Contes de Fées.* Romance Monographs no. 30. Oxford, Miss.: University of Mississippi, 1978.

Neumann, Erich. *Amor and Psyche: The Psychic Development of the Feminine, a Commentary on the Tale by Apuleius.* Translated from the German by Ralph Manheim. New York: Pantheon, 1956.

O'Suilleabhain, Sean, and Reidar Th. Christiansen. *The Types of the Irish Folktale.* Helsinki: Suomalainen Tiedakatemia, 1967.

Oneal, Zibby. "In Summer Light," *Horn Book* 63, no. 1 (January/February, 1987): 32.

Ord, Priscilla A., ed. *Proceedings of the Eighth Annual Conference of the Children's Literature Association,* University of Minnesota, March 1981. Boston: Children's Literature Association, 1982.

Pallottino, Paola. "La Bestia Della Bella." *Linea Grafica* (6 Novembre, 1987): 4–13.

Pentikäinen, Juha. *Oral Repertoire and World View: An Anthropological Study of Marina Takalo's Life History.* Folklore Fellows Communications no. 219. Helsinki: Suomalainen Tiedeakatemia, 1978.

Pop, Mihai. "Die Funktion der Anfangs- und Schlussformeln in rumäischen Märchen" In *Volksüberlieferung: Festschrift für Kurt Ranke.* Edited by Fritz Harbort, Karel C. Peeters, and Robert Wildhaber, 321–326. Göttingen: Verlag Otto Schwartz & Co., 1968.

Pope, Kenneth S. and associates. *On Love and Loving: Psychological Perspectives on the Nature and Experience of Romantic Love.* San Francisco, Washington and London: Jossey-Bass Publishers, 1980.

Propp, Vladimir. "Morphology of the Folktale." *International Journal of American Linguistics* 24, no. 4 (October 1958). Bloomington: Indiana University Research Center in Anthropology, Folklore, and Linguistics, no. 10. Edited by Svatava Pirkova-Jakobson and translated by Laurence Scott.

———. *Morphology of the Folktale.* 2d ed. Revised and edited with a preface by Louis A. Wagner; new introduction by Alan Dundes. Austin, Tex.: University of Texas Press, 1968.

Ralston, W. R. S. "Beauty and the Beast." *The Nineteenth Century* (December 1878): 990–1012.

Rambaux, Claude. *Trois analyses de l'amour.* Paris: Société d'édition "Les belles lettres," 1985.

Röhrich, Lutz. "Metamorphosen des Märchens heute." In *Über Märchen für Kinder von heute: Essays zu ihren Wandel und ihrer Funktion.* Edited by Klaus Doderer. Weinheim und Basel: Beltz Verlag, 1983.

Rooth, Anna Brigitta. *The Cinderella Cycle.* Lund: Gleerup, 1951.

Sale, Roger. *Fairy Tales and After: From Snow White to E. B. White.* Cambridge: Harvard University Press, 1978.

Schlam, C. C. "The Scholarship on Apulieus since 1938," *Classical World* 64, no. 9 (May 1971): 285–308.

Segel, Elizabeth. "Feminists and Fairy Tales." *School Library Journal* (January 1983): 30–31.

Singer, Irving. *The Nature of Love.* 2d ed. Chicago and London: University of Chicago Press, 1984.

Singer, June. *Energies of Love: Sexuality Re-visioned.* Garden City, New York: Anchor Press/Doubleday, 1983.

Stone, Kay. "Things Walt Disney Never Told Us." In *Women and Folklore.* Edited by Claire R. Farrer, 42–50. Austin: University of Texas Press, 1975.

Storer, Mary Elizabeth. *Un épisode littéraire de la fin du XVII siècle: La mode des contes de fées (1685–1700).* Paris: Librarie Ancienne Honoré Champion, 1928.

Swahn, Jan-Öjvind. *The Tale of Cupid and Psyche.* Lund: Gleerup, 1955.

Tagore, Rabindranath. *The King of the Dark Chamber.* New York: Macmillan, 1916.

Taylor, Archer. "The Predestined Wife," *Fabula* 2 (1959): pp. 45–82.

Thompson, Stith. *Motif-Index of Folk-Literature: A Classification of Narrative Elements in Folktales, Ballads, Myths, Fables, Mediaeval Romances, Exempla, Fabliaux, Jest-books, and Local Legends.* 6 vols. Bloomington: Indiana University Press, 1956.

———. *The Folktale.* Berkeley: University of California Press, 1977.

Todoroff, Tzvetan. *The Fantastic: A Structural Approach to a Literary Genre.* Translated from the French by Richard Howard. Ithaca, N. Y.: Cornell University Press, 1975.

Toelken, Barre. "The 'Pretty Languages' of Yellowman: Genre, Mode, and Texture in Navaho Coyote Narratives." In *Folklore Genres.* Edited by Dan Ben-Amos. Austin: University of Texas Press, 1983.

Tolkien, J. R. R. "Tree and Leaf." In *The Tolkien Reader.* New York: Ballantine Books, 1966.

Travers, Pamela L. *About the Sleeping Beauty.* Illustrated by Charles Keeping. New York: McGraw-Hill, 1975.

Ulanov, Ann, and Barry Ulanov. *Cinderella and Her Sisters: The Envied and the Envying.* Philadelphia: Westminster Press, 1983.

Von Franz, Marie-Louise. *A Psychological Interpretation of the Golden Ass of Apuleius.* Irving, Tex.: Spring Publications, University of Dallas, 1980.

Yolen, Jane. *Touch Magic: Fantasy, Faerie and Folklore in the Literature of Childhood.* New York: Philomel Books, 1981.

Zipes, Jack David. *Breaking the Magic Spell: Radical Theories of Folk and Fairy Tales.* New York: Methuen, 1984.

———. "The Dark Side of Beauty and the Beast: The Origins of the Literary Fairy Tale for Children." In *Proceedings of the Eighth Annual Conference of the Children's Literature Association.* Edited by Priscilla A. Ord. University of Minnesota, March 1981. Boston: Children's Literature Association, 1982.

———. *Fairy Tales and the Art of Subversion: The Classical Genre for Children and the Process of Civilization.* New York: Wildman Press, 1983.

———. "Klassische Märchen im Zivilisationsprozess: Die Schattenseite von 'La Belle et la Bête.'" In *Uber Märchen für Kinder von heute: Essays zu ihrem Wandel und ihrer Funktion.* Edited by Klaus Doderer, 57–77. Weinheim und Basel: Beltz Verlag, 1983.

———. *The Trials and Tribulations of Little Red Riding Hood: Versions of the Tale in Sociocultural Context.* South Hadley, Mass.: J. F. Bergin Publishers, 1983.

——— *Don't Bet on the Prince: Contemporary Feminist Fairy Tales in North America and England.* New York: Methuen, 1986.

Sample Sources Treating the Relationship between
Folklore and Children's Literature

Babbitt, Natalie. "Fantasy and the Classic Hero." *School Library Journal* 34, no. 2 (1987): 25–29.

Children's Books International 4, *Folklore, Unique and Universal.* Proceedings. Boston: Boston Public Library, 1979.

Egoff, Sheila. "Folklore, Myth, and Legend." *Thursday's Child: Trends and Patterns in Contemporary Children's Literature,* 193–220. Chicago: American Library Association, 1981.

Gose, Elliott. *Mere Creatures: A Study of Modern Fantasy Tales for Children.* Toronto: University of Toronto Press, 1988.

Gough, John. "Patricia Wrightson's Wirrun: A Modern Aboriginal Mythic Hero." *Review Bulletin* 2 (1987): 17–21.

Halpert, Herbert. "Folktales in Children's Books: Some Notes and Reviews." *Midwest Folklore* 2, no. 1 (Spring 1952): 59–71.

Hamilton, Virginia. "The Known, the Remembered and the Imagined: Celebrating Afro-American Folktales," *Children's Literature in Education* 18:2, 1987, pp. 67–75.

The Lion and the Unicorn: A Critical Journal of Children's Literature. The Fairy Tale. December, 1988.

MacDonald, Margaret Read. "An Analysis of Children's Folktale Collections with an

Accompanying Motif-Index of Juvenile Folktale Collections." 2 vols. Ph.D. dissertation, Indiana University, 1979.

Norton, Eloise S., ed. *Folk Literature of the British Isles: Readings for Librarians, Teachers, and Those Who Work with Children and Young Adults.* Metuchen, N.J.: Scarecrow, 1978.

Ord, Priscilla, ed. "Special Section: Folklore." *Children's Literature Association Quarterly* 6, no.2 (Summer 1981): 11–33.

Philip, Neil. "Children's Literature and the Oral Tradition." In *Further Approaches to a Research in Children's Literature*, 5–22. Edited by Peter Hunt. Proceedings of the Second British Research Seminar in Children's Literature, Cardiff, September 1981. Cardiff: University of Wales, Institute of Science and Technology, Dept. of English, 1982.

Saxby, Maurice, ed. *Through Folklore to Literature.* Papers presented at the Australian National Section of the IBBY Conference on Children's Literature, Sydney, 1978. Sidney: IBBY Australia Publications, 1979.

Whalley, June. "The Cinderella Story 1724–1919." *Signal* (May 1972): 49–62.

Winslow, David J. "Children's Picture Books and the Popularization of Folklore." *Keystone Folklore Quarterly* 14 (Winter 1969): 142–157.

Index